VIRTUE, VICE, AND PERSONALITY

VIRTUE, VICE, AND PERSONALITY

THE COMPLEXITY OF BEHAVIOR

Edited by

Edward C. Chang and Lawrence J. Sanna

American Psychological Association • Washington, DC

Published by
American Psychological Association
750 First Street, NE
Washington, DC 20002
www.apa.org

To order
APA Order Department
P.O. Box 92984
Washington, DC 20090-2984
Tel: (800) 374-2721; Direct: (202) 336-5510
Fax: (202) 336-5502; TDD/TTY: (202) 336-6123
Online: www.apa.org/books/
E-mail: order@apa.org

In the U.K., Europe, Africa, and the Middle East, copies may be ordered from
American Psychological Association
3 Henrietta Street
Covent Garden, London
WC2E 8LU England

Typeset in Goudy by Page Grafx, Inc., St. Simons Island, GA

Printer: Data Reproductions Corporation, Auburn Hills, MI
Cover Designer: Naylor Design, Washington, DC
Technical/Production Editor: Rosemary Moulton

The opinions and statements published are the responsibility of the authors, and such opinions and statements do not necessarily represent the policies of the American Psychological Association.

Library of Congress Cataloging-in-Publication Data
Virtue, vice, and personality : the complexity of behavior / edited by Edward C. Chang and Lawrence J. Sanna.
  p. cm.
 Includes bibliographical references and index.
 ISBN 1-59147-013-7 (alk. paper)
 1. Personality. I. Chang, Edward C. (Edward Chin-Ho) II. Sanna, Lawrence J.

 BF698.V57 2003
 155.2—dc21

                  2003006516

British Library Cataloguing-in-Publication Data
A CIP record is available from the British Library.

Printed in the United States of America
First Edition

To my loving parents, Tae Myung-Sook and Chang Suk-Choon,
who continue to nurture my passion to reach for unreachable goals.
To my adoring wife, Stephanie, who has never been short on
offering love and support in my life.
And finally, to my precocious two-year-old daughter, Olivia Dae,
who offers me priceless opportunities each and every passing day
to live, laugh, and love like a child again.
—*Edward C. Chang*

To my parents, John and Marie,
who continuously tried to guide me to recognize virtue.
—*Lawrence J. Sanna*

CONTENTS

CONTRIBUTORS

Glenn Affleck, PhD, Graduate Program in Public Health, Community Medicine and Health Care, University of Connecticut Health Center, Farmington

Chad M. Burton, BA, Department of Psychological Sciences, University of Missouri, Columbia

Alex Casillas, MA, Department of Psychology, University of Iowa, Iowa City

Edward C. Chang, PhD, Department of Psychology, University of Michigan, Ann Arbor

Jennifer A. Clarke, MS, Department of Psychology, University of North Carolina, Chapel Hill

J. Scott Hanson, PhD, MA, Department of Psychology, Washington University, St. Louis, MO

Michael H. Kernis, PhD, Department of Psychology, University of Georgia, Athens

Laura A. King, PhD, Department of Psychological Sciences, University of Missouri, Columbia

Laurel Newman, BA, Department of Psychology, Washington University, St. Louis, MO

Julie K. Norem, PhD, Department of Psychology, Wellesley College, Wellesley, MA

Christopher Peterson, PhD, Department of Psychology, University of Michigan, Ann Arbor

Lawrence J. Sanna, PhD, Department of Psychology, University of North Carolina, Chapel Hill

Robert J. Sternberg, PhD, Yale University, PACE Center, New Haven, CT

Shevaun L. Stocker, BA, Department of Psychology, University of North Carolina, Chapel Hill

Michael J Strube, PhD, Department of Psychology, Washington University, St. Louis, MO

Howard Tennen, PhD, Department of Community Medicine and Health Care, University of Connecticut Health Center, Farmington

Robert S. Vaidya, BA, Department of Psychology, University of Michigan, Ann Arbor

David Watson, PhD, Department of Psychology, University of Iowa, Iowa City

FOREWORD

FROM SIMPLICITY TO COMPLEXITY: EXTREMES, PENDULUMS, AND MATURATION

C. R. SNYDER

As the years roll by and I learn more about the world and myself, I sometimes wonder whether my ancestors went through the same developmental lessons. Ontogeny knowledge, so to speak, replicates phylogeny insight. Likewise, my experiences over the years have helped me to better understand *accretion*—how one piece of information helps to build an aggregate formed of several pieces of information. Similar to these developmental insights, I believe that good books offer insights into what we previously recognized as separate pieces of information but had not integrated into a coherent whole. In reading this book, I initially sensed a vague familiarity—a feeling of déja vu—regarding the contents. As the chapters unfolded, however, clear take-home messages emerged, messages that have implications for views about one's life and the science of personality psychology more generally.

EXTREMES AND THE SWINGING PENDULUM

In this book, the reader is exposed to a verity about our field; namely, that it is a budding science that has been prone to extremes. For a variety of reasons, much of 20th-century personality psychology has focused on the negative in humankind. The pages of previous books and journals were filled with harsh portrayals of people who were thinking and doing things that varied from the slightly bad to the downright horrific. It was as if the area of personality became a psychology circus sideshow involving the aberrant and terrible. Weaknesses and pathology were the foci, and analyses centered on human vices.

As we entered the 21st century, however, personality psychology became enamored of what has been called *positive psychology*, a view that turned the lens toward people who were doing things that ranged from the mildly positive to the heroic. As this new strengths approach gained followers, there developed a tendency to portray the previous pathology model as being completely wrongheaded and, to some degree, mean-spirited in its scholarly endeavors. Articles and books began to proliferate on this new approach, there were conventions of like-minded positive psychologists, and scholars began to chart the turf of all matters pertaining to human strengths. Likewise, the previous pathology vocabulary was supplanted with terms that sang tributes to positive human capacities and actions. From their perspective, *virtue* became the password.

MATURATION

In this volume, the reader is treated to views about both of these camps—the vice and virtue scholars, so to speak. I caution the reader, however, to realize that this book is ahead of the curve temporally. By this I mean that the various authors present enlightened views that borrow content from both camps. This eventuality represents a logical and desired progression for the field, but the field at present has not made it to this point. Instead, the positive psychologists appear to be enjoying the limelight, and they are publishing furiously about the many strengths of human beings.

For the reader who is interested in having a glimpse of where this scholarly psychological debate about the bad and the good in people will be going, I highly recommend this book. It argues for a perspective that aptly includes both parts—the vices and the virtues—as being crucial for a full understanding of the human condition.

SIMPLICITY TO COMPLEXITY

To effect a maturation of our understanding, we psychologists must abandon any simplistic notions and replace them with more complex views about the nature of human beings. People are not "good" or "bad"; they are both, and such an admission demands a more sophisticated level of analysis than has heretofore been applied. In addition, even within a given positive characteristic, there may be good and not-so-good aspects.

The field of personality must embrace such complexity in its theorizations and methodologies in order to mature as a science. This is precisely the message that the chapter authors are sending. A serious scientific field must be willing to expound complex models to capture the realities of that field. So too must genuine science, over time, take seemingly disparate pieces of information to build a more accurate and thorough understanding. We face the same process in our own lives as we continually are challenged to remain open to new information and to make it part of our working model of reality. Personality scholars and researchers must do the same for their field, and this volume provides a cogent roadmap for this important journey.

PREFACE

Like many readers, we have become increasingly aware of a growing focus on what many refer to as the *positive psychology* movement. In fact, one of us (Chang) participated a few years ago in what was the first positive psychology conference, held in Akumal, Mexico. Although we appreciated the importance of this new (or renewed) focus on the positive (e.g., "What makes people healthy?"), we were also concerned that the shift to a positive psychology may leave the field overly skewed; it may leave many of the things we have gained from the study of the negative at the wayside (e.g., "What makes people unhealthy?"). Although neither of us believed that the study of dysfunction should be the primary focus of our endeavors, we felt that there was a pressing need to emphasize a more balanced approach, one that incorporated both the positive and the negative.

In thinking about this further, we realized that one important approach to studying the positive or the negative has been to link personality with adjustment or maladjustment, respectively. Therefore, based in part on our own research on personality over the years, we wondered if different personality variables might each possess both adaptive and maladaptive qualities (a question that was the focus of a recent volume on optimism and pessimism edited by one of the present editors [Chang]). It seemed quite clear—to us, anyway—that available evidence indicated that a more balanced view of human behavior was warranted. We also wondered if other researchers felt as we did, and accordingly surveyed some of the leading experts on personality. These experts expressed a ready appreciation for the idea that what are conventionally viewed as adaptive personality constructs may in some circumstances function maladaptively and, conversely, the idea that what are conventionally viewed as maladaptive personality constructs may in some circumstances function adaptively. Consequently, we became even more enthusiastic about the utility of sharing this view of balance, not only with researchers who had already actively been studying personality but also with those in other fields who could similarly see the benefit of a more comprehensive appreciation and understanding of what is both good and bad about various personality variables.

Our goal was to produce a volume that reflected the thoughts of some of the leading personality experts, as they challenge themselves (and, we hope, challenge the reader) to consider alternative ways for understanding some of the personality variables that have garnered a great deal of attention over the years because of their presumed association with adjustment or maladjustment. The present volume is unique in that it will be an important resource for researchers, practitioners, educators, and students, among others, in helping to break us out of our tendency to dichotomize our conceptions of personality. We build on the ideas of the German philosopher Frederich Nietzsche (1844–1900), who more than a century ago in his work *Beyond Good and Evil* implored his readers to develop a higher meta-morality that went beyond the convention of determining morality as a function of what was deemed good versus evil. In that spirit, we ask readers to go beyond a view of personality as either a virtue or a vice.

As with any book, we simply could not include everything. We chose to be illustrative, thought provoking—and, dare we hope, action provoking—by including chapters from leading experts in their respective areas, who have researched prominent personality constructs. It is likely that our general ideas, however, could have just as easily applied to other personality variables that were not included in this book. Balance, we think, is key. It is thus not our goal either to promote a shift away from a positive psychology (indeed, some of our contributors would probably consider themselves positive psychologists); neither was our goal to promote a shift back toward a negative psychology. Rather, our goal was to make salient to ourselves and to others that such shifting exists, and will continue to exist, as history has always shown us, and that by considering both the positive and the negative we may become less vulnerable (or more resilient) to transient biases that may limit our fullest understanding of personality.

We greatly acknowledge the support, guidance, and insights proffered by the contributors of this volume as responsible for any success the book attains. Without their courage and enthusiasm to think outside of what has become routine and conventional, this book simply would not have been possible. The existence of this book provides us much hope that we can thoughtfully appreciate the complexity of personality as multifaceted and as multifunctional and, in a more general sense, appreciate the rich complexity of our everyday existence with others. We also thank Susan Reynolds at the American Psychological Association (APA) for giving us the opportunity to edit this volume and for her encouragement and support when it was not much more than a rough idea. Relatedly, we are most thankful to Anne Woodworth at APA for her support and guidance as development editor on this volume, and to Rosemary Moulton for her excellent work as production editor of this volume. Finally, we thank the many individuals, including the contributors to this book, who continue to help shape and guide our sensibility and appreciation for going beyond the virtue and vice of personality.

INTRODUCTION

BEYOND VIRTUE AND VICE IN PERSONALITY: CLASSICAL THEMES AND CURRENT TRENDS

Everything in excess is opposed to nature.

—*Hippocrates*

Let the states of equilibrium and harmony exist in perfection, and a happy order will prevail throughout heaven and earth, and all things will be nourished and flourish.

—*Confucius*

In the time of ancient Greece, people believed that the world could be understood in terms of four basic elements, namely, earth, water, air, and fire. Hippocrates, the Greek father of medicine, took this metaphysical view of four elements one step further and argued that people also could be understood as a function of four humors, namely, black bile, yellow bile, blood, and phlegm. In attempting to understand differences in personality and adjustment more than 500 years later, Galen, the great Roman physician, held that it was the excess of a given humor that resulted in one of four distinct temperaments. For example, a person with excessive black bile was considered to be melancholic or temperamentally depressive. A person with excessive yellow bile was considered to be choleric or temperamentally irritable. A person with excessive blood was considered sanguine or temperamentally optimistic. Finally, a person with excessive phlegm was considered to be phlegmatic or temperamentally calm. Thus, it is clear that people have long been fascinated with the link between personality and adjustment. Across history in the West, especially over the past several decades, there has been a growing tendency to consider certain personality characteristics as more beneficial or adaptive than others, insofar as some have been associated with adjustment rather than maladjustment.

PERSONALITY, STRATEGY, AND ADJUSTMENT: DISTINGUISHING VIRTUE AND VICE

In studying personality over the years, psychologists have come to look at how various characteristics relate to adjustment and have drawn some general conclusions about the value of these characteristics for individuals. For example, because personality attributes such as optimism and pessimism have come to be associated with adjustment and maladjustment, respectively, there is a tendency to appraise optimism as beneficial and pessimism as costly (Chang, 2001). In a sense, we have come to see optimism as a virtue and pessimism as a vice.

In the *Nicomachean Ethics*, Aristotle (1908/350 BC) attempted to provide a comprehensive ethical theory of how people should live the good life and obtain what we all seek at the end of this process, namely, happiness or *eudaimonia*. According to Aristotle, to live a good life and attain happiness, a person should live by virtues and not by vices. Virtue (*areté*) was defined by the mean (*to meson*), whereas vice (*kakia*) was defined by deficiency or excess. As summarized by Aristotle:

> Virtue, then, is a state of character concerned with choice, lying in a mean, i.e., the mean relative to us, this being determined by a rational principle, and by that principle by which the man of practical wisdom would determine it. Now it is a mean between two vices, that which depends on excess and that which depends on defect; and again it is a mean because the vices respectively fall short of or exceed what is right in both passions and actions, while virtue both finds and chooses that which is intermediate. (Book 3, Section 6, 1106b37–1107a5)

Thus, courage was considered by Aristotle to represent a virtuous mean, whereas cowardice (deficiency) and rashness (excess) represented its vices. However, what is novel about Aristotle's notion of the mean is that he well recognized the importance of choosing a specific behavior or strategy based on the particular context at hand. Thus, the mean did not represent some absolute mathematical point between two extremes but rather a relative point based on the context as a person of "practical wisdom would determine it."

Although Aristotle's theory of virtue remains crucial in contemporary discussions on ethics and morality, the notion that there are virtuous ways of being that are associated with and lead to happiness is particularly important to us. In many ways, it would seem as if psychologists over the decades have attempted to study dispositions that have some theoretical or practical implication for attaining happiness. Accordingly, the study of personality has often been grounded in attempts to identify personality characteristics that are helpful or hurtful in trying to live a full and happy life. To that end, the study of various personality variables in modern psychology can be viewed as a continuation of a classic theme. In other words, much of the research on personality may be not unreasonably viewed as attempts to directly and indirectly identify and distinguish virtuous dispositions from vicious dispositions, human strengths from human weaknesses. However, by viewing personality simply in terms of dichotomies, the field as a whole may be unintentionally colluding to an oversimplification of personality characteristics and ignoring their important complexities.

A key point for us in developing the present volume was to provide some examples of why psychologists need to refrain from viewing personality characteristics as either a virtue or a vice and instead view characteristics involving both good and bad qualities depending on the specific context at hand and the choices or actions taken by an individual. It is not surprising that the handful of personality variables that have captured the attention of psychologists in recent decades have been those with relatively clear and direct implications for adjustment or maladjustment. For example, individual differences in self-esteem and optimism have primarily been considered as adaptive or virtuous, whereas pessimism and perfectionism have primarily been considered as maladaptive or vices. However, as Aristotle noted centuries ago, virtue and vice are relative. What may be a virtue to one individual may be a vice to another, and what may be a virtue to one individual at one time and place may be a vice for that individual at another time and place.

The notion that personality may serve as a vice for some individuals and as a virtue for others has support in the empirical literature. For example, studies on defensive pessimism have shown that some people harbor what is typically deemed as a vice, namely, negative expectations of the future (Norem & Cantor, 1986; Sanna, 1996). Yet if one takes the view that individuals may *use* their personalities as strategies to obtain certain outcomes (Cantor, 1990), then it is no surprise that pessimism gets some people motivated and results in obtaining desired goals. In short, pessimism is maintained and nurtured, not as a vice, but as a virtue (Norem, 2001).

As noted earlier, Aristotle defined virtues and vices as a function of personal agency. Thus, we believe that personalities, as strategies, do not possess any inherent quality but rather do acquire and maintain relative value for an individual based on how personally useful a given strategy was and is across situations. For some individuals, given their unique context, the use of pessimism may be a very useful and effective strategy to obtain certain desired goals, whereas it may be ineffective and associated with disengagement and depression for others.

Another way in which it would be helpful to get beyond an either–or view of personality utility is the growing realization that some personality characteristics embody facets that are both virtuous and vicious, or, in more lay terms, facets that are both helpful and harmful. To give one other example, studies on perfectionism over the past decade have focused on a negative view of this personality characteristic; that is, perfectionism has been seen as a vice rather than as a virtue. However, there is a growing literature suggesting that perfectionism may entail facets that are both adaptive and maladaptive. Hence, a given personality characteristic may engender more than one quality. In this way, we believe that other personality characteristics can also be most fruitfully understood to map the complexities and dynamics of human existence.

OVERVIEW OF THE PRESENT VOLUME

The present volume is broken down into two major sections. The first focuses on some of the personality variables that have traditionally been viewed as positive or as virtues. The general point of the chapters in this section is that a personality virtue can also be a personality vice. Kernis discusses in chapter 1 how recent studies on self-esteem, a popular and routinely viewed as positive personality variable, have indicated that there may be more than one type. In fact, Kernis intriguingly identifies eight different varieties of high self-esteem, ranging from defensive high self-esteem to stable high self-esteem. Beyond a consideration of these variations, Kernis also argues that varieties of self-esteem that are secure tend to be adaptive, whereas varieties that are fragile tend to be maladaptive.

Following the idea that what is generally viewed as a positive personality variable may not always be adaptive, Peterson and Vaidya focus on the study of optimism in chapter 2. They provide an excellent review of the literature on optimism from both a dispositional framework and from an attributional style framework. In addition, drawing from their own research and from other recent studies on unrealistic optimism, Peterson and Vaidya provide a critical discussion about the ways in which optimism may not be beneficial. As these authors make very clear, although optimism may in fact be positive in situations where a person can exert some control, it may not be adaptive to hold an optimistic stance in situations over which one has little or no control.

In chapter 3, Sternberg takes a closer look at intelligence. Beginning with a very lively and thoughtful appraisal of recent studies of intelligence, he argues that too much intelligence may not always be useful or adaptive. Sternberg outlines a balance theory of wisdom that reconciles some of the potential problems of being too intelligent. Within this insightful framework, intelligence is at best only one facet of wisdom. Once again, Sternberg points out that what is normally viewed as a virtue can also be a vice under certain circumstances.

Chapter 4 focuses on the many and varied potential hazards associated with personal striving and goal pursuits. King and Burton discuss in detail several ways in which personal goal pursuits may be hampered and ways in which this may not lead to reaching one's goal. Moreover, although these authors acknowledge that the negative aspects of goal pursuits are to some extent inevitable, they also argue that these aspects of goal pursuits are valuable if one is to appreciate the complexities and challenges that exist in the everyday world and in one's efforts to pursue personally relevant goals.

In chapter 5, Strube, Hanson, and Newman examine personal control. In providing a critical review of the literature on personal control, beginning with early studies on Type A behavior patterns to more recent studies on desire for control, these authors show that personal control involves both benefits and costs depending on the circumstances. As they note, there are many factors, some good and some bad, associated with the need to seek, exert, and maintain personal control in one's life.

The second section of this volume focuses on some personality variables that have traditionally been viewed as negative or as vices. The section begins with Norem's thoughtful examination of pessimism in chapter 6. Although pessimism is often viewed as a negative personality variable, Norem considers recent research on pessimism and, more specifically, reviews important works on defensive pessimism conducted by her and other researchers over the past decade. Norem clearly shows that defensive pessimism may actually serve as an adaptive and effective strategy to help regulate negative mood and increase performance for some individuals, depending on the specific context and conditions that are involved.

In chapter 7, Sanna, Stocker, and Clarke provide a critical examination of rumination. In reviewing the literature in this area, these authors point out that although ruminations have traditionally been thought of as negative, some research actually suggests that they can be functional for problem solving and other reasons. They outline several varieties of ruminative thoughts, some reactive and some goal based, and attempt to reconcile divergent findings in terms of their imagination, goals, and affect model.

In chapter 8, Chang critically examines the common notion that perfectionism is maladaptive. He looks at different models and measures used to study perfectionism and argues that although past studies have shown that perfectionism is maladaptive, more recent studies have begun to show that perfectionism may have both adaptive and maladaptive dimensions. As with each of the preceding perspectives, what has normally been viewed as a vice can also be viewed as a virtue.

In chapter 9, Watson and Casillas look carefully and insightfully at the prominent and broad dimension of neuroticism. They begin with a thoughtful review of past and current conceptualizations of neuroticism as a multifaceted biologically based personality variable. Watson and Casillas continue their chapter with a critical survey of the literature pointing to the costs of high neuroticism, followed by a thought-provoking discussion on the potential pitfalls of low neuroticism. Using a states-of-mind framework, they argue for the value and adaptiveness of moderate amounts of neuroticism in one's life.

We end the book with a context for understanding personality as virtue and vice. In chapter 10, Tennen and Affleck provide a very thoughtful discussion on the many different factors that need to be considered by researchers and scholars in viewing and studying personality as a virtue. They also make clear an implicit theme throughout this volume, namely, a critical need to exercise restraint and caution given recent efforts by some researchers to identify and promote human strengths or virtues. Following these thoughtful cautions, we conclude the book in chapter 11 with an appeal for researchers and scholars to appreciate the greater context in which personality has been studied in the past and present; we argue that it is only with an appreciation of the broader historical context, and balance, that the study of personality and adjustment may be best understood.

Of course, as with any volume of this nature, it becomes impossible to provide readers with an exhaustive survey of each and every personality variable that has been the object of some study or examination. Rather, our quite modest goal was to provide readers with a sampling of some of the personality variables that have had a major impact on our understanding of ourselves and of others over the years and to show readers how each may serve as both a virtue and a vice. Our underlying assumption is that many of the specific arguments offered in this volume for understanding the present sample of personality variables as virtue and as vice can also be equally applied to other personality variables that we did not include. The fact that particular variables were not included in the present volume also should not be taken to indicate that we presumed that they were of lesser importance in some way. Instead, we decided to sample personality variables that have received a good deal of recent attention, and in a way that would minimize overlap between the chapters. For example, one personality variable not included in the present volume, but which has gained considerable attention in recent years, has been hope. According to Snyder (2000), hope represents a personality variable that is believed to be associated with goal attainment and adjustment. Because the constructs of hope and optimism are related, at least to a certain degree, we believe that many of the thoughts raised in Peterson and Vaidya's chapter (chap. 2) on optimism can be meaningfully applied to our understanding of hope.

We planned this volume with a broad audience in mind. It is our expectation that this book will provoke new ways of thinking (and possibly doing something) about personality from a more balanced perspective among our research colleagues as well as among students just beginning to venture into the study of personality. We would be delighted to see as a consequence of this volume researchers asking with greater frequency questions such as "When might it be maladaptive to be optimistic?" or "Under what conditions is it good to be perfectionistic?" We hope that this volume also offers a useful resource for informing practitioners and educators of the rich complexities of personality in their work with others. Appreciating the rich diversity of personality as both a virtue and a vice may help prevent us from developing overly biased or unbalanced clinical or educational formulations and profiles and, in contrast, may help foster a genuine empathic connection with the clients and students we are privileged to serve. However, one does not need to be a researcher, a practitioner, or an educator to appreciate the broad theme running throughout this volume, namely, that personality variables can be both virtue and vice.

FINAL REMARKS: BALANCING THE WORLD AND OURSELVES

This volume focuses on a few of the most notable personality variables that have garnered the attention of researchers and scholars over the past several decades. As noted earlier, our goal was not to provide an exhaustive treatise on the virtue and vice of every personality variable known in modern personality theory; rather, our goal was to make explicit that personality variables that are presumed to be adaptive may also be maladaptive and that personality variables that are presumed to be maladaptive may also be adaptive. Our view lies in the utility of taking a more balanced perspective. Indeed, at a point in time in which some psychologists have become quite interested in identifying and studying human strengths (McCullough & Snyder, 2000; Seligman & Csikszentmihalyi, 2000), we present this volume to express our concerns over any unbalanced efforts to delineate what human virtues and vices are or should be. As Aristotle noted long ago, it is difficult to live a virtuous life because it is often difficult to determine the virtuous mean between its extremes. In that regard, we hope that this book provides a useful call for greater care and sensitivity in trying to understand human behavior in context and for appreciating the real complexities and challenges we all face in trying to live virtuous lives.

REFERENCES

Aristotle. (1908). *Nicomachean ethics* (W. D. Ross, Trans.). Oxford, England: Clarendon Press. (Original work written 350 BC)

Cantor, N. (1990). From thought to behavior: "Having" and "doing" in the study of personality and cognition. *American Psychologist, 45,* 735–750.

Chang, E. C. (2001). Optimism and pessimism: Moving beyond the most fundamental question of all. In E. C. Chang (Ed.), *Optimism and pessimism: Implications for theory, research, and practice* (pp. 3–12). Washington, DC: American Psychological Association.

McCullough, M. E., & Snyder, C. R. (2000). Classical sources of human strength: Revisiting an old home and building a new one. *Journal of Social and Clinical Psychology, 19,* 1–10.

Norem, J. K. (2001). *The positive power of negative thinking: Using "defensive pessimism" to harness anxiety and perform at your peak.* New York: Basic Books.

Norem, J. K., & Cantor, N. (1986). Defensive pessimism: Harnessing anxiety as motivation. *Journal of Personality and Social Psychology, 51,* 1208–1217.

Sanna, L. J. (1996). Defensive pessimism, optimism, and simulating alternatives: Some ups and downs of prefactual and counterfactual thinking. *Journal of Personality and Social Psychology, 71,* 1020–1036.

Seligman, M. E. P., & Csikszentmihalyi, M. (2000). Positive psychology: An introduction. *American Psychology, 55,* 5–14.

Snyder, C. R. (Ed.). (2000). *Handbook of hope: Theory, measures, and applications.* San Diego, CA: Academic Press.

I

POSITIVE PERSONALITIES: WHEN VIRTUE CAN BECOME VICE

1

HIGH SELF-ESTEEM:
A DIFFERENTIATED PERSPECTIVE

MICHAEL H. KERNIS

A few years ago, if someone had questioned the positive features of seeking and possessing high self-esteem, he or she may have been considered silly, stupid, or worse. After all, what could be wrong with liking oneself and thinking that one is a person of worth and value? Now, however, questions about the universal adaptiveness of high self-esteem are common. Is one's high self-esteem overinflated (Baumeister, Smart, & Boden, 1996)? Is one's high self-esteem fragile or contingent on the achievement of specific outcomes (Crocker & Wolfe, 2001; Kernis & Paradise, 2002b)? Is seeking high self-esteem a basic psychological need, the fulfillment of which is related to optimal psychological functioning (i.e., the self-enhancement motive)? Or, can seeking high self-esteem be so important to an individual that it interferes with need satisfaction and psychological adjustment? In this chapter I consider these and related questions with the goal of presenting a balanced view of high self-esteem and the motive to achieve and maintain it.

Preparation of this chapter and much of the research reported herein were supported by National Science Foundation Grant SBR-9618882. I thank Brian Goldman for his critical contributions to the conceptualization of authenticity offered here.

TWO DIFFERENT KINDS OF HIGH SELF-ESTEEM

As I have described elsewhere (e.g., Kernis, 2003; Kernis & Paradise, 2002a), two different perspectives have emerged on the nature of high self-esteem. One perspective is espoused mostly by social psychologists, whereas the other perspective is espoused mostly by clinical and personality psychologists with a humanistic orientation. Rather than view one perspective as correct and the other as incorrect, I believe that each perspective is correct in that it characterizes some individuals with high self-esteem. I first present these two broad perspectives. Then, I discuss four different ways to distinguish between them and the evidence supportive of each. Much of this evidence is recent; some of it has yet to be published. However, taken as a whole, it offers strong support for understanding high self-esteem as differentiated, rather than monolithic, in nature.

Secure High Self-Esteem

One view of high self-esteem is that it reflects positive feelings of self-worth that are well anchored and secure and that positively relate to a wide range of psychological health and well-being indexes. Its roots lie in the writings and research of clinical and personality psychologists with humanistic inclinations (e.g., Rogers, 1959). From this vantage point, people with high self-esteem like, value, and accept themselves, "warts and all." They do not feel a need to be superior to others; instead, they are satisfied with being on an equal plane with others (Rosenberg, 1965). Attempts to bolster their feelings of worth through self-promoting or self-protective strategies are rare, given that their feelings of self-worth are not easily challenged. In essence, these individuals typically experience everyday positive and negative outcomes in ways that do not implicate their global feelings of worth or value. Throughout this chapter, I refer to this perspective as describing *secure* high self-esteem.

Fragile High Self-Esteem

The second, contrasting, view of high self-esteem is that it reflects positive feelings of self-worth that are fragile and vulnerable to threats and that relate to many different types of self-protective or self-enhancement strategies. This view is reflected in much of the self-esteem research conducted by social and personality psychologists in recent years. Studies have shown, for example, that individuals with high self-esteem may take great pride in their successes ("I am a genius") yet deny any involvement in their failures ("The test was unfair"; Fitch, 1970), that they denigrate individuals who threaten their (or their group's) sense of value and worth (Crocker, Thompson, McGraw, & Ingerman, 1987), and that they create obstacles to successful performance so that their competencies will seem especially noteworthy should they subsequently succeed anyway (Tice, 1991). Also, people with high self-esteem whose egos have been threatened engage in maladaptive self-regulatory processes (e.g., taking excessive risks by overestimating their competency) that result in unnecessary slumps in performance (Baumeister, Heatherton, & Tice, 1993). Findings such as these suggest that individuals with high self-esteem are especially caught up in how they feel about themselves and that they will go to great lengths to bolster, maintain, and enhance these self-feelings. Throughout this chapter, I refer to this perspective as describing *fragile* high self-esteem (cf. Horney, 1950).

A Resolution

A few researchers seem to have dismissed the existence of *secure* high self-esteem (e.g., Baumeister, Tice, & Hutton, 1989), claiming instead that high self-esteem reflects an aggressively self-enhancing presentational style. I disagree with this dismissal and instead argue that both secure and fragile forms of high self-esteem exist. To acknowledge their existence, however, raises the difficult issue of how to determine which form is operative. As I have noted elsewhere (Kernis, in press; Kernis & Paradise, 2002a), traditional measures of self-esteem are ill suited for this purpose. Rosenberg's (1965) Self-Esteem Scale, one of the most widely used and well-validated measures of self-esteem (Blascovich & Tomaka, 1991), includes items such as "I feel that I have a number of good qualities" and "I feel that I am a person of worth, at least on an equal basis with others." High self-esteem is reflected by strong agreement to these items. However, taken alone, this agreement does not inform one whether the person's high self-esteem is secure or fragile. The same is true for other self-esteem measures. Fortunately, recent theory and evidence suggest four ways to distinguish between secure and fragile high self-esteem. Each way is based on the notion that multiple forms of high self-esteem exist that vary in the extent to which they relate to psychological adjustment and well-being. After giving a brief overview of these multiple forms of high self-esteem, I discuss each in greater detail.

DISTINGUISHING SECURE FROM FRAGILE HIGH SELF-ESTEEM

Table 1.1 provides a brief description of the multiple forms of high self-esteem that I discuss in this chapter.[1] A common theme these forms share is that although two people may report high self-esteem, the nature of their self-esteem and how it relates to their psychological functioning may

---

[1]Narcissism may reflect another form of fragile high self-esteem. I discuss this issue elsewhere (Kernis, 2001) and therefore do not consider it here.

TABLE 1.1
Varieties of High Self-Esteem

Variety	Description
Defensive high	Report positive feelings of self-worth, but inside harbor negative feelings.
Genuine high	Report and feel positive feelings of self-worth.
High explicit	Conscious feelings of positive self-worth.
Implicit positive	Nonconscious feelings of positive self-worth.
Contingent high	Positive feelings of self-worth that are dependent on achieving specific outcomes, meeting expectations, matching standards, etc.
True high	Secure, positive feelings of self-worth that do not need continual validation.
Unstable high	Typical feelings of positive self-worth accompanied by immediate feelings of self-worth that exhibit considerable short-term fluctuations.
Stable high	Typical feelings of positive self-worth accompanied by immediate feelings of self-worth that exhibit little or no short-term fluctuations.

be quite different. For example, people who report high self-esteem may or may not be masking negative feelings that they are unwilling to acknowledge (*defensive* high self-esteem) or of which they are unaware they possess (*high explicit/low implicit* self-esteem). In other instances, people may or may not be basing their high self-esteem on the extent to which they are successful at achieving specific outcomes. If they are, their high self-esteem is much more tenuous (*contingent* self-esteem) than if they are not (*true* self-esteem). Finally, people who report that they typically have high self-esteem may have immediate feelings of self-worth that fluctuate considerably (*unstable* self-esteem) or little, if at all (*stable* self-esteem).

These forms of high self-esteem are not mutually exclusive. In fact, possessing self-esteem that is always totally without aspects that are defensive, contingent, unstable, and so forth, is probably rare. Put differently, although people may desire high self-esteem that is true, genuine, and stable, it is unlikely that all will be completely and permanently successful. Recognizing this can help each of us to learn more about ourselves and the ways that we deal with threatening information. For example, it can help us to understand that reacting to a perceived insult with an intense and anger-laden counterattack does not necessarily come from strength or satisfaction with oneself; instead, it may reflect damage control to protect fragile, defensive, or contingent self-esteem.

Research on these components of self-esteem is still in its infancy. Nonetheless, I believe that they provide considerable insight into the nature of high self-esteem. As noted previously, one perspective suggests that individuals with high self-esteem will go to great lengths to bolster and promote their positive self-feelings, that is, that high self-esteem can be fragile and vulnerable to challenge. As I describe shortly, existing theory and research suggest that engaging in self-aggrandizing and self-protective strategies (e.g., boasting and excuse making, derogating others, easily getting angry) are associated with high self-esteem that is accompanied by defensive, contingent, nonconscious negative, or unstable components. A second perspective suggests that individuals with high self-esteem are not especially defensive or self-promoting because they are happy and content with themselves and accepting of their weaknesses. As I describe, existing theory and research suggest that secure high self-esteem reflects the relative absence of hidden or nonconscious negativity, contingencies, or instability. I turn now to discussions of these various forms of fragile and secure high self-esteem.

Is the Person Telling the Truth?

One way to distinguish between secure and fragile high self-esteem is to determine whether respondents misrepresented their self-feelings when completing the self-esteem measure. Some people, out of immense desires to be accepted by others, are unwilling to admit to possessing negative self-feelings. Called *defensive* high self-esteem many years ago (Horney, 1950; Schneider & Turkat, 1975), it is believed to trigger heightened efforts to undermine self-threatening information and to magnify claims of personal strengths in domains unrelated to the content of the threat (Schneider & Turkat, 1975). Qualities such as these suggest that defensive high self-esteem is one manifestation of fragile high self-esteem. In contrast, *genuine* high self-esteem reflects the honest reporting of one's inner positive self-feelings. Without the concerns about social acceptance that characterize their defensive counterparts, individuals with genuine high self-esteem are less threatened by negative evaluative information. Genuine high self-esteem is thus considered one manifestation of secure high self-esteem. Although genuine and defensive high self-esteem are appealing constructs, they have not generated a large body of empirical findings. The findings that do exist, however, support the distinction (e.g., Schneider & Turkat, 1975).

Do the Person's Conscious and Nonconscious Feelings of Self-Worth Match?

A second way to distinguish secure from fragile high self-esteem involves a consideration of both conscious and nonconscious feelings of self-worth. Specifically, some individuals with high self-esteem may report favorable feelings of self-worth yet simultaneously hold negative self-feelings of which they are unaware (and not just that they are unwilling to report). Although the notion of nonconscious self-feelings is not new, only in recent years has it received substantive attention, aided by the development of sophisticated computer-based methodologies.

Epstein and Morling (1995) suggested that when people possess high explicit (conscious) self-esteem, but negative implicit (nonconscious) self-esteem, they often will react very defensively to potentially negative evaluative information. Elsewhere, my colleagues and I (Abend et al., 2002; Kernis, 2003; Kernis & Goldman, 1999; Kernis & Paradise, 2002a) have suggested that *high explicit self-esteem* coupled with *negative implicit self-esteem* is fragile and so may relate to defensive and self-aggrandizing strategies without explicit threats. In contrast, when explicit and implicit self-esteem both are favorable, one's high self-esteem is secure, making it less necessary to defend against real or imagined threats or to flaunt one's strengths.

A variety of techniques have been used to examine individual differences in implicit self-esteem and its implications for psychological functioning (for descriptions, see Farnham, Greenwald, & Banaji, 1999; Hetts, Sakuma, & Pelham, 1999; Koole, Dijksterhuis, & van Knippenberg, 2001). Surprisingly, these techniques have been shown not to correlate highly with one another (Bosson, Swann, & Pennebaker, 2000). An alternative approach is to manipulate implicit self-esteem by exposing people to positive or negative self-esteem relevant stimuli (e.g., words such as *worthless*, *capable*, *likeable*, *insecure*) at speeds too fast to be consciously recognized.

My colleagues and I used this alternative approach in two recent studies (Abend et al., 2002). In the first study, we examined whether manipulating implicit self-esteem so that it was discrepant with individuals' explicit self-esteem would heighten self-serving responses (compared with congruent explicit and implicit self-esteem). As anticipated, self-serving responses were greater among individuals with high self-esteem who were presented with negative self-relevant words (high explicit/negative implicit self-esteem), compared with those who were presented with positive self-relevant words (high explicit/positive implicit self-esteem). It is interesting that low explicit/positive implicit self-esteem also related to more self-serving responses than did low explicit/negative implicit self-esteem. This pattern was reflected in a significant Explicit Self-Esteem × Implicit Self-Esteem interaction (neither main effect was significant).

In a second study, we examined whether manipulating implicit self-esteem so that it was discrepant with individuals' explicit self-esteem would heighten out-group derogation (as compared with congruent implicit and explicit self-esteem). This pattern would be expected if discrepancies between implicit and explicit self-esteem reflect fragility that can be bolstered by derogating out-group members (Fein & Spencer, 1996; Greenberg, Solomon, & Pyszczynski, 1997). In this study, Christian women rated a Jewish "job applicant's" personality and job suitability. As anticipated, applicant ratings were lower among individuals with high explicit self-esteem who were presented negative self-relevant words (high explicit/negative implicit) compared with those who were presented positive words (high explicit/positive implicit). Conversely, among individuals with low self-esteem, ratings of the applicant were lower among those exposed to positive words (low explicit/positive explicit) compared with those exposed to negative words (low explicit/negative explicit). Thus, compared with congruent implicit and explicit self-esteem, discrepant implicit and explicit self-esteem was associated with greater derogation of an out-group member. As in the first study, this pattern was reflected in an Explicit Self-Esteem × Implicit Self-Esteem interaction (in the absence of any significant main effects).

The findings from the Abend et al. (2002) studies are among the first demonstrations that discrepant explicit/implicit self-esteem is associated with heightened self-serving and self-protective responses. With respect to the present discussion, they support the contention that some forms of high self-esteem can be characterized as fragile whereas other forms can be characterized as secure. Specifically, whereas high explicit self-esteem that is accompanied by negative implicit self-esteem is fragile, high explicit self-esteem that is accompanied by positive implicit self-esteem is secure.

Is the Person's High Self-Esteem Dependent on Certain Outcomes?

A third way to distinguish between fragile and secure high self-esteem is to determine the extent to which individuals' feelings of self-worth are dependent on the achievement of certain outcomes (Deci & Ryan, 1995). For someone with *contingent* high self-esteem, preoccupations with one's standings on specific evaluative dimensions (e.g., "How attractive am I?") and how one is viewed by others ("Do people think I am competent?"), together with engagement in a continual process of setting and meeting evaluative standards, constitute a core aspect of everyday life. High self-esteem that is contingent is fragile because it is highly dependent on the individual's success at satisfying relevant criteria. If one is continually successful, then high self-esteem may seem secure and well anchored. As Deci and Ryan (1995) emphasized, however, it is not, because the need for continual validation drives the person to attain more and more successes. Furthermore, should these successes cease, the person's self-esteem may plummet.

In contrast, Deci and Ryan (1995) proposed that *true* high self-esteem reflects feelings of self-worth that are well-anchored and secure, that do not depend on the attainment of specific outcomes, and that do not require continual validation. Furthermore, they suggested that true high self-esteem develops when one's actions are self-determined and congruent with one's inner, core self rather than a reflection of externally imposed or internally based demands. Activities are chosen and goals are undertaken because they are of interest and importance. In addition, true self-esteem is fostered by relationships with others that are characterized by mutual acceptance, intimacy, and understanding (Ryan, 1993).

Kernis and Paradise (2002b) reasoned that people with highly contingent self-esteem would be easily threatened by an insulting evaluation and would deal with this threat by becoming especially angry and hostile. To test this hypothesis, they used a measure of contingent self-esteem (the Contingent Self-Esteem Scale, Paradise & Kernis, 1999) that focuses on matching standards, attaining performance outcomes, and receiving positive evaluations from others. Through random assignment, some women received an evaluation that contained insulting statements about their appearance and mannerisms, whereas other women received a generally positive evaluation. The results showed that the more contingent women's self-esteem, the more intense their anger in response to the insulting treatment. This effect emerged with the impact of self-esteem level controlled.

Neighbors, Larimer, Geisner, and Knee (2001) found that among college students, the more contingent their self-esteem (as assessed by the Paradise & Kernis, 1999, measure), the more they reported drinking alcohol to enhance their mood, improve their social functioning, prevent peer rejection, and cope with their problems. In addition, contingent self-esteem was related to greater frequency of alcohol consumption and to alcohol-related problems.

Other research suggests that people may vary in the specific contingencies on which they base their self-esteem. Crocker, Sommers, and Luhtanen (2002) examined the relation between domain-specific contingent self-esteem and college seniors' reactions to being accepted or rejected from graduate schools to which they had applied. Their findings indicated that the state self-esteem of individuals whose self-esteem was contingent on academic competence was especially likely to rise with news of acceptance and decline with news of rejection. None of the other contingencies showed similar effects, suggesting that the match between life events and particular self-esteem contingencies can be important (for further discussion of this issue, see Crocker & Park, 2002). Crocker (2002) reported findings that the contingencies of social approval and physical attractiveness were predictive of depressive symptoms among college freshman. Crocker and Wolfe (2001) found that common domains of contingencies among college students include academic competence, social acceptance, physical appearance, God's love, power over others, and self-reliance. Among children and young adolescents, common contingency domains include physical appearance, social acceptance, and competence (Harter, 1998).

Existing research and theory offer encouraging initial support for the construct of contingent self-esteem, its assessment, and its implications for distinguishing between fragile and secure high self-esteem. However, it remains for future researchers to uncover many of these implications. The findings reported here reflect main effects of contingent self-esteem (and not an interaction with self-esteem level), raising the possibility that contingent self-esteem may have uniform effects among individuals with either high or low self-esteem. At least two measurement instruments are available (Crocker & Wolfe, 2001; Paradise & Kernis, 1999). Paradise and Kernis's (1999) measure emphasizes the overall degree of contingent self-esteem per se, whereas Crocker and Wolfe's (2001) measure focuses on specific domains of self-esteem contingencies. Both are likely to be useful to investigators as they pursue the implications of contingent self-esteem for various aspects of psychological functioning and well-being (for further discussion of this issue, see Kernis, in press).

Do the Person's Current, Contextually Based Feelings of Self-Worth Fluctuate?

A fourth way to distinguish between secure and fragile high self-esteem is based on the extent to which a person's current feelings of self-worth fluctuate across time and situations. These short-term fluctuations in one's immediate, contextually based feelings of self-worth reflect the degree to which one's self-esteem is unstable; the greater the fluctuations, the more unstable one's self-esteem. *Stability* of self-esteem is distinct from *level* of self-esteem in that the latter refers to the positivity of one's typical or general feelings of self-worth (for reviews, see Greenier, Kernis, & Waschull, 1995; Kernis, 1993; Kernis & Goldman, 2002; Kernis & Waschull, 1995).

Past research has shown that compared with people who have stable self-esteem, people with unstable self-esteem (a) experience greater increases in depressive symptoms when faced with daily hassles (Kernis et al., 1998), (b) have self-feelings that are more affected by everyday negative and positive events (Greenier et al., 1999), (c) take a more self-esteem protective (therefore, less mastery oriented) stance toward learning (Waschull & Kernis, 1996), (d) focus relatively more on the self-esteem threatening aspects of aversive interpersonal events (Waschull & Kernis, 1996), (e) have more impoverished self-concepts (Campbell et al., 1996; Kernis, Paradise, Whitaker et al., 2000), and (f) consume alcohol more so as a function of the frequency of daily events that occur (Paradise, 2002).

More important for the present purposes, other findings point to the utility of using stability of self-esteem to distinguish between fragile and secure forms of high self-esteem. Specifically, research has shown that people with unstable high self-esteem are more defensive and self-aggrandizing than are their stable high self-esteem counterparts, yet they are lower in psychological health and well-being. Kernis, Grannemann, and Barclay (1989) reported that individuals with unstable high self-esteem scored the highest on several well-validated anger and hostility inventories, individuals with stable high self-esteem scored the lowest, and stable and unstable low self-esteem individuals scored between these two extremes. Other research has shown that compared with individuals with stable high self-esteem, people with unstable high self-esteem say that they would be more likely to boast about a success to their friends (Kernis, Greenier, Herlocker, Whisenhunt, & Abend, 1997); after an actual success, they were also more likely to claim that they did so in spite of the operation of performance inhibiting factors (Kernis, Grannemann, & Barclay, 1992).

As expected if unstable high self-esteem is fragile, these enhanced tendencies to engage in self-protective and self-enhancing strategies do not translate into greater psychological well-being. Paradise and Kernis (2002) administered Ryff's (1989) measure of psychological well-being to a sample of college students who also completed measures of level and stability of self-esteem. Their findings showed that compared with individuals who possess stable high self-esteem, individuals with unstable high self-esteem reported lower autonomy, environmental mastery, purpose in life, self-acceptance, and positive relations with others. Stated differently, whereas individuals with stable high self-esteem reported that they functioned autonomously, possessed a clear sense of meaning in their lives, related effectively within both their physical and social environments, and were highly self-accepting, the same was less true of individuals with unstable high self-esteem.

One interpretation of these findings is that whereas possessing secure feelings of self-positive worth may provide the basis for functioning effectively in various realms, fragile self-feelings may undermine effective functioning. This undermining may occur directly or indirectly via heightened defensiveness, anger, and emotional reactivity (Greenier et al., 1999; Kernis, Brown, & Brody, 2000; Kernis & Paradise, 2002b). Stated differently, individuals with unstable high self-esteem who frequently use self-aggrandizing and self-protective strategies may overshadow more effective responses, strain interpersonal relations, and curtail a sense of meaning and purpose (cf. Tennen & Affleck, 1993). A second interpretation is that whereas effective functioning in a variety of domains may foster well-anchored self-feelings, ineffective functioning may undermine the security and favorableness of one's self-feelings. In this regard, Deci and Ryan (1995) argued that true high self-esteem develops naturally out of the satisfaction of one's needs for self-determination, competence, and relatedness. Consistent with this view, Paradise and Kernis's (2002) findings indicate that individuals with stable high self-esteem report better functioning in domains related to the satisfaction of these needs than do individuals with unstable high self-esteem. A third interpretation emphasizes the reciprocal influences that self-esteem and other aspects of psychological well-being may have on each other.

Other researchers have found that self-esteem stability has important implications for relationship quality. A considerable amount of research has shown that low self-esteem individuals are prone to act in ways that are detrimental to their intimate relationships (Murray & Holmes, 2000). Although this work is very important, the analysis offered here suggests that fragile high self-esteem may also be associated with suboptimal relationship functioning. Specifically, being in a relationship with someone with fragile high self-esteem may be akin to "walking on eggs"; even the hint of a slight may be blown out of proportion and result in defensiveness and hurt feelings.

A recent study conducted by Kernis, Paradise, and Goldman (2003) substantiates this claim. In addition to measures of stability and level of self-esteem, participants completed a questionnaire designed to assess their reactions to relatively innocuous positive and negative behaviors that their partners might engage in (the Relationship Reaction Inventory, RRI). The RRI consists of 15 scenarios: 9 negative and 6 positive. Respondents rate the likelihood that they would engage in each of four possible responses. An example scenario is as follows: "Your partner gives you a nice birthday present, but it isn't what you subtly let him or her know that you really wanted. How likely is it that you would . . . ?" Two response options reflect heightened self-investment in the event. Of these, one (*personalizing*) involves magnifying the event's positive or negative implications for the self (e.g., "Think that you must not be important enough to him/her"). The other (*reciprocating*) involves getting even to deal with the self-esteem threatening aspects of negative events (e.g., "In the future give him/her a present other than what you know he or she clearly wants"). For positive events, the intent was to create *reciprocating* items that captured anxiety- or insecurity-driven attempts to "even things." The two remaining response options were designed to capture reactions or interpretations that did not involve the "investment of self." Of these, one (*benign*) involves a transient external (usually partner-based) explanation (e.g., "Think that circumstances beyond his or her control must have prevented it"). The other (*minimize*) involves taking the event at face value, that is, not making a big deal of it (e.g., "Enjoy the present you got").

The results strongly supported the predictions. Significant (or marginally so) Self-Esteem Level × Self-Esteem Stability interactions emerged on seven of eight response option indexes. For negative scenarios, predicted values indicated that among individuals with high self-esteem, the more unstable their self-esteem, the more they endorsed reciprocating and personalizing responses, and the less they endorsed benign or minimizing responses; individuals with low self-esteem, regardless of self-esteem stability, fell within these two extremes. With respect to positive scenarios, the results were no less interesting, although they were a bit more complex. For benign and minimizing reactions, the results conceptually replicated those found for negative events. Specifically, among individuals with high self-esteem, the more unstable their self-esteem, the less they endorsed minimizing and benign explanations. Contrary to expectations, however, a marginal Self-Esteem Stability × Self-Esteem Level interaction emerged for reciprocating reactions, suggesting that among individuals with high self-esteem, the more stable their self-esteem, the more they endorsed reciprocating partners' positive behaviors. Close examination of our items suggested that they focused primarily on communally based behaviors. Although a strict interpretation of the communal orientation would suggest that reciprocation is unnecessary (and, in fact, detrimental in some contexts), our participants may have interpreted the scenarios differently. No effects emerged for personalizing explanations for positive events (Kernis et al., 2003).

The defensive and hostile reaction styles displayed by individuals with unstable high self-esteem presumably had cumulative adverse effects on the development of intimacy, trust, and security in their relationships. Individuals with unstable high self-esteem presumably felt barriers to increased intimacy with their partners, although they may have been unaware that these barriers were partly of their own making. Moreover, these barriers could have undermined their relationship quality and satisfaction. Consistent with this line of reasoning, additional findings indicated that individuals with unstable high self-esteem rated their relationship quality lower than did individuals with stable high self-esteem. In addition, Kernis et al. (2003) obtained support for the mediating role of personalizing and reciprocating responses to negative scenarios on the RRI. Specifically, when responses on these items were controlled, the Self-Esteem Stability × Self-Esteem interaction that in part was reflected in lower relationship quality among individuals with unstable as compared with stable high self-esteem no longer was significant (Kernis et al., 2003). An important direction for future research is to incorporate partners into the analysis. Many provocative questions can then be addressed. For example, are partners of individuals with unstable high self-esteem more likely to engage in potentially threatening behaviors than are partners of individuals with stable high self-esteem? Do the former partners generally treat their mates with less respect than do the latter, so that Kernis et al.'s (2003) participants' responses reflected reality to some extent? That is, do partners get caught up in the cycle of overreaction and defensiveness that characterizes individuals with fragile high self-esteem and become active participants themselves? Answers to questions such as these will provide important information about how processes associated with fragile and secure high self-esteem may undermine or promote the development of mutually satisfying intimate relationships.

Striving for High Self-Esteem

People have at their disposal many pre-emptive and reactive strategies to ward off the unfavorable implications of potential threats or to accentuate the favorable implications of positive events (Hoyle, Kernis, Leary, & Baldwin, 1999). *Pre-emptive strategies* are those used in advance either to reduce the likelihood of potential threats or to maximize the likelihood of positive events. Included in this category is *defensive pessimism* (Norem & Cantor, 1986), which refers to excessively lowering one's performance expectations to avoid being disappointed by failure, and *self-handicapping*, which refers to creating or claiming impediments to personal success so that subsequent failure can be attributed to the impediment whereas subsequent success can be attributed more strongly to one's talents or skills (Berglas, 1985).

The research and theory reviewed in this chapter suggest that use of these strategies may be linked to the possession of fragile as opposed to secure high self-esteem. Does this mean that engaging in protecting and enhancing one's self-esteem are necessarily maladaptive and negatively related to psychological functioning and well-being? I agree with Crocker and Park (in press; see also Tennen & Affleck, 1993), who argued that although such strategies may be adaptive in the short run by helping to alleviate distress, they are likely to be maladaptive over time by interfering with learning and creativity, undermining relationships with others, and promoting unhealthy behaviors. Moreover, they are likely to reflect the lack of (and even interfere with the) satisfaction of one's basic needs for competence, self-determination, and relatedness (Deci & Ryan, 2000; Kernis, 2000).

In much of the social psychology literature, defensive and self-promoting strategies are viewed as markers of healthy psychological functioning (Taylor & Brown, 1988; see also Tennen & Affleck, 1993). At first blush, then, research showing that fragile high self-esteem is associated with heightened use of such strategies may seem to contradict research that links unstable high self-esteem to less than optimal psychological functioning. It is important to note that this apparent contradiction can be resolved by viewing heightened use of defensive and self-promoting strategies as compensatory reactions to fundamental need thwarting. In other words, rather than viewing defensive and self-promotion strategies as reflecting normal, healthy functioning, an understanding of fragile self-esteem and its relation to substitute needs and compensatory activities suggests another, more compelling, interpretation. Namely, Deci and Ryan (2000) identified heightened use of these strategies as stemming from insecurity, fragility, and suboptimal functioning that emerges when satisfaction of one's fundamental needs for competence, self-determination, and relatedness are thwarted. In short, the quest for high self-esteem may reflect a substitute need rather than a basic or fundamental one. I am not suggesting that wanting to feel good about oneself is wrong; I am suggesting that when feeling good about oneself becomes a *prime directive*, then excessive self-protection and self-promotion are likely to follow, and the resultant self-esteem is likely to be fragile rather than secure (see also Kernis, 2000).

I believe that a more fruitful approach to achieving secure high self-esteem is to foster what Brian Goldman and I refer to as *authenticity* (Goldman & Kernis, 2002; Kernis, in press). We characterize authenticity as the unobstructed operation of one's true, or core self in one's daily enterprise. In our view, authenticity has four discriminable components, each of which we measure with our Authenticity Inventory (Goldman & Kernis, 2001): (a) awareness, (b) unbiased processing, (c) behavior, and (d) relational orientation. The *awareness* component involves awareness of, and trust in, one's motives, feelings, desires, and self-relevant cognitions. It includes, but is not limited to, being aware of one's strengths and weaknesses, trait characteristics, and emotions (e.g., "I find it important to recognize my true feelings even if they are unpleasant"). The *unbiased processing* component involves objectivity and acceptance of one's positive and negative aspects. It involves *not* denying, distorting, or ignoring private knowledge, internal experiences, and externally based self-evaluative information (e.g., "I do not exaggerate my strengths to myself; I tend to find it easy to pretend that I do not have any faults" [reversed]). The *behavior* component involves acting according to one's values, preferences, and needs as opposed to acting merely to please others, attain rewards, or avoid punishments (e.g., "I am willing to wear the right social mask for the right social occasion if it will get me what I want" [reversed]). The *relational orientation* component involves valuing and achieving openness and truthfulness in one's close relationships (e.g., "I place a great deal of importance on close others understanding who I truly am").

Although the scale is still in development, I can report initial data involving a sample of approximately 70 individuals (Goldman & Kernis, 2002). Total authenticity scores were positively related to life satisfaction and high self-esteem and negatively related to contingent self-esteem and negative affect. Subscale analyses revealed that life satisfaction was positively related to the Awareness, Unbiased Processing (marginally), and Relational subscales; self-esteem level was positively related to the Awareness and Behavioral subscales; contingent self-esteem was negatively related to the Behavior subscale; and negative affect was negatively related to the Awareness and Relational subscales.

Goldman and I (Goldman & Kernis, 2002; Kernis, in press) believe that authenticity is reciprocally related to optimal self-esteem in that it provides both the foundation for achieving optimal self-esteem and the processes through which optimal self-esteem relates to psychological and interpersonal adjustment. Elsewhere (Kernis, in press), I have suggested that optimal self-esteem involves favorable feelings of self-worth that naturally arise from dealing successfully with life challenges, incorporating one's authentic self as a source of input to behavioral choices, and possessing relationships in which one is valued for whom one is, not for one's achievements. It is characterized by the relative absence of defensiveness, that is, the unwillingness to divulge negative behaviors or self-aspects out of strong desires to be liked. Moreover, it is characterized by favorable implicit feelings of self-worth, built up from years of positive associations between self and one's actions, contextual factors, and one's interpersonal relationships. Conversely, optimal self-esteem is characterized by not being dependent on specific outcomes or achievements (it is not contingent) and its contextual component does not exhibit substantial fluctuations (it is stable). As noted, my colleagues and I are developing a measure of individual differences in authenticity, and we will examine its implications for optimal self-esteem processes and psychological well-being.

CONCLUDING COMMENTS

The literature reviewed in this chapter reinforces the view that self-esteem has multiple components. I believe that all of these components must be taken into account for self-esteem theory and research to progress. Specifically, I believe that they are of particular importance in distinguishing between fragile and secure forms of high self-esteem. One question deserving future attention is the extent to which these various forms of high self-esteem covary within individuals. Other important questions pertain to the extent to which these various components have similar implications for interpersonal relations, psychological health, and well-being.[2]

Is high self-esteem an asset or a liability? I have attempted to answer this question on the basis of whether high self-esteem is predominantly secure or fragile. High self-esteem that is secure is an asset; high self-esteem that is fragile too often is a liability. Furthermore, I believe that the construct of authenticity will be of great value in understanding the processes and mechanisms that make high self-esteem an asset. My hope is that simple views on the nature and value of self-esteem will give way to more complex, differentiated views, such as those discussed in this chapter.

REFERENCES

Abend, T., Kernis, M. H., Paradise, A. W., Goldman, B. M., Shrira, I., & Hampton, C. (2002). *Discrepancies between explicit and implicit self-esteem and self-serving responses*. Manuscript submitted for publication.

---

[2]Historically, defensive high self-esteem has been considered a variant of high self-esteem (i.e., false high self-esteem) and it is treated as such in this chapter. However, it can also be characterized as a variant of low self-esteem given that individuals' privately held true negative feelings are replaced publicly by false positive feelings. Likewise, high explicit/negative implicit self-esteem can be thought of as a variant of either high or low self-esteem, depending on one's interpretive framework. I do not believe that this is the case for unstable and contingent high self-esteem, however. Unstable high self-esteem reflects favorable typical feelings of self-worth that are accompanied by fluctuations in current, contextually based feelings of self-worth. It is important to note that these fluctuations may involve differing degrees of positive self-feelings and not negative self-feelings (Greenier et al., 1999). Likewise, contingent high self-esteem may involve continually high levels of self-esteem provided that contingencies are continually satisfied. What differentiates these fragile forms of high self-esteem from their secure counterparts (stable or true self-esteem, respectively) is that they are not well anchored and secure; instead, they require continual validation. These considerations suggest another reason that it is important for future research to incorporate the measures of self-esteem fragility discussed in this chapter. Specifically, if findings obtained for defensively high and high explicit/negative implicit self-esteem are comparable to those obtained for unstable and contingent high self-esteem, my confidence that the former reflect variants of high self-esteem will be bolstered. In addition, examination of these various self-esteem components may shed light on whether some forms of low self-esteem are more adaptive than others.

Baumeister, R. F., Heatherton, T. F., & Tice, D. M. (1993). When ego threats lead to self-regulation failure: Negative consequences of high self-esteem. *Journal of Personality and Social Psychology, 64,* 141–156.

Baumeister, R. F., Smart, L., & Boden, J. M. (1996). Relation of threatened egotism to violence and aggression: The dark side of high self-esteem. *Psychological Review, 103,* 5–33.

Baumeister, R. F., Tice, D. M., & Hutton, D. G. (1989). Self-presentation motivations and personality differences in self-esteem. *Journal of Personality, 57,* 547–579.

Berglas, S. (1985). Self-handicapping and self-handicappers: A cognitive/attributional model of interpersonal self-protective behavior. In R. Hogan & W. H. Jones (Eds.), *Perspectives in personality* (Vol. 1, pp. 235–270). Greenwich, CT: JAI Press.

Blascovich, J., & Tomaka, J. (1991). Measures of self-esteem. In J. P. Robinson, P. R. Shaver, & L. S. Wrightsman (Eds.), *Measures of personality and social psychological attitudes* (Vol. 1, pp. 115–160). New York: Academic Press.

Bosson, J. K., Swann, W. B. Jr., & Pennebaker, J. W. (2000). Stalking the perfect measure of implicit self-esteem: The blind men and the elephant revisited? *Journal of Personality and Social Psychology, 79,* 631–642.

Campbell, J. D., Trapnell, P. D., Heine, S. J., Katz, I. M., Lavallee, L. F., & Lehman, D. R. (1996). Self-concept clarity: Measurement, personality correlates, and cultural boundaries. *Journal of Personality and Social Psychology, 70,* 141–156.

Crocker, J. (2002). Contingencies of self-worth: Implications for self-regulation and psychological vulnerability. *Self and Identity, 1,* 143–149.

Crocker, J., & Park, L. E. (2002). Seeking self-esteem: Construction, maintenance, and protection of self-worth. In M. Leary & J. Tangney (Eds.), *Handbook of self and identity* (pp. 291–313). New York: Guilford Press.

Crocker, J., Sommers, S. R., & Luhtanen, R. K. (2002). Hopes dashed and dreams fulfilled: Contingencies of self-worth and admissions to graduate school. *Personality and Social Psychology Bulletin, 28,* 1275–1286.

Crocker, J., Thompson, L. L., McGraw, K. M., & Ingerman, C. (1987). Downward comparison, prejudice and evaluations of others: Effects of self-esteem and threat. *Journal of Personality and Social Psychology, 52,* 907–916.

Crocker, J., & Wolfe, C. T. (2001). Contigencies of self-worth. *Psychological Review, 108,* 593–623.

Deci, E. L., & Ryan, R. M. (1995). Human agency: The basis for true self-esteem. In M. Kernis (Ed.), *Efficacy, agency, and self-esteem* (pp. 31–50). New York: Plenum.

Deci, E. L., & Ryan, R. M. (2000). The "what" and "why" of goal pursuits: Human needs and the self-determination of behavior. *Psychological Inquiry, 11,* 227–268.

Epstein, S., & Morling, B. (1995). Is the self motivated to do more than enhance and/or verify itself? In M. H. Kernis (Ed.), *Efficacy, agency, and self-esteem* (pp. 9–30). New York: Plenum.

Farnham, S. D., Greenwald, A. G., & Banaji, M. R. (1999). Implicit self-esteem. In D. Abrams & M. A. Hogg (Eds.), *Social cognition and social identity* (pp. 230–248). London: Blackwell.

Fein, S., & Spencer, S. J. (1996). *Readings in social psychology: The art and science of research.* Williamstown, MA: Williams College.

Fein, S., & Spencer, S. J. (1997). Prejudice as self-image maintenance: Affirming the self through derogating others. *Journal of Personality and Social Psychology, 73,* 31–44.

Fitch, G. (1970). Effects of self-esteem, perceived performance, and choice on causal attributions. *Journal of Personality and Social Psychology, 16,* 311–315.

Goldman, B. M., & Kernis, M. H. (2001). *Development of the Authenticity Inventory.* Unpublished data, University of Georgia, Athens.

Goldman, B. M., & Kernis, M. H. (2002). The role of authenticity in optimal psychological functioning and subjective well-being. *Annals of Psychotherapy Association, 5,* 18–20.

Greenberg, J., Solomon, S., & Pyszczynski, T. (1997). The role of self-esteem and cultural worldviews in the management of existential terror. In M. Zanna (Ed.), *Advances in experimental social psychology.* New York: Academic Press.

Greenier, K. G., Kernis, M. H., & Waschull, S. B. (1995). Not all high (or low) self-esteem people are the same: Theory and research on stability of self-esteem. In M. H. Kernis (Ed.), *Efficacy, agency, and self-esteem* (pp. 51–71). New York: Plenum.

Greenier, K. G., Kernis, M. H., Whisenhunt, C. R., Waschull, S. B., Berry, A. J., Herlocker, C. E., & Abend, T. (1999). Individual differences in reactivity to daily events: Examining the roles of stability and level of self-esteem. *Journal of Personality, 67,* 185–208.

Harter, S. (1998). *The construction of the self: A developmental perspective.* New York: Guilford Press.

Hetts, J., Kuwano, M., & Pelham, B. (2000). Two roads to positive regard: Implicit and explicit self-evaluation and culture. *Journal of Experimental Social Psychology, 35,* 512–559.

Hetts, J., Sakuma, M., & Pelham, B. W. (1999). Two roads to positive regard: Implicit and explicit self-evaluation and culture. *Journal of Experimental Social Psychology, 35,* 512–559.

Horney, K. (1950). *Neurosis and human growth: The struggle toward self-realization.* New York: Norton.

Hoyle, R. H., Kernis, M. H., Leary, M. R., & Baldwin, M. W. (1999). *Selfhood: Identity, esteem, regulation.* Boulder, CO: Westview Press.

Kernis, M. H. (1993). The roles of stability and level of self-esteem in psychological functioning. In R. F. Baumeister (Ed.), *Self-esteem: The puzzle of low self-regard* (pp. 167–182). New York: Plenum.

Kernis, M. H. (2000). Substitute needs and fragile self-esteem. *Psychological Inquiry, 11,* 298–300.

Kernis, M. H. (2001). On the trail from narcissism to fragile self-esteem. *Psychological Inquiry, 12*, 223–225.

Kernis, M. H. (2002, February). Fragile self-esteem and intimate relationships. In K. Stein (Chair), *Recent development in research on stability of self-esteem*. Symposium conducted at the annual conference of the Society for Personality and Social Psychology, Savannah, GA.

Kernis, M. H. (in press). Toward a conceptualization of optimal self-esteem. *Psychological Inquiry*.

Kernis, M. H., Brown, A. C., Brody, G. H. (2000). Fragile self-esteem in children and its associations with perceived patterns of parent-child communication. *Journal of Personality, 68*, 225–252.

Kernis, M. H., & Goldman, B. M. (2002). Stability and variability in self-concept and self-esteem. In M. Leary & J. Tangney (Eds.), *Handbook of self and identity* (pp. 106–127). New York: Guilford Press.

Kernis, M. H., & Goldman, B. N. (1999). Self-esteem. In D. Levinson, J. Ponzetti, & P. Jorgensen (Eds.), *Encyclopedia of human emotions* (pp. 593–600). New York: Macmillan Library Reference.

Kernis, M. H., Grannemann, B. D., & Barclay, L. C. (1989). Stability and level of self-esteem as predictors of anger arousal and hostility. *Journal of Personality and Social Psychology, 56*, 1013–1023.

Kernis, M. H., Grannemann, B. D., & Barclay, L. C. (1992). Stability of self-esteem: Assessment, correlates, and excuse making. *Journal of Personality, 60*, 621–644.

Kernis, M. H., Grannemann, B. D., & Mathis, L. C. (1991). Stability of self-esteem as a moderator of the relation between level of self-esteem and depression. *Journal of Personality and Social Psychology, 61*, 80–84.

Kernis, M. H., Greenier, K. D., Herlocker, C. E., Whisenhunt, C. W., & Abend, T. (1997). Self-perceptions of reactions to positive and negative outcomes: The roles of stability and level of self-esteem. *Personality and Individual Differences, 22*, 846–854.

Kernis, M. H., Jadrich, J., Stoner, P., & Sun, C. R. (1996). Stable and unstable components of self-evaluations: Individual differences in self-appraisal responsiveness to feedback. *Journal of Social and Clinical Psychology, 15*, 430–448.

Kernis, M. H., & Paradise, A. W. (2002a). Distinguishing between fragile and secure forms of high self-esteem. In E. L. Deci & R. M. Ryan (Eds.), *Handbook of self-determination* (pp. 339–360). Rochester, NY: University of Rochester Press.

Kernis, M. H., & Paradise, A. W. (2002b). *Fragile self-esteem and anger reactions*. Manuscript submitted for publication, University of Georgia, Athens, GA.

Kernis, M. H., Paradise, A. W., & Goldman, B. N. (2003). *Overinvestment of self in relationships: Implications of fragile self-esteem*. Manuscript in preparation.

Kernis, M. H., Paradise, A. W., Whitaker, D., Wheatman, S., & Goldman, B. (2000). Master of one's psychological domain?: Not likely if one's self-esteem is unstable. *Personality and Social Psychology Bulletin, 26*, 1297–1305.

Kernis, M. H., & Waschull, S. B. (1995). The interactive roles of stability and level of self-esteem: Research and theory. In M. P. Zanna (Ed.), *Advances in experimental social psychology* (Vol. 27, pp. 93–141). San Diego, CA: Academic Press.

Kernis, M. H., Whisenhunt, C. R., Waschull, S. B., Greenier, K. D., Berry, A. J., Herlocker, C. E., & Anderson, C. A. (1998). Multiple facets of self-esteem and their relations to depressive symptoms. *Personality and Social Psychology Bulletin, 24*, 657–668.

Koole, S. L., Dijksterhuis, A., & van Knippenberg, A. (2001). What's in a name: Implicit self-esteem and the automatic self. *Journal of Personality and Social Psychology, 80*, 669–685.

Murray, S. L., & Holmes, J. G. (2000). Seeing the self through a partner's eyes: Why self-doubts turn into relationship insecurities. In A. Tesser, R. B. Felson, & J. Suls (Eds.), *Psychological perspectives on self and identity* (pp. 173–198). Washington, DC: APA Books.

Neighbors, C., Larimer, M. E., Geisner, I. M., & Knee, C. R. (2001). *Self-determination, contingent self-esteem, and drinking motives among college students.* Unpublished manuscript, University of Washington, Seattle.

Norem, J., & Cantor, N. (1986). Defensive pessimism: "Harnessing" anxiety as a motivation. *Journal of Personality and Social Psychology, 52*, 1208–1217.

Paradise, A. W. (2002). Fragile high self-esteem and alcohol use. (Doctoral dissertation, University of Georgia, 2002). *Dissertation Abstracts International: Section B: The Sciences and Engineering, 62* (8–B), 3851.

Paradise, A. W., & Kernis, M. H. (1999). [Development of the Contingent Self-Esteem Scale]. Unpublished raw data.

Paradise, A. W., & Kernis, M. H. (2002). Self-esteem and psychological well-being: Implications of fragile self-esteem. *Journal of Social and Clinical Psychology, 21*, 345–361.

Rogers, C. R. (1959). A theory of therapy, personality, and interpersonal relationships, as developed in the client-centered framework. In S. Koch (Ed.), *Psychology: A study of science* (Vol. 3, pp. 184–256). New York: McGraw-Hill.

Rosenberg, M. (1965). *Society and the adolescent self-image.* Princeton, NJ: Princeton University Press.

Ryan, R. M. (1993). Agency and organization: Intrinsic motivation, autonomy, and the self in psychological development. In J. Jacobs (Ed.), *Nebraska Symposium on Motivation: Vol. 40. Developmental perspectives on motivation* (pp. 1–56). Lincoln: University of Nebraska Press.

Ryff, C. (1989). Happiness is everything, or is it? Explorations on the meaning of psychological well-being. *Journal of Personality and Social Psychology, 57*, 1069–1081.

Schneider, D. J., & Turkat, D. (1975). Self-presentation following success or failure: Defensive self-esteem models. *Journal of Personality, 43*, 127–135.

Taylor, S. E., & Brown, J. D. (1988). Illusion and well-being: A social psychological perspective on mental health. *Psychological Bulletin, 103*, 193–210.

Tennen, H., & Affleck, G. (1993). The puzzles of self-esteem: A clinical perspective. In R. F. Baumeister (Ed.), *Self-esteem: The puzzle of low self-regard* (pp. 37–54). New York: Plenum.

Tice, D. M. (1991). Esteem protection or enhancement? Self-handicapping motives and attributions differ by trait self-esteem. *Journal of Personality and Social Psychology, 60,* 711–725.

Waschull, S. B., & Kernis, M. H. (1996). Level and stability of self-esteem as predictors of children's intrinsic motivation and reasons for anger. *Personality and Social Psychology Bulletin, 22,* 4–13.

2

OPTIMISM AS VIRTUE AND VICE

CHRISTOPHER PETERSON AND ROBERT S. VAIDYA

Too much of a good thing is wonderful.

—*Mae West*

Of late, an optimism bandwagon of considerable magnitude has developed, in psychology and popular U.S. culture. Tapping into long-standing American traditions of positive thinking and buttressed by contemporary psychological research demonstrating the benefits of optimistic expectations, this modern bandwagon asks everyone to emphasize the positive and downplay the negative. Internet Web sites advertise optimism trainers. Candidates for public office fall over themselves in a no-holds-barred optimism competition. People in unprecedented numbers play the lottery and visit casinos. Children are told to be positive, to maintain high self-esteem, and to reach for the stars. Science seems on the verge of curing AIDS, Alzheimer's disease, and cancer. The "problem" of old age will presumably be solved shortly as well. Even in the wake of unprecedented national tragedy, we hear calls for hope and expectations of progress.

But can there be too much of a good thing? Does optimism have a downside? Less dramatic, but just as important, are there circumstances in which optimism pays no particular benefits, in which what is crucial is not thinking pessimistically? Our invitation to contribute to this volume is timely because of the optimism bandwagon. We are among the researchers who have fueled society's current obsession with positive thinking, but we are also struggling to be even handed about optimism. Optimism is beneficial under certain conditions yet costly under others. Optimism and pessimism deserve to be unpacked, both conceptually and empirically, because they are complex and nuanced.

We believe that optimism is neither a virtue nor a vice, that its moral status depends on other considerations. Indeed, we believe that this is generally the case for ostensible virtues and the psychological states that stand in for them in modern discourse. If taken out of context and pushed to an extreme, almost all virtues become vices. Conscientiousness writ large is perfectionism; bravery without bounds is foolhardiness; too much empathy makes one codependent; and so on. The ease with which one can generate the lunatic extreme of an apparent virtue suggests that this slippery slope is close to a general principle.

SOME HISTORY

The history of optimism and pessimism suggests that each psychological stance has costs and benefits (Peterson, 2000; Peterson & Bossio, 2001; Peterson & Chang, 2003; Peterson & Steen, 2002). The term *optimism* is a relatively recent arrival on the historical scene, as is its cousin *pessimism* (Siçinski, 1972). In the 1700s, Leibniz characterized optimism as a mode of thinking, and Voltaire popularized the term in his 18th-century novel *Candide*, which was highly critical of the shallowness of an optimistic perspective. Pessimism appeared a century later, independently introduced by Schopenhauer and Coleridge. In their original forms, optimism and pessimism were not symmetric. Optimism was cognitive in its emphasis, reflecting a reasoned judgment that good would predominate over evil, even if goodness were sometimes associated with suffering. In contrast, pessimism had an emotional reference: The pessimistic individual was one for whom suffering outweighed happiness. Someone can be optimistic in the cognitive Leibniz sense yet pessimistic in the emotional Schopenhauer–Coleridge sense.

The original definitions of optimism and pessimism introduced distinctions still worth taking seriously by everyday people and researchers. An optimistic person, as described by Leibniz, is one who has arrived at a *reasoned* conclusion that eventually good will outweigh bad. Optimism is not accepted on blind faith; it is not happiness; it is not freedom from setbacks and disappointments. Indeed, Voltaire's *Candide* is anything but a good example of optimism. A pessimistic person, as characterized by Schopenhauer and Coleridge, was simply one who suffered. By these views, optimism and pessimism are hardly opposites. We can attempt to alleviate pessimism without urging optimism. At least theoretically, we can encourage optimism but leave pessimism in place.

More recent discussions of optimism by social scientists tend to take two forms (Peterson, 2000). In the first, it is posited as an inherent part of human nature, either to be praised or decried. Early approaches to optimism as human nature were decidedly critical. This negative view of positive thinking lies at the heart of Freud's influential writings on the subject. In *The Future of an Illusion*, Freud (1928) decided that optimism was widespread but illusory. For Freud, optimism helps make civilization possible, particularly when institutionalized in the form of religious beliefs about an afterlife. However, optimism requires the denial of one's instinctual nature and hence the denial of reality. As psychodynamic ideas became popular in the 20th century, Freud's formula equating (religious) optimism and illusion had widespread impact. Although no mental health professional asserted that extreme pessimism should be the standard of health, most theorists pointed to the *accurate* perception of reality as the epitome of good functioning: "The perception of reality is called mentally healthy when what the individual sees corresponds to what is actually there" (Jahoda, 1958, p. 49).

Matters began to change in the 1960s and 1970s in light of research evidence showing that most people are not strictly accurate in how they think. Cognitive psychologists documented an array of shortcuts that people take as they process information. Matlin and Stang (1978) surveyed hundreds of studies showing that language, memory, and thought are selectively positive. For example, in free recall, people produce positive memories sooner than negative ones. Most people evaluate themselves positively, and even more positively than they evaluate others. Apparently, in our minds, we are all the children of Lake Woebegone, where everyone is above average.

Another turning point in the view of optimism was Taylor and Brown's (1988) review of research on positive illusions. They described a variety of evidence showing that people are biased toward the positive and that the only exceptions are individuals who are anxious or depressed. Taylor (1989) elaborated these ideas in her book *Positive Illusions*, in which she proposed that people's pervasive tendency to see themselves in the best possible light is a sign of well-being.

Perhaps the strongest statement that optimism is an inherent aspect of human nature is found in Tiger's (1979) book *Optimism: The Biology of Hope*. He located optimism in the biology of the human species and argued that it is one of our most defining and adaptive characteristics. For Tiger, optimism was selected for in the course of evolution, developing along with cognitive abilities and indeed the human capacity for culture.

At the same time that optimism as general human nature was being discussed in positive terms, other psychologists interested in individual differences began to address optimism as a characteristic that people possess to varying degrees. These two approaches are compatible. Human nature provides a baseline optimism, of which individuals show more versus less, and a person's experiences influence the degree to which he or she is relatively optimistic or pessimistic vis-à-vis this baseline.

CONTEMPORARY APPROACHES
TO OPTIMISM (AND PESSIMISM)

At present, there are two particularly well-known approaches within psychology to optimism as an individual difference. Each line of work has an associated self-report measure; each usually has focused on the consequences of the individual difference as opposed to the antecedents; and each has spawned a large empirical literature demonstrating that optimism (or at least the absence of pessimism) is usually associated with all manner of desirable outcomes. Each proposes a process model of how optimism influences behavior, which means that each has the potential to identify when optimism has good consequences and when it does not. So, contemporary approaches write a new chapter in the history of optimism because they do not force a monolithic view of the construct as always a virtue or always a vice.

Dispositional Optimism

Carver and Scheier (1981, 1990, 2001) have studied *dispositional optimism*: the global expectation that good things will be plentiful in the future and bad things scarce. Carver and Scheier's overriding perspective is in terms of how people pursue *goals*, defined as desirable values. To them, virtually all realms of human activity can be cast in goal terms, and people's behavior entails the identification and adoption of goals and the regulation of actions vis-à-vis these goals. They therefore refer to their approach as a *self-regulatory model*. Optimism enters into self-regulation when people ask themselves about impediments to the achievement of the goals they have adopted. In the face of difficulties, do people nonetheless believe that goals will be achieved? If so, they are optimistic—if not, pessimistic. Optimism leads to continued efforts to attain the goal, whereas pessimism leads to giving up.

Optimistic Explanatory Style

Seligman and his colleagues have approached optimism in terms of an individual's *explanatory style*—how he or she explains the causes of bad events (Buchanan & Seligman, 1995; Gillham, Shatté, Reivich, & Seligman, 2001; Peterson, Maier, & Seligman, 1993). Those who explain bad events in a circumscribed way—with external, unstable, and specific causes—are described as optimistic, whereas those who favor internal, stable, and global causes are described as pessimistic. The notion of explanatory style emerged from the attributional reformulation of the learned helplessness model (Abramson, Seligman, & Teasdale, 1978). In brief, the original helplessness model proposed that after experience with uncontrollable aversive events, animals and people become helpless—passive and unresponsive—presumably because they have "learned" that there is no contingency between actions and outcomes (Maier & Seligman, 1976). This learning is represented as a generalized expectancy that future outcomes will be unrelated to actions. It is this generalized expectation of response–outcome independence that produces later helplessness. However, the helplessness/explanatory style research tradition has infrequently looked at expectations. Rather, researchers measure explanatory style and correlate it with outcomes thought to revolve around helplessness. In contrast to dispositional optimism, explanatory style is a construct concerning agency.

Correlates and Consequences of Optimism

The correlates and consequences of these two modern incarnations of optimism (and pessimism) have been extensively studied. We do not attempt to review this research literature here. We instead refer readers to Table 2.1, in which the major findings are summarized (Buchanan & Seligman, 1995; Chang, 2001; Peterson et al., 1993): Studies with a variety of operationalizations and designs show that when people are placed along a continuum from pessimistic to optimistic and examined with respect to measures of adaptation drawn from a variety of domains—cognition, mood, behavior, physical health, and social relations—"optimism" is often associated with good outcomes and "pessimism" with bad outcomes.

When Optimism Does Not Matter

These conclusions must be qualified by recognizing the casual treatment by most researchers of optimism and pessimism as simple opposites (Peterson & Chang, 2003). Indeed, this approach has been reified in the research strategy of measuring these constructs with the same scale, anchored at one end with optimism and at the other with pessimism. Nearly all optimism research then looks at the overall relationship among variables without examining the full distribution of data. What this means is that we do not know the actual source of ostensible benefits: in optimism ("the power of positive thinking"), in the absence of pessimism ("the power of non-negative thinking"), or in both. Another qualification of the generalizations in Table 2.1 is that most of the summarized studies used middle-class White Americans as research participants; whether these findings apply, for example, to Asian populations is largely unknown (Chang, Asakawa, & Sanna, 2001).

In any event, researchers should closely scrutinize their data. When researchers study dispositional optimism, it is a simple matter to look at optimism and pessimism separately, because the typical measure—the Life

TABLE 2.1
Correlates and Consequences of Optimism

Outcome variable	Correlation w/dispositional optimism and/or optimistic explanatory style
Cognition	
Accurate risk perception	Negative (see text)
Perception of hassle-free life	Positive
Personal control	Positive
Mood	
Absence of anxiety, depression	Positive
Absence of suicide	Positive
Behavior	
Achievement (academic, athletic, military, political, vocational)	Positive
Active (problem-focused) coping	Positive
Perseverance	Positive
Delay of gratification	Positive
Maladaptive persistence	Negative (see text)
Health	
Absence of illness	Positive
Immunocompetence	Positive
Speed of recovery from illness	Positive
Survival time with illness	Positive
Longevity	Positive
Freedom from traumatic accidents	Positive
Health-promoting lifestyle	Positive
Social relations	
Absence of loneliness	Positive
Attractiveness to others	Positive
Friendships	Positive

Orientation Test (LOT; Scheier & Carver, 1985)—contains separate Optimism and Pessimism subscales. The Optimism subscale of the LOT negatively correlates with the Pessimism subscale but not so highly that the overall LOT is unidimensional. Furthermore, optimism and pessimism so measured have somewhat different correlates (Chang, Maydeu-Olivares, & D'Zurilla, 1997). However, researchers do not routinely report results separately for the Optimism and Pessimism subscales of the LOT. Instead, they report results for a composite that combines the subscales, making it impossible to advance conclusions about possible differences between the correlates of optimism and pessimism.

When researchers study explanatory style, a more subtle analysis is needed to tease apart optimism and pessimism: Examine the linearity of the association between explanatory style and the outcome of interest. We can illustrate this strategy by describing data combined from eight different college student samples (total $N = 1,009$). The relationship between a catastrophizing explanatory style (i.e., the explanation of bad events with stable and global causes) and depressive symptoms (measured by the Beck Depression Inventory, BDI; Beck, Ward, Mendelson, Mock, & Erbaugh, 1961) was notably nonlinear; the overall correlation between explanatory style and depression was $r = .32$, $p < .001$, and the quadratic trend was $F = 28.74$, $p < .001$. If an individual were below the midpoint on the 7-point explanatory measure, the degree of his or her pessimism was related to BDI scores. However, above the midpoint, the degree of optimism did not matter. In an additional college student data set ($N = 1,263$), we found the same nonlinear relationship between globality of explanatory style and self-reported history of psychological difficulties; the overall correlation between explanatory style and depression was $r = .25$, $p < .001$, and the quadratic trend was $F = 7.19$, $p < .007$.

It is tempting to conclude from these exploratory analyses that a pessimistic explanatory style is more relevant to bad outcomes than is an optimistic explanatory style, but we really have no idea whether this pattern holds across diverse outcomes; neither do we have even a hint about the linearity of relationships between explanatory style and good outcomes, because so few studies have looked at these. The important point is that we did not have to search through too many data sets to find examples of nonlinear relationships. We urge other researchers to explore (in samples of sufficient size) the linearity of relations between explanatory style and outcomes. The optimism bandwagon may not always be traveling along a straight line.

When Optimism Is Problematic

Let us move from the cases in which optimism pays no benefit or pessimism incurs no cost to those in which optimism seems to have drawbacks. Several of these cases can be deduced from the typical benefits summarized in Table 2.1. Optimism is associated with active coping, persistence, and delay of gratification. These are laudable characteristics so long as the world cooperates. However, at least in principle, optimism can be associated with maladaptive persistence. There is not much of a research literature here, because investigators have been biased toward studying outcomes that are attainable through perseverance. Regardless, an inflexible optimism is sometimes linked to the pursuit of the unattainable (Slusher & Anderson, 1989), perhaps because optimists overlook or ignore information that contradicts their positive expectations (Metcalfe, 1998). Certainly, constructs like perfectionism, John Henry-ism, mania, and the Type A coronary-prone behavior pattern are flavored with a problematic optimism (Peterson, 1999).

Reality matters, and one's expectations about the future cannot be too much at odds with this reality. As Taylor (1989) phrased it, a beneficial optimism is illusory but not delusional. When reality smacks the optimistic individual alongside the face, his or her optimism is no longer a virtue. Consider findings described by Isaacowitz and Seligman (2001) that among elderly people, an optimistic explanatory style predicts depression in the wake of stressful events. Perhaps extreme optimism among elderly people is unrealistic because an indefinitely extended future orientation does not square with what will be. The occurrence of something terrible can therefore devastate optimistic older individuals when they realize that their optimism must be wrong, a realization that is much more infrequent for younger individuals.

Clarifying these conclusions is research by Aspinwall and Richter (1999) showing that research participants high in dispositional optimism were more likely than pessimistic individuals to disengage themselves from tasks that could not be solved, if solvable tasks were available as an alternative. The interpretation seems to be that optimists are better than pessimists at recognizing productive pursuits and channeling their efforts in these directions. In discussing these results, Aspinwall, Richter, and Hoffman (2001) proposed that optimists are better information processors than pessimists and thus more likely to attend to cues that tasks cannot be solved. However, these cues must exist, and alternatives must be present. Consider again the elderly optimists studied by Isaacowitz and Seligman (2001); no alternative to being old exists, and their exceedingly positive expectations can thus produce difficulties.

Here is another downside to optimism that we can deduce: The growing literature on optimism and physical well-being (see Table 2.1) is creating a popular worldview in which people blame the victims of illness—including themselves—for thinking negatively and thereby producing poor health. This is of course insidious. Two centuries ago, the germ model of illness rescued us from magical thinking about the causes of disease and death, and the positive-thinking movement now threatens to return us to this era, apparently with empirical support. Remember the original characterization of optimism from the beginning of this chapter: a *reasoned* judgment. Blaming individuals with cancer or AIDS for their health status is unreasoned and immoral.

Optimism as an individual difference is associated with what has been dubbed in the public health literature as an *optimistic bias in risk perception* (Weinstein, 1989). It is not surprising that optimistic people exaggerate the tendency of most individuals to see themselves as "below average" for such dire health outcomes as heart disease (Peterson & de Avila, 1995). This bias can be a problem when reality matters and a person neglects preventive or remediative actions. Optimistic expectations about health do not always lead one to ignore threats to well-being, especially if the individual believes that good health is something he or she can control (Aspinwall & Brunhart, 1996), but there are circumstances in which optimism results in the neglect of health promotion (Davidson & Prkachin, 1997; Rutter, Quine, & Albery, 1998; Schwarzer, 1994).

Our own recent research documented the optimistic bias among first-year college students and explored its relationship to dispositional optimism.

Our major goal was to extend research on the optimistic bias beyond physical health perceptions. If asked to estimate their risks for the academic and social setbacks that can occur during college, are first-year students realistic in their appraisals? And do these students overestimate the likelihood of academic and social triumphs?

To sharpen our conclusions, we also administered to research participants measures of depression and of study habits, in an attempt to estimate the "reality" of an individual's social and academic expectations. Depressed students should realistically expect social setbacks, and students with poor study habits should realistically expect academic difficulties. Does the link between dispositional optimism and unrealistic expectations hold even when these reality markers are taken into account?

The research participants were 156 first-year college students from the University of Michigan introductory psychology subject pool. In October 1998, 86 first-semester students participated, and in February 1999, 70 second-semester students participated. The sample was mainly female (79%) and mainly White (76%). Mean age was 18.1 years, with a range from 17 to 20 years. There were no demographic differences between students from the two semesters, except of course age (18.0 years vs. 18.2 years), $t(154) = 2.68$, $p < .01$. Gender, ethnicity, and age did not influence the results. In small groups of 3 to 10 individuals, research participants in single sessions completed several questionnaires.

First, they provided demographic information. Next, they completed the LOT, an eight-item measure of dispositional optimism versus pessimism (Scheier & Carver, 1985). Four items reflect an optimistic orientation to the future, and four items reflect a pessimistic orientation; respondents express their degree of agreement with these items on a 5-point scale. In the present sample, internal consistency of the overall LOT, estimated by Cronbach's (1951) coefficient alpha, was .82. As typically found, the Optimism and Pessimism subscales were negatively correlated ($r = -.50$, $p < .001$). The subscale reliabilities were .70 for optimism and .82 for pessimism.

Respondents were next presented with a list of 16 good events and the instructions to place a mark in each case along a 90-cm line anchored by 0% and 100% (with the intermediate points of 25%, 50%, and 75% also indicated) to estimate the chances, compared with other first-year students at the university, that the given event would happen to them during the next year. Events were drawn from both the psychosocial ("you will meet the true love of your life") and academic ("you will receive A grades in your courses") domains. Responses were coded by measuring to the nearest 5% where they fell along the line. Internal consistency of this measure of specific expectations for good events was .79.

The next questionnaire was an analogous measure of expectations for bad events. Fourteen bad events were used, again drawn from both the psychosocial ("you will end up in a terrible living situation") and academic ("you will wind up on academic probation") domains. Internal consistency of this measure of specific expectations for bad events was .79.

Expectations for bad events were negatively correlated with expectations for good events ($r = -.31$, $p < .01$). An overall measure of expectations was created for each respondent by subtracting "bad" expectation scores from "good" scores. The internal consistency of this composite was .82.

Twelve items were chosen from the Motivated Strategies for Learning Questionnaire that reflected study habits that beginning students arguably had brought with them (or not) to college (Pintrich, Smith, Garcia, & McKeachie, 1993). In each case, respondents use a 5-point scale to indicate how true of them is the learning strategy. Representative items included "I usually study in a place where I can concentrate on my coursework" and "I set goals for work each day." Scores were averaged, and in the present sample the internal consistency of the resulting composite was .79.

Respondents next completed the brief version of the BDI (Beck, Rial, & Rickels, 1974). This self-report measure presents respondents with 13 common symptoms and asks them to use 0 to 3 scales to indicate the degree to which they have experienced each during the past week. Scores are summed. In the present sample, the internal consistency of this measure was .83.

Even by stringent criteria—requiring that the mean expectation be greater (or less) than 50% at the .001 level and that the majority of individual respondents report above (or below) average expectations—the hypothesized optimistic bias was robustly present for almost all events, especially the bad ones. The majority of college students believed that they were above average in the likelihood of experiencing good events (M = 63%, SD = 11%), and they believed that they were below average in the likelihood of experiencing bad events (M = 15%, SD = 9%). In terms of the composite measure of overall expectations (good–bad), only one respondent out of 156 had a negative score.

Although the optimistic bias was the norm, its degree was nonetheless associated with our individual-difference measures. So, the composite expectations (good–bad) measure was predicted by depressive symptoms ($r = -.49$, $p < .001$), by learning strategies ($r = .32$, $p < .01$), and by the LOT composite ($r = .51$, $p < .001$). The link between dispositional optimism and expectations remained significant even when depressive symptoms and learning strategies were partialed from the correlation ($pr = .38$, $p < .001$), implying that this association did not simply reflect reality. Indeed, semester (first or second) was unrelated to expectations ($r = -.07$, ns), suggesting that experience did not make the students more realistic.

We followed our own advice and looked separately at the Optimism and Pessimism subscales of the LOT and their associations with expectations for good events and expectations for bad events. As it turned out, there were no differential patterns (Peterson & Vaidya, 2001). The four different measures were substantially intercorrelated ($Mdn \, |r| = .35$), an impression confirmed by a principal-components factor analysis with varimax rotation. There was only one factor with an eigenvalue greater than 1.00, and this factor (eigenvalue = 2.14) accounted for 53% of the variance in the scores. All the conclusions advanced here apply to optimism and pessimism and to expectations for good events and expectations for bad events.

Overall, our first-year college students evidenced an optimistic bias vis-à-vis academic and social events analogous to that shown in the public health literature. Dispositional optimists particularly showed this bias, and it is apparently not the result of superior learning strategies used by these students or the absence of problematic depressive symptoms. Furthermore, the bias was unaffected by experience.

When the optimistic bias shows itself as a belief that one is immune to cancer, heart disease, or AIDS, there is reason to be alarmed, because people may not behave in ways known to reduce the risk of these illnesses. A good dose of reality is indicated. But what about optimistic expectations concerning college events, academic and social? In some cases, these expectations can be self-fulfilling, which means that one should be cautious in deeming them unrealistic for all individuals (Peterson & de Avila, 1995). College students who expect to find concerned instructors may well create such faculty members by their enthusiasm and interest. College students with good study habits are well served by positive expectations because they lead to appropriate efforts (Peterson & Barrett, 1987). In other cases, however, these expectations are likely to produce eventual disappointment because they are for most students flat out wrong. Grade inflation notwithstanding, very few college students will receive all A grades, and they may become demoralized and even depressed in the wake of a less-than-perfect grade-point average (cf. Metalsky, Abramson, Seligman, Semmel, & Peterson, 1982).

CONCLUSIONS

Optimism has many benefits and a few notable drawbacks. Optimism can be either a virtue or a vice, depending on the circumstances in which it is deployed. Optimism is to be urged on an individual when it is a realistic stance or when the future is indefinite and positive expectations can shape what comes to pass. Optimism is suspect if it leads to pointless persistence. It is dangerous if it provides a roadmap of the future that leads one off the edge of a cliff—and then to blaming oneself for not being able to fly.

The moral resolution, as it were, is to adopt what Seligman (1991) called *flexible optimism* or what Armor and Taylor (1998) called *situated* or *strategic optimism*: a psychological strategy to be exercised when appropriate as opposed to a reflex or habit over which one has no control and into which one has no insight. As noted earlier, contemporary research traditions have looked much more at the consequences of optimism and pessimism than at their causes, and even when the origins of optimism and pessimism are studied, the focus has been on factors over which individuals seem to have little control: genetics, trauma, early childhood experience, culture, and the like (Peterson & Steen, 2002).

A different focus is indicated, perhaps along the lines of the Penn Prevention Program (aka the Penn Resiliency Project; Seligman, Reivich, Jaycox, & Gillham, 1995). Schoolchildren are taught basic cognitive–behavioral strategies, especially disputation and decatastrophizing, for thinking about the causes of events. In its original form, the Penn Prevention Program attempted to boost children's optimism across the board as a means of preventing later depression and anxiety, but the current version of the intervention conceptualizes its intent differently (K. Reivich, personal communication, January 8, 2001). Optimism should be in the toolbox of life, but one needs to know its uses and, just as important, its misuses.

Years ago, we characterized an optimistic explanatory style as traitlike (Peterson & Seligman, 1984). In the context of the present discussion, we are pleased with this description because it allows us enough wiggle room to conclude that optimism is also un-traitlike in the sense that one can (and must) exercise choice over its use. As Aristotle (1908/350 BC) observed in *The Nichomachean Ethics*, if one cannot speak of ostensibly virtuous activity as chosen, then it is only behavior masquerading as virtue. Optimism is a virtue (as opposed to a trait) when someone selects it from among alternative cognitive stances and then uses it in appropriate circumstances. Once again, we see that optimism as a *reasoned* judgment is the version we should label a virtue. Said another way, optimism is a virtue when coupled with metacognitive skills concerning its appropriate use.

REFERENCES

Abramson, L. Y., Seligman, M. E. P., & Teasdale, J. D. (1978). Learned helplessness in humans: Critique and reformulation. *Journal of Abnormal Psychology, 87,* 49–74.

Aristotle. (1908). *Nicomachean ethics* (W. D. Ross, Trans.). Oxford, England: Clarendon Press. (Original work written 350 BC)

Armor, D. A., & Taylor, S. E. (1998). Situated optimism: Specific outcome expectations and self-regulation. In M. P. Zanna (Ed.), *Advances in experimental social psychology* (Vol. 30, pp. 309–379). New York: Academic Press.

Aspinwall, L. G., & Brunhart, S. M. (1996). Distinguishing optimism from denial: Optimistic beliefs predict attention to health threats. *Personality and Social Psychology Bulletin, 22,* 993–1003.

Aspinwall, L. G., & Richter, L. (1999). Optimism and self-mastery predict more rapid disengagement from unsolvable tasks in the presence of alternatives. *Motivation & Emotion, 23,* 221–245.

Aspinwall, L. G., Richter, L., & Hoffman, R. R. (2001). Understanding how optimism works: An examination of optimists' adaptive moderation of belief and behavior. In E. C. Chang (Ed.), *Optimism and pessimism: Implications for theory, research, and practice* (pp. 217–238). Washington, DC: American Psychological Association.

Beck, A. T., Rial, W. Y., & Rickels, K. (1974). Short form of Depression Inventory: Cross-validation. *Psychological Reports, 34*, 1184–1186.

Beck, A. T., Ward, C. H., Mendelson, M. N., Mock, J., & Erbaugh, J. (1961). An inventory for measuring depression. *Archives of General Psychiatry, 4*, 561–571.

Buchanan, G. M., & Seligman, M. E. P. (Eds.). (1995). *Explanatory style*. Hillsdale, NJ: Erlbaum.

Carver, C. S., & Scheier, M. F. (1981). *Attention and self-regulation: A control-theory approach to human behavior*. New York: Springer-Verlag.

Carver, C. S., & Scheier, M. F. (1990). Origins and functions of positive and negative affect: A control-process view. *Psychological Review, 97*, 19–35.

Carver, C. S., & Scheier, M. F. (2001). Optimism, pessimism, and self-regulation. In E. C. Chang (Ed.), *Optimism and pessimism: Implications for theory, research, and practice* (pp. 31–51). Washington, DC: American Psychological Association.

Chang, E. C. (Ed.). (2001). *Optimism and pessimism: Implications for theory, research, and practice*. Washington, DC: American Psychological Association.

Chang, E. C., Asakawa, K., & Sanna, L. J. (2001). Cultural variations in optimistic and pessimistic bias: Do Easterners really expect the worst and Westerners really expect the best when predicting future life events? *Journal of Personality and Social Psychology, 81*, 476–491.

Chang, E. C., Maydeu-Olivares, A., & D'Zurilla, T. J. (1997). Optimism and pessimism as partially independent constructs: Relations to positive and negative affectivity and psychological well-being. *Personality and Individual Differences, 23*, 433–440.

Cronbach, L. J. (1951). Coefficient alpha and the internal structure of tests. *Psychometrika, 16*, 297–334.

Davidson, K., & Prkachin, K. (1997). Optimism and unrealistic optimism have an interacting impact on health-promoting behavior and knowledge changes. *Personality and Social Psychology Bulletin, 23*, 617–625.

Freud, S. (1928). *The future of an illusion*. London: Hogarth.

Gillham, J. E., Shatté, A. J., Reivich, K. J., & Seligman, M. E. P. (2001). Optimism, pessimism, and explanatory style. In E. C. Chang (Ed.), *Optimism and pessimism: Implications for theory, research, and practice* (pp. 53–75). Washington, DC: American Psychological Association.

Isaacowitz, D. M., & Seligman, M. E. P. (2001). Is pessimism a risk factor for depressive mood among community-dwelling older adults? *Behaviour Research and Therapy, 39*, 13–30.

Jahoda, M. (1958). Current concepts of positive mental health. New York: Basic Books.

Maier, S. F., & Seligman, M. E. P. (1976). Learned helplessness: Theory and evidence. *Journal of Experimental Psychology: General, 105,* 3–46.

Matlin, M., & Stang, D. (1978). *The Pollyanna principle.* Cambridge, MA: Schenkman.

Metalsky, G. I., Abramson, L. Y., Seligman, M. E. P., Semmel, A., & Peterson, C. (1982). Vulnerability to depressive mood reactions: Life events in the classroom. *Journal of Personality and Social Psychology, 43,* 612–617.

Metcalfe, J. (1998). Cognitive optimism: Self-deception or memory-based processed heuristics? *Personality and Social Psychology Review, 2,* 100–110.

Peterson, C. (1999). Personal control and well-being. In D. Kahneman, E. Diener, & N. Schwarz (Eds.), *Well-being: The foundations of hedonic psychology* (pp. 288–301). New York: Russell Sage Foundation.

Peterson, C. (2000). The future of optimism. *American Psychologist, 55,* 44–55.

Peterson, C., & Barrett, L. C. (1987). Explanatory style and academic performance among university freshmen. *Journal of Personality and Social Psychology, 53,* 603–607.

Peterson, C., & Bossio, L. M. (2001). Optimism and physical well-being. In E. C. Chang (Ed.), *Optimism and pessimism: Implications for theory, research, and practice* (pp. 127–145). Washington, DC: American Psychological Association.

Peterson, C., & Chang, E. C. (2003). Optimism and flourishing. In C. L. M. Keyes & J. Haidt (Eds.), *Flourishing: Positive psychology and the life well-lived* (pp. 55–79). Washington, DC: American Psychological Association.

Peterson, C., & de Avila, M. E. (1995). Optimistic explanatory style and the perception of health problems. *Journal of Clinical Psychology, 51,* 128–132.

Peterson, C., Maier, S. F., & Seligman, M. E. P. (1993). *Learned helplessness: A theory for the age of personal control.* New York: Oxford University Press.

Peterson, C., & Seligman, M. E. P. (1984). Causal explanations as a risk factor for depression: Theory and evidence. *Psychological Review, 91,* 347–374.

Peterson, C., & Steen, T. A. (2002). Optimistic explanatory style. In C. R. Snyder (Ed.), *Handbook of positive psychology.* New York: Oxford University Press.

Peterson, C., & Vaidya, R. S. (2001). Explanatory style, expectations, and depressive symptoms. *Personality and Individual Differences, 31,* 1217–1223.

Pintrich, P. R., Smith, D. A., Garcia, T., & McKeachie, W. J. (1993). Reliability and predictive validity of the Motivated Strategies for Learning Questionnaire (MSLQ). *Educational and Psychological Measurement, 53,* 801–813.

Rutter, D. R., Quine, L., & Albery, I. P. (1998). Perceptions of risk in motorcyclists: Unrealistic optimism, relative realism and predictions of behaviour. *British Journal of Psychology, 89,* 681–696.

Scheier, M. F., & Carver, C. S. (1985). Optimism, coping, and health: Assessment and implications of generalized outcome expectancies. *Health Psychology, 4,* 219–247.

Schwarzer, R. (1994). Optimism, vulnerability, and self-beliefs as health-related cognitions: A systematic overview. *Psychology and Health, 9,* 161–180.

Seligman, M. E. P. (1991). *Learned optimism*. New York: Knopf.

Seligman, M. E. P., Reivich, K., Jaycox, L., & Gillham, J. (1995). *The optimistic child*. Boston: Houghton Mifflin.

Siçinski, A. (1972). Optimism versus pessimism (Tentative concepts and their consequences for future research). *Polish Sociological Bulletin, 25–26,* 47–62.

Slusher, M. P., & Anderson, C. A. (1989). Belief perseverance and self-defeating behavior. In R. C. Curtis (Ed.), *Self-defeating behaviors* (pp. 11–40). New York: Plenum.

Taylor, S. E. (1989). *Positive illusions*. New York: Basic Books.

Taylor, S. E., & Brown, J. D. (1988). Illusion and well-being: A social psychological perspective on mental health. *Psychological Bulletin, 103,* 193–210.

Tiger, L. (1979). *Optimism: The biology of hope*. New York: Simon & Schuster.

Weinstein, N. D. (1989, December 8). Optimistic biases about personal risks. *Science, 246,* 1232–1233.

3

INTELLIGENCE:
CAN ONE HAVE
TOO MUCH OF A GOOD THING?

ROBERT J. STERNBERG

Some years ago, I was seated at lunch with the chair of my department, who has since gone on to bigger and better things as a top administrator at a leading university. In the course of our conversation, it came out that we both had independently come to the same conclusion: Although we both felt fortunate to be reasonably intelligent, in the traditional sense of the term, at the same time we also felt fortunate never to have been intellectual superstars—the kind who receive straight As and sky-high standardized test scores. This chapter is about why we came to this conclusion.

Before proceeding to the body of the chapter, however, I should make clear that when I refer to *intelligence* in this chapter, unless noted otherwise, I refer to it in its traditional sense, as the ability to learn and to adapt to the environment. This conventional definition is what I refer to elsewhere as

Preparation of this chapter was supported by Grant REC-9979843 from the National Science Foundation, Grant R206R000001 from the U.S. Office of Educational Research and Improvement, and a grant from the W. T. Grant Foundation. This support does not imply acceptance or endorsement of the positions taken in this chapter.

analytical intelligence—the ability to analyze, compare and contrast, evaluate, judge, and critique (Sternberg, 1997, 1999b). It also corresponds roughly to the amalgamation of what Gardner (1983, 1999) has referred to as *linguistic intelligence* and *logical–mathematical intelligence*.

THE BENEFITS OF INTELLIGENCE

Virtually everyone knows the benefits of intelligence, and U.S. society values intelligence so much that, at times, discussions of it seem to separate with only the thinnest line intelligence and the value of a person (e.g., Herrnstein & Murray, 1994). Experts and laypeople alike see higher levels of intelligence as preferable to lower levels of it, whether in the United States (Sternberg, 1985b; Sternberg, Conway, Ketron, & Bernstein, 1981) or elsewhere (Berry, 1994; Grigorenko et al., 2001; Serpell, 1974; Sternberg & Kaufman, 1998; Yang & Sternberg, 1997).

Intelligence is correlated with many positive life outcomes, such as generalized socioeconomic status, being employed, income from employment, various kinds of evaluations of job success, prestige of job, marital stability, and freedom from criminal record (Herrnstein & Murray, 1994). For example, the average IQ of accountants and lawyers was reported in one study to be 128; that for machinists to be 110; and that for laborers and truck drivers to be 96 (Harrell & Harrell, 1945). More intelligent people generally tend to have greater degrees of education (Jencks, 1972; Mackintosh, 1998; McCall, 1977), although this effect may derive in part from the fact that formal schooling increases one's level of measured intelligence (Ceci, 1996). Moreover, the correlation between IQ and job success seems to hold across virtually all jobs (Schmidt & Hunter, 1998). The effect cannot be totally due to IQ driving schooling, however, because IQ measured at an earlier age predicts *later* educational attainment (e.g., Horn & Packard, 1985; Mackintosh & Mascie-Taylor, 1986; Vernon, 1947)—and, of course, people with higher measured intelligence perform better in school (Mackintosh, 1998; see also Mayer, 2000).

Given all of these benefits of higher intelligence, it might seem odd that anyone would question the value of intelligence. Yet there seem to be circumstances in which intelligence as conventionally defined may not be advantageous. What are some of these circumstances?

THE CHANGING NATURE OF
THE SOCIETAL REWARD SYSTEM

I have argued that intelligence as conventionally defined accounts for only one part of the phenomenon as a whole (Sternberg, 1985a, 1997,

1999b). According to the triarchic theory of human intelligence, intelligence—or what I sometimes call *successful intelligence*, to distinguish it from the narrow sense of intelligence—comprises not only memory and analytical abilities measured by conventional tests but also creative and practical abilities, which typically are not measured by conventional tests. Often, these additional abilities are not particularly valued by schools either, despite the fact that once individuals leave school and enter the world of work, such abilities are probably as important as or more important than memory and analytical abilities. With respect to creative intelligence, for example, one important aspect of job success is the creative flexibility to keep up with a rapidly changing set of expectations, technologies, social mores, and so forth. With respect to practical intelligence, an important aspect of job success is being able to relate effectively to colleagues and supervisors and being able to figure out the kinds of behavior that lead to salary increases and job promotions.

This situation creates a problem. In school, students are largely rewarded for memory and analytical abilities. Such abilities lead to approbation on the part of teachers, higher grades, placement in more advanced classes, admission to more prestigious colleges and universities, enhanced possibilities for financial aid in education, and so forth. The result is that students who show high levels of memory and analytical abilities are continuously reinforced for their pattern of abilities. Reinforcement theory suggests, of course, that continuous reinforcement is very effective for acquiring new patterns of behavior. One such pattern is the development and display of memory and analytical abilities.

When students have graduated from school, they face a situation in which memory and analytical abilities are of somewhat lesser relative importance and creative and practical abilities are of somewhat higher relative importance. It is not that memory and analytical abilities stop mattering; of course they continue to matter. They just matter less, relatively speaking, than they did before. As a result, individuals stop being continuously reinforced for these abilities and start being intermittently (partially) reinforced. The problem is that whereas continuous reinforcement is particularly effective for acquiring patterns of behavior, intermittent reinforcement is particularly effective for sustaining already-acquired patterns of behavior (e.g., gambling at slot machines). As a result, even though the individuals' memory and analytical abilities may no longer be functioning as effectively for the individuals as they did in the past, nevertheless, the individuals are likely to continue and even increase their use of these abilities, to their own detriment.

A mechanism is thereby put into place that may actually result in people with very high levels of conventional intelligence performing worse than their lower IQ counterparts. Indeed, there is evidence that success as an adult shows a curvilinear rather than linear relation to various measures of success (Simonton, 1994), with people at the highest levels of IQ not necessarily living up to their expected levels of success. Of course, what constitutes success differs for different people (Sternberg, 1999b). Nevertheless, one is sometimes puzzled by the way people use their abilities to achieve success.

LEADERSHIP

There also is evidence that conventional intelligence may not be particularly helpful for leadership. For example, some evidence suggests that the most effective leaders are not much smarter than the individuals they follow, but rather, a little smarter (Simonton, 1994). Leaders who are much smarter conventionally than those they are supposed to lead may find that they simply are not well understood by their flock. Other problems also are associated with intelligence in leadership.

Fred Fiedler and his colleagues (e.g., Fiedler & Link, 1994) have studied the relationship between intelligence and experience on the one hand and leadership success on the other. They have been particularly interested in how stress mediates the relationship between intelligence and leadership success. They have found that the relationship is complex: Under conditions of low stress, intelligence is positively associated with leadership; under conditions of high stress, however, intelligence is negatively associated with success in leadership (whereas experience is positively associated with leadership success).

Why might such a relationship appear? Under conditions of low stress, leaders have the luxury of reflecting on the situations they confront and of leisurely using their intellectual abilities to solve problems. Under conditions of high stress, however, the leaders may not have the time or the state of mind to use their intellectual processing to solve problems; rather, they may have to react quickly and even automatically. It is under such conditions that a solid base of experience and automatized routines for handling many different kinds of problems may be particularly useful in solving leadership problems.

BEING TOO SMART FOR YOUR OWN GOOD

Are some people too smart for their own good? I believe that such cases tend to arise not so much because the individual is too smart but because he or she becomes intellectually arrogant. In particular, very high levels of conventional intelligence and the reinforcement that go with them can tend to produce feelings of invulnerability, of much the same kind that Janis (1972) observed among victims of groupthink.

Bill Clinton in the Lewinsky scandal, Boris Yeltsin in a series of scandals, and Lyndon Johnson in the Vietnam fiasco highlight kinds of mistakes that characterize many individuals who are intelligent, even brilliant, but at the same time unwise and even foolish. These mistakes—of placing the perceived short-term interests of oneself, (significant) others, and institutions over the needs of all three of these entities considered in balance—may suggest why intelligence is not enough to make one's life, others' lives, and the world, a better place.

Perhaps intelligence is not the one-size-fits-all solution that U.S. society wishes to make it. Might there be another construct that would provide a better basis not only for evaluating people but also for developing in people? I believe wisdom is such a construct.

WISDOM AS A SOLUTION TO CERTAIN PROBLEMS OF INTELLIGENCE

Wisdom is not just a story about great leaders of the world. It is something anyone can show. *Wisdom* can be defined as the "power of judging rightly and following the soundest course of action, based on knowledge, experience, understanding, etc." (*Webster's New World College Dictionary*, 1997, p. 1533). Thus, wisdom is related to intelligence, but it is more than intelligence. This is a characteristic open to anyone, and there are several reasons to understand wisdom beyond saving the world. A second reason is to provide people with a means to achieving happiness and contentment in their lives, not just success. Intelligence, ambition, and sheer drive may be keys to success of certain kinds, but the history of our times shows they provide no keys to happiness. Wisdom, I argue, does. A third reason to study wisdom is that it is open to anyone. It is not some unreachable attribute that only the few can share. Some societies have become obsessed with intelligence—conventional intelligence, multiple intelligences, emotional intelligence, and even the successful intelligence I have proposed (e.g., Sternberg, 1997). These societies would do more for themselves and the people within them if they paid more attention to wisdom and if they nurtured and valued wisdom.

Wisdom is related to, but different from, intelligence. Other researchers and I have conducted a number of studies of people's conceptions of intelligence and of wisdom, and although the elements of wisdom and intelligence overlap, they are not identical. A critical difference is that wisdom must involve serious life problems and some role of values (Sternberg, 1998). Intelligence, in contrast, can be applied to problems that have nothing to do with life issues and that are essentially value free. Many so-called brilliant people are intelligent, but not wise, just as wise people need not be brilliant.

Many industrialized societies today, and notably the United States, place a premium on conventionally defined intelligence—the kind that leads to high scores on conventional aptitude tests and to stellar grades in school. They sort their youth through an elaborate ritual of tests and school grades to ensure that the "best and the brightest" have the opportunity to excel in society and that the intellectually impoverished are not provided with opportunities of which they are unable to take advantage.

Society sorts children by their test scores, and so, of course, children with better test scores are more likely to be able to advance to more lucrative jobs. Those who do not have elevated test scores have great difficulty gaining admission to the preparatory programs (prestigious colleges, and then law schools, medical schools, business schools, graduate schools, and so on) that will enable them to get the inside track to the best jobs. So the system may seem to be reflecting an invisible hand of nature, when in fact it is of society's own creation. This fact is shown by fluctuations in test scores at top universities such as Harvard between the 1950s and the 1960s. Average test scores rose about 100 points (1 SD), reflecting not any invisible hand of nature but the decision on the part of admissions offices at prestigious universities such as Harvard to use SAT scores rather than socioeconomic class as a primary basis for admission. Last name, social connections, and parental wealth started to count less, and test scores started to count more.

One might argue that the system of using testing is better than the system of using wealth. Perhaps. Typically, however, whatever group benefits from a given system tends to view the system as desirable. Thus, when people with high test scores attain positions of power, they look for others like themselves; when wealthy or well-connected people reach positions of power, they do the same. From time to time, other methods of sorting have been used as well (Sternberg, 1997, 1999a): race, religion, caste, and gender, to name a few. These methods of sorting individuals in society are ill chosen. Indeed, they are foolish. The reason they are so predominant and yet so foolish is that once any of these systems is in place, it tends to become self-perpetuating, as people chosen for a certain attribute choose more of the same to enter the elite. What was the preferred method of sorting? It was always wisdom. It still is.

THE BALANCE THEORY OF WISDOM

The balance theory of wisdom holds that a wise person can be identified on the basis of the way he or she forms judgments and solves significant problems. Wisdom involves several components.

Wisdom starts with tacit knowledge, or what a person needs to know to adapt to or shape an environment that is not explicitly taught and that usually is not even verbalized. *Tacit knowledge* is knowledge of how to negotiate the environment and hence is usually learned from experience. For example, knowledge of how effectively to supervise one's subordinates or to maintain cordial relations with one's peers is usually tacit. Research shows that there is no necessary or even likely relation between tacit knowledge, on the one hand, and formal knowledge, on the other (Sternberg et al., 2000).

So-called "practical intelligence," like wisdom, starts with tacit knowledge. What distinguishes wisdom from practical intelligence is how the tacit knowledge is used. A typical application of practical intelligence is to benefit oneself or one's significant others. Wisdom, in contrast, is used when people use their tacit knowledge in the service of a common good. They seek the best possible outcome not just for themselves, but rather for all. They believe that in the long run, what is best for all truly is best for them too. The common good takes into account the interests of anyone who might potentially be affected by a judgment or decision. A judge is someone whose job is prototypical in its requirement of wise judgments, a fact allegedly illustrated long ago by King Solomon when he decided how to judge which of two women truly was the mother of a particular baby.

The common good is not a concept that most people readily grasp. Because many people are egocentric in nature, they may view the common good as being what is good for them. They are like the young, preoperational children (roughly ages 2–7) studied by Piaget (see, e.g., Piaget, 1972), who are able to see things only from their own perspective. Other people go one step further and take others into account. However, these others may be only members of their own group, tribe, or other entity.

How do wise people go about seeking a common good? They do so by balancing their own interests with the interests of others and of institutions (e.g., an organization, a community, or a society). Thus wisdom always involves a balancing act, and it is for this reason that the theory is called a *balance theory of wisdom* (Sternberg, 1998, 1999a). In the theory, these three interests are referred to as *intrapersonal* interests (one's own interests), *interpersonal* interests (the interests of others), and *extrapersonal* interests (the interests of institutions and society).

It is easy to find cases of individuals exercising their practical intelligence (or emotional intelligence, for that matter) not in the service of wisdom but at its expense. A fairly common example is in negotiations between management and unions, or sometimes between countries. Each side may employ negotiators whose task is to produce an agreement that maximizes the unilateral advantages for their own side. Often, the more ruthless the negotiators are, the more competent they are considered to be. The problem is that in antagonizing the other side, the result is a strike, in the case of the union, or a war, in the case of the countries. Sometimes there is an agreement between the sides, but if it is one-sided, smoldering resentments lead to flare-ups of bad feelings on the part of the side that feels it has been treated inequitably.

The three kinds of interests mentioned above are distributed through *space*; that is, they refer to people and institutions in various places. Wise decisions also balance interests over time. In particular, they balance the long term with the short term. Many acts of foolishness arise because people only think for the short-term and not for what the long-term future may bring. Most cases of AIDS, for example, are the wholly preventable result of foolish behavior that was pleasurable in the short term but probably fatal in the long term. Desperate acts of violence and depravity also often bring about some perceived short-term gain at the expense of the long term.

Intrapersonal, interpersonal, and extrapersonal interests are balanced over the short and the long term to adapt to, shape, and select environments. These three responses to the environment must be balanced as well, so that the theory as a whole comprises three balancing operations: (a) of interests, (b) of the term (short or long) over which the interests apply, and (c) of response to the environment.

Adaptation occurs when individuals modify themselves to suit their environments. People adapt when they enter new jobs, move to new communities, or start new relationships. Adaptation is important because without it, a person or any other organism would not survive for very long, as Darwin and his successors have shown in the biological domain. Societies as people know them could not exist unless individuals were willing to obey laws and follow customs. However, adaptation in itself does not provide a basis for wisdom. Sometimes people need to shape their environment. Instead of modifying themselves to suit the environment, they need to modify the environment to suit them.

For example, many people find their jobs not to be everything they had hoped these jobs would be. The working conditions may not be ideal, the ethics of what they are doing may be shady, their colleagues may not be that for which they had hoped. People need to balance adaptation to the environment by shaping it to mold it into what they ideally would like it to be. Of course, such shaping is more apparent in the case of people in high-level positions who are placed in roles of leadership, but shaping can occur at any level. Teachers, for example, are often strait-jacketed with textbooks that they would never have adopted if left to their own devices. They may decide that it is in the best interests of the children they teach to supplement these texts with additional enriching material of their own. Members of an organization may find that the same entrenched bureaucracy has been running the organization for many years and shows no signs of wanting to give up its authority. These individuals may then decide to run for office or to serve on committees to revive the organizations. At a more profound level, individuals such as Oscar Schindler work in the context of a government whose mandates they have found to be unprincipled and immoral. Schindler did what he could to save Jews who otherwise would have been consigned to death camps. Similarly, Anne Frank survived as long as she did because a family was willing to hide her and her loved ones, although ultimately she was found and sent to her death.

At times, one realizes that the wise thing to do is neither to adapt nor to shape an environment but to get out of it. The values of a community may be so at odds with one's own values that one can view the choice of the community only as a mistake. Having realized that one has nothing to offer nor be offered by such a community, one may decide to leave it, even at one's peril, as in the case of certain religious cults. Such a decision may represent the realization that one made a mistake in the first place, or the realization that whatever the community once had to offer one, it no longer has the same attraction.

Wise selection of teachers and mentors in the course of attaining expertise also requires a certain level of wisdom. Research shows that extremely talented musicians usually start off with one teacher but then outgrow that teacher. Sometimes the teacher realizes that he or she no longer has much to offer the student, and sometimes the student or the student's parents have this realization (Bloom, 1985; Sosniak, 1985). At this point, neither the student, the teacher, nor the musical field will benefit from the continued association, and the student does well to select another teacher. Of course, the same painful realization often occurs in intimate relationships, when one realizes one has outgrown the intimate relationship in which one is involved and that the relationship seems to be unable to grow to fit one's needs.

In sum, then, wisdom involves applying tacit knowledge in the service of a common good by balancing intrapersonal, interpersonal, and extrapersonal interests over the short and long terms to adapt to, shape, and select environments. However, all balancing acts involve values.

It is impossible to speak of wisdom outside the context of a set of values, which in combination may lead one to a moral stance—or, in Kohlberg's (1969, 1983) view—stage. The same can be said of all practical intelligence: Behavior is viewed as practically intelligent as a function of what is valued in a societal–cultural context. Values mediate how one balances interests and responses and collectively contribute even to how one defines a common good. I believe the intersection of wisdom with the moral domain can be seen in the fact that there is some overlap in the notion of wisdom presented here and the notion of moral reasoning as it applies in the two highest stages (4 and 5) of Kohlberg's (1969) theory. At the same time, wisdom is broader than moral reasoning. It applies to any human problem involving a balance of intrapersonal, interpersonal, and extrapersonal interests, regardless of whether moral issues are at stake.

In our research in different cultures, my colleagues and I have found a surprising coincidence of values across cultures, although the expression of these values may differ from one culture to another. Values such as honesty, sincerity, helpfulness, respect for oneself and others, and forthrightness seem to be important almost wherever one goes. I thus believe that it is possible to specify a set of values that will be relevant to the attainment of wisdom in any culture.

Wisdom may sound like a construct relevant only to adults. Nothing could be further from the case. We need to start developing wisdom in children. Moreover, we need to start developing a valuing and appreciation of wisdom and what it can bring to society. The devaluing of older people in many societies reflects as well a devaluing of the wisdom that these people can bring to the societies.

Wisdom can be developed in several ways. First, providing students with problems that require wise thinking is a start. Helping them through the balancing operations of wisdom is important, too. Third, valuing wise information processing and solutions is essential. Without rewards for wise behavior, whatever wisdom children show may be extinguished quickly. Fourth, providing examples of wise thinking from history and analyzing them would seem to be important. Fifth, role modeling is essential. If one wants children to act wisely, one must show them how by acting wisely oneself. Sixth, wisdom probably is best developed through the incorporation of dialectical thinking (Hegel, 1807/1931) into one's processing of problems (Basseches, 1984; Labouvie-Vief, 1990; Pascual-Leone, 1990; Riegel, 1973; Sternberg, 1999a). The essence of dialectical thinking is that most problems in the world do not have right or wrong answers, but better or worse ones, and what is seen as a good answer can vary with time and place. With respect to time, it involves the recognition that ideas evolve over time through an ongoing, unending process of thesis followed by antithesis followed by synthesis, with the synthesis in turn becoming the next thesis (Hegel, 1807/1931). When dialectical thinking occurs with respect to place (or space), it involves the recognition that at a given point in time, people may have diverging viewpoints on problems that seem uniquely valid or at least reasonable to them. The values one espouses today or in the United States cannot immediately be applied to other times or other places without considering the context in which others live and have lived.

It is past time for a radical paradigm shift in our values and our educational system. Intelligence is important; so is traditional school achievement, but neither will "save the world." Individuals and societies would achieve great benefits by attuning themselves to the importance of wisdom. First, they would create happier individuals. Second, they would create more productive individuals. Third, they would create a better society and a better world.

Luis Alberto Machado, once Minister for the Development of Intelligence in Venezuela, argued that the key to a better society is intelligence. In the 1980s, he oversaw massive intervention programs in Venezuela to improve the intelligence of Venezuelan schoolchildren. His political party lost the next election, and with the loss of the election came the loss of the intervention programs, so the world never got to see whether his intervention program would have worked. However, a natural experiment has taken place: Over the last few generations, IQs around the world have been rising (Flynn, 1987; Neisser, 1998), even though the conditions of the world seem not to be a whole lot better. Maybe this is because the answer is not and never was in increased intelligence but in increased wisdom.

REFERENCES

Basseches, J. (1984). *Dialectical thinking and adult development*. Norwood, NJ: Ablex.

Berry, D. C. (1994). Implicit learning: Twenty-five years on. A tutorial. In C. Umilta & M. Moscovitch (Eds.), *Attention and performance 15: Conscious and nonconscious information processing* (pp. 755–782). Cambridge, MA: MIT Press.

Bloom, B. (1985). *Developing talent in young people*. New York: Ballantine.

Ceci, S. J. (1996). *On intelligence* (expanded ed.). Cambridge, MA: Harvard University Press.

Fiedler, F. E., & Link, T. G. (1994). Leader intelligence, interpersonal stress, and task performance. In R. J. Sternberg & R. K. Wagner (Eds.), *Mind in context: Interactionist perspectives on human intelligence* (pp. 152–167). New York: Cambridge University Press.

Flynn, J. R. (1987). Massive IQ gains in 14 nations. *Psychological Bulletin, 101*, 171–191.

Gardner, H. (1983). *Frames of mind: The theory of multiple intelligences*. New York: Basic Books.

Gardner, H. (1999). *Intelligence reframed: Multiple intelligences for the 21st century*. New York: Basic Books.

Grigorenko, E. L., Geissler, P. W., Prince, R., Okatcha, F., Nokes, C., Kenny, D. A., et al. (2001). The organization of Luo conceptions of intelligence: A study of implicit theories in a Kenyan village. *International Journal of Behavioral Development, 25*, 367–378.

Harrell, T. W., & Harrell, M. S. (1945). Army General Classification Test scores for civilian occupations. *Educational and Psychological Measurement, 5*, 229–239.

Hegel, G. W. F. (1931). *The phenomenology of the mind* (2nd ed., J. D. Baillie, Trans). London: Allen & Unwin. (Original work published 1807)

Herrnstein, R. J., & Murray, C. (1994). *The bell curve*. New York: Free Press.

Horn, W. F., & Packard, T. (1985). Early identification of learning problems: A meta-analysis. *Journal of Educational Psychology, 77*, 597–607.

Janis, I. L. (1972). *Victims of groupthink*. Boston: Houghton Mifflin.

Jencks, C. (1972). *Inequality: A reassessment of the effect of family and schooling in America*. New York: Basic Books.

Kohlberg, L. (1969). Stage and sequence: The cognitive–developmental approach to socialization. In G. A. Goslin (Ed.), *Handbook of socialization theory and research* (pp. 347–380). Chicago: Rand McNally.

Kohlberg, L. (1983). *The psychology of moral development*. New York: Harper & Row.

Labouvie-Vief, G. (1990). Wisdom as integrated thought: Historical and developmental perspectives. In R. J. Sternberg (Ed.), *Wisdom: Its nature, origins, and development* (pp. 52–83). New York: Cambridge University Press.

Mackintosh, N. J. (1998). *IQ and human intelligence*. Oxford, England: Oxford University Press.

Mackintosh, N. J., & Mascie-Taylor, C. G. N. (1986). The IQ question. In C. Bagley & G. K. Verma (Eds.), *Personality, cognition and values* (pp. 77–131). London: Macmillan.

Mayer, R. E. (2000). Intelligence and education. In R. J. Sternberg (Ed.), *Handbook of intelligence* (pp. 519–533). New York: Cambridge University Press.

McCall, R. B. (1977). Childhood IQs as predictors of adult educational and occupational status. *Science, 197*, 482–483.

Neisser, U. (Ed.). (1998). *The rising curve*. Washington, DC: American Psychological Association.

Pascual-Leone, J. (1990). A chapter on wisdom: Toward organismic processes that make it possible. In R. J. Sternberg (Ed.), *Wisdom: Its nature, origins, and development* (pp. 244–278). New York: Cambridge University Press.

Piaget, J. (1972). *The psychology of intelligence*. Totowa, NJ: Littlefield Adams.

Riegel, K. F. (1973). Dialectical operations: The final period of cognitive development. *Human Development, 16*, 346–370.

Schmidt, F. L., & Hunter, J. E. (1998). The validity and utility of selection methods in personnel psychology: Practical and theoretical implications of 85 years of research findings. *Psychological Bulletin, 124*, 262–274.

Serpell, R. (1974). Aspects of intelligence in a developing country. *African Social Research, 17*, 576–596.

Simonton, D. K. (1994). *Greatness: Who makes history and why?* New York: Guilford Press.

Sosniak, L. (1985). Learning to be a concert pianist. In B. Bloom (Ed.), *Developing talent in young people* (pp. 19–67). New York: Ballantine.

Sternberg, R. J. (1985a). *Beyond IQ: A triarchic theory of human intelligence*. New York: Cambridge University Press.

Sternberg, R. J. (1985b). Implicit theories of intelligence, creativity, and wisdom. *Journal of Personality and Social Psychology, 49*, 607–627.

Sternberg, R. J. (1997). *Successful intelligence*. New York: Plume.

Sternberg, R. J. (1998). A balance theory of wisdom. *Review of General Psychology, 2*, 347–365.

Sternberg, R. J. (1999a). Creativity is a decision. In A. L. Costa (Ed.), *Teaching for intelligence II* (pp. 83–106). Arlington Heights, IL: Skylight Training and Publishing.

Sternberg, R. J. (1999b). The theory of successful intelligence. *Review of General Psychology, 3*, 292–316.

Sternberg, R. J., Conway, B. E., Ketron, J. L., & Bernstein, M. (1981). People's conceptions of intelligence. *Journal of Personality and Social Psychology, 41*, 37–55.

Sternberg, R. J., Forsythe, G. B., Hedlund, J., Horvath, J., Snook, S., Williams, W. M., et al. (2000). *Practical intelligence in everyday life*. New York: Cambridge University Press.

Sternberg, R. J., & Kaufman J. C. (1998). Human abilities. *Annual Review of Psychology, 49*, 479–502.

Vernon, P. E. (1947). Research on personnel selection in the Royal Navy and the British Army. *American Psychologist, 2*, 35–51.

Webster's new world college dictionary (3rd ed.). (1997). New York: Simon & Schuster.

Yang, S., & Sternberg, R. J. (1997). Taiwanese Chinese people's conceptions of intelligence. *Intelligence, 25*, 21–36.

4

THE HAZARDS OF GOAL PURSUIT

LAURA A. KING AND CHAD M. BURTON

One of the ways human beings attach themselves to the events of everyday life—one way that daily life gains meaning—is through the pursuit of goals. Goals are ways of mattering, ways that one invests in daily activities and imbues them with personal meaning.

In the mid-1980s, personological approaches to the study of personality and well-being embraced the idea that the relation between a person and the events of his or her life can be understood through everyday goals. Daily goals are highly contextualized motivational units that are assumed to be available to awareness and that are fairly easily measured by simply asking people what they are typically trying to do. Daily goals might include desires such as "to do my best at whatever I attempt," "to be viewed as an intelligent person," and "to deepen my understanding of human life." Various research programs focusing on daily goals have emerged, all converging on the important role of everyday goals in human functioning. Working toward valued goals is an important aspect of psychological (e.g., Brunstein, 1993; Emmons, 1989, 1999; King, Richards, & Stemmerich, 1998; Omodei & Wearing, 1990) and physical (Emmons & King, 1988; Sheldon & Kasser, 1995) well-being. Goals have been shown to

Preparation of this chapter was supported in part by funding from the Templeton Foundation as well as Grant 54142 from the National Institute of Mental Health.

organize daily experience and mediate the relationship between events and daily emotional life (Cantor, Norem, Langston, & Zirkel, 1991). There is no question that daily goal pursuit has positive value. Daily goals have been viewed as instantiations of agency in everyday life (e.g., Harlow & Cantor, 1995; King, 1998).

The appeal of the goal construct is such that successful self-regulation has often been described as making satisfactory progress toward valued ends (Carver & Scheier, 1990; King et al., 1998). Yet to an extent, models of self-regulation make sense only if they assume that the level of commitment to these goals is appropriate; that the goals are structurally optimal; and that, ultimately, the goals are well chosen. Problems in goal identification and articulation are essentially avoided or disregarded if one assumes that goal direction is simply a property of well-functioning systems. Furthermore, it is difficult, in talking abstractly about goal-directed behavior, to retain the dynamic character of goals. The changing circumstances of human life indicate that goals must change. However, there is also no denying that goals have a kind of psychic gravity—typically they surrender their places in one's life only begrudgingly.

Inasmuch as goal pursuits provide a sense of purpose in life and identify idiosyncratic sources of meaning, it may be difficult to consider that such pursuits may have negative consequences. One reason for the difficulty involved in pinpointing the vices attached to the virtue of goal pursuit is that research in this area typically has focused (and rightly so) on the positive consequences of goal pursuit. Even some of the more generic results—for example, that goal relevance determines mood reactions to life events—have been interpreted in positive ways, as demonstrating, for instance, the coherence of human life. The very notion of the human being as a goal-directed organism is associated with more positive views of human nature (e.g., Adler, 1927; Allport, 1961; Rogers, 1961). Yet a consideration of the research literature reveals that the very properties of goals that indicate the large role they play in daily life also suggest their potentially destructive character.

Given the relations of goals to thoughts, behaviors, mood, and well-being, it is perhaps worthwhile to consider that goals are actually somewhat ambiguous in terms of their benefits or pitfalls; that is, with their level of importance in the person's life, their relation to others' goals, and their content unspecified, goals are simply structures that attach the self to daily life. Simply knowing someone has a goal tells one little about the role of that goal in that person's life. If goals are viewed as the glue that attaches one to the events of the day, then the impact of goal pursuit on an individual can be good, bad, or indifferent. The actual impact of a goal on a person's life depends on the level of commitment experienced; the amount of success attained; the structural properties of the goal; and, of course, the content of the goal itself. In this chapter, we consider empirical evidence that reveals the potential negative aspects of goals in human life. These studies indicate that goal investment, goal structure, and goal content may all lead to negative outcomes.

CAN GOALS MATTER TOO MUCH?

Setting a goal typically means having some interest in how that goal turns out. One of the positive features of goals is that they provide a means for one to engage in one's daily life, which is a correlate of superior functioning throughout the life span (Cantor & Sanderson, 1999). Yet simply making one's endeavors matter may mean not only enjoying the experience of striving and accomplishment but also risking the experience of concern and worry over those events.

Goals and Worry: An Inevitable Combination?

Pomerantz, Saxon, and Oishi (2000) found that individuals who were highly invested in their goals were also more likely to report worrying about those goals. Participants listed their personal goals and then rated those goals on their importance, the degree to which they worried about those goals, and the level of disappointment they would experience in response to failure. The results indicated that goal investment was associated with lowered depression but greater worry. Analyses at the level of goal, controlling for individual differences, showed that it was the very goals in which individuals were most invested about which they also tended to worry. In addition, individuals tended to worry about goals that were seen as requiring great effort and those goals in which failure was perceived as having larger impact on the self. These findings are not surprising if one thinks of goals as mechanisms of mattering, but they do indicate that goal pursuit—a source of personal satisfaction—may have its costs. Mediational analyses revealed that the more individuals perceived failure as having impact, the more they worried about their deeply invested goals. Results with regard to perceived success were particularly interesting. Perceived success was negatively associated with worry and positively associated with positive affect. These results seem to indicate that goal investment is beneficial to one's emotional life only when one is pursuing goals that are relatively easy or high in perceived success. When individuals take on difficult tasks, they may be setting themselves up for preoccupation.

Indeed, the relation of goals to everyday thoughts might well indicate that goals are likely to be the source of considerable worry. For instance, a commonly cited finding is that goals are more likely to occur in spontaneous thought if they are important, if a deadline is approaching, or if substantial obstacles are encountered in the pursuit of the goal (e.g., Emmons & King, 1988, Klinger, 1977). These results not only indicate evidence of the power of goals in directing thought but also demonstrate the potential place of goals in preoccupation. Indeed, some characteristics of thoughts about goals render these thoughts particularly susceptible to anxiety. Goals attach one's present behavior to future outcomes. This attachment to a fictitious future suggests that goal-related thoughts may concern consequences and future expectations, including potential disasters and failures. These are the very topics that Ingram and Kendall (1987) suggested as cognitive aspects of anxiety. Repetitive thoughts about negative possible outcomes or worrying is associated with anxiety and spreading of anxious meanings (Borkovec, Ray, & Stober, 1998). Rumination has also been linked to depression (Nolen-Hoeksema, 1996). Although King and Pennebaker (1997) contrasted rumination with goal-relevant thought, it is notable that Martin and Tesser's (1996) model of rumination includes repetitive thought about goals as one form of rumination. Goals, although potentially imbued with the promise of a more meaningful existence, also serve as avenues to anxiety and worry (although cf. chap. 7, this volume).

One of the central concerns of the worried goal seeker is likely to be the possibility of failure and the possible negative consequences likely to accompany failure. It certainly is fairly obvious that goal pursuit might sometimes lead to failure. Failure by definition is undesirable to the pursuer of a goal (given a reasonable level of psychological adjustment). Failing at a valued goal may be a source of some misery and increased preoccupation. The Zeigarnick effect (1938) is a classic example of the power of interrupted goals on thought and behavior. Brunstein and Gollwitzer (1996) found that failure was likely to lead to rumination. Thus, the already-preoccupied goal seeker becomes even more so after goal failure. Affective reactions to failure may be even more severe for individuals who are more invested in those goals.

One way to think about goals as potentially negative preoccupations is to think about the extent to which individuals "put themselves on the line" in goal pursuit. The degree to which one's ultimate happiness or self-esteem is wagered against goal success may influence the level of overall well-being a person experiences.

This idea certainly resonates with James's notion that individuals who invest in their goals may experience their self-esteem as contingent on accomplishing those goals (cf. Pelham, 1991). Perhaps it would make sense to limit the potentially negative aspects of goal failure, yet evidence for a kind of limited impact of goal-relevant events is difficult to come by (cf. Marsh, 1995). Research has certainly demonstrated the negative consequences of having one's self-esteem depend on particular life events.

Contingent Self-Esteem

Contingent self-esteem is just plain bad for you. A large body of evidence amassed by Kernis and his colleagues has shown that individuals whose self-esteem varies depending on how things are going tend to show a variety of maladaptive responses to life (see chap. 1, this volume). Kernis, Paradise, Whitaker, Wheatman, and Goldman (2000) described individuals with unstable self-esteem as having "fragile, vulnerable feelings of self worth influenced by internally generated (e.g., reflecting on one's progress toward important goals) and externally provided . . . evaluative events" (p. 1297). Thus, they not only pointed out the difficulty faced by individuals whose "feelings of self worth are continually on the line" (p. 1298) but also noted the role of goal pursuit in such a deleterious situation. Individuals with unstable, contingent self-esteem tend to focus on threatening aspects of events (Waschull & Kernis, 1996), show greater increases in depressive symptoms when faced with hassles (Kernis et al., 1998), have self-feelings that are affected by positive and negative events (Greenier et al., 1999), and have a less mastery-oriented stance toward learning (Waschull & Kernis, 1996) and show greater anger and hostility (Kernis et al., 1989) and self-doubt in response to failure (Kernis, Cornell, Sun, Berry, & Harlow, 1993). In a sense, the degree to which goals attach the self to life events and guide emotional reactions, goals may be the means by which one makes one's self-esteem contingent on life events.

"Linking"

Thematically similar ideas are apparent in a program of research conducted by McIntosh and colleagues, who have examined individuals who tend to link their personal happiness to the fulfillment of certain values or the accomplishment of certain goals. These "linkers" believe that attaining certain goals will make them happy. Nonlinkers tend to be less outcome focused. McIntosh, Harlow, and Martin (1995) found that linkers were more likely to experience rumination, depression, physical complaints and repeated long-term negative affect and were more tuned to negative affect. McIntosh, Martin, and Jones (2001) found that linkers were more susceptible to sadness. McIntosh et al. (2001) found that linkers demonstrated heightened sensitivity to feedback of potential failure—once again demonstrating the relation between aspects of goal pursuit and negative outcomes (see chap. 7, this volume).

NEUROTIC PERSEVERANCE: NOT KNOWING WHEN TO GIVE UP

In addition to the potentially negative outcomes of simply caring about what happens in one's goal pursuits, high dedication to goals may lead to a variety of other negative consequences, particularly in the face of failure. One potential negative of caring too much about one's goals is the inability to disengage from hopeless situations. Individuals who are unable to disengage from goals that no longer hold the possibility of fulfillment are likely to fall into patterns of negative behavior. The issue of unrealistic, self-defeating goals is certainly a common theme in cognitive–behavioral interventions (e.g., Ellis, 1997). A hallmark of successful self-regulation may be the ability to flexibly pursue goals and to disengage from life goals that no longer include the possibility of fulfillment (King, 1996, 1998). Films and literature teem with examples of individuals who obsessively pursue some potentially insane goal, including Don Quixote, Ahab, Heathcliff, and Dr. Frankenstein. Individuals who refuse to give up on lost goals may be seen variously as pathetic, potentially deluded, irritating, or even frightening.

It would be comforting to think that a great deal of rationality goes into the selection of life goals, such that people will value what they are good at. According to this ideal, goals will optimally map onto one's talents. In reality, however, such a relationship is not always apparent (cf. Marsh, 1993, 1995; Rosenberg, 1979). An interesting case in point is provided by participants in a study conducted by Bell (1997), in which premed students were asked to describe self-defining memories that led them to adopt the goal of becoming a doctor. Many of the memories included incidents such as calling 911 during a medical emergency as a child, having a broken limb treated by a compassionate doctor, and having a family member suffer from a serious illness. None of these memory elements was related to success at science courses in college or even with overall academic success (Bell, 1997). The high percentage of rejection letters mailed out by graduate school admissions committees each year would seem to support the idea that goals may not be selected with a realistic eye toward actual skills. What happens when beloved goals are the subject of negative performance feedback?

Research typically indicates that in the face of negative feedback goal seekers do not forsake their goals but rather redouble their efforts. For instance, Brunstein and Gollwitzer (1996) found that high involvement in a task was associated with even more involvement after failure. Emmons, Colby, and Kaiser (1998) found that the typical response to life change was not goal change but rather a redoubling of effort on existing goals. Similarly, King and Williams (2001) found that goal investment led to persistence at goals even in the face of failure feedback. In that study, premed students were asked to list their personal strivings. These strivings were content analyzed for relevance to the ultimate goal of becoming a doctor. King and Williams found that seeking goals related to getting into medical school was associated with persistence in premed coursework, even controlling for grade-point average. Although these results might be taken as evidence of heroic or admirable goal persistence, feedback about one's academic performance clearly is relevant to the probability of ultimate success at one's goal. For participants who were doing poorly, high goal investment was associated with persistence even in the face of apparent failure (King & Williams, 2001).

If goal investment leads to maladaptive persistence, then such investment may be problematic. Sometimes quitting is a good idea. However, stories of heroic persistence at a life goal and the glorification of goal pursuit per se may inspire individuals to "dream the impossible dream." To be sure, some individuals who undertake seemingly impossible goals do succeed; unfortunately, it is not really possible to predict in advance whose investment is foolish and whose is the beginning of a heroic tale of accomplishment. Stories of achievement in the face of apparently inevitable failure might inspire individuals to doggedly pursue their "impossible dreams" when, in fact, another life path might promise greater fulfillment.

Klinger (1975, 1977) has suggested that failure to disengage from unattainable goals is linked to depressive symptoms. Although this distress is considered a normal part of the process of letting go of valued goals, Klinger (1977) suggested that reduced daily goal functioning and increased psychological distress may result from expending daily thought and emotion toward unfulfilled goals. Kuhl and Helle (1986) experimentally demonstrated that individuals who failed to disengage from unattainable goals tended to show depressive symptoms and limited opportunities for new goals.

Unfulfilled ambitions may also become the seeds of eventual regret. Ryff (1991) found that regrets were a predictor of lowered psychological well-being in midlife. A goal-directed youth that meets with little success may well be looked back on as a wasted youth, unless one is able to recognize the nobility of striving even without success.

The issues discussed thus far all pertain to goal pursuit in general, yet more specific aspects of goals also warrant discussion. Although goal pursuit per se may be a potentially treacherous endeavor, other characteristics of goals, including their structure and content, may also exacerbate these potential problems.

THE HAZARDS OF GOAL STRUCTURE

Most research on personalized goal constructs has focused on the relations of goal characteristics to psychological and physical health. Some of these aspects of goals have been shown to be particularly problematic for individuals. We focus on three structural properties of goals that have been shown to be predictors of psychological as well as physical problems: (a) difficulty; (b) conflict; and, perhaps most troubling, (c) avoidance goals.

"Too Hard" Versus "Too Easy": There May Be No "Just Right"

A classic issue in the study of motivation has been the question of level of aspiration. Should one reach for the stars or for something less stellar but more realistic? Are there differing implications of these two strategies for the individual? Goal research has typically found that pursuing particularly difficult goals is a negative predictor of daily well-being. The daily-goal literature has tended to advocate instead setting modest goals that are doable (e.g., King et al., 1998; Locke, 2001). Yet, when one places the concept of goals in the grand scheme of human life, is it not the grander pursuits that one thinks of as most meaningful (i.e., those in which one is most invested, which are most challenging, and in which failure *is* an option)? Is pursuing loftier ambitions necessarily bad for the person?

Vallacher and Wegner (2000) presented a classic examination of the importance of the level at which individuals identify their behavior for task performance, behavioral maintenance, and so forth. There is no doubt that the level of identification (from quite concrete to quite abstract) shares a delicate relation with its ultimate completion. How might one's typical or habitual goalsetting levels relate to overall goal performance and well-being? Emmons (1992) examined the daily personal strivings generated by participants across a variety of samples. There were clear differences among individuals in their typical level of goal striving. Some individuals set very high level goals, such as "treat others with dignity" and "increase my knowledge of the world," while others pursue lower level goals, such as "clean the house," or "buy some new luggage." High-level strivers tended to be higher in negative affect and depression. Low-level strivers tended to be more likely to suffer physical illness, measured by means of peer and spouse ratings of illness as well as number of health center visits. Emmons (1992) suggested that low-level strivers may be engaging in repressive coping and are therefore focusing on low-level concrete aspects of life. Conversely, high-level strivers seem to use a more confrontational coping style. These results seem to indicate a kind of trade-off so that a person is left with a choice: feeling sad or being sick. However, it may well be that individuals must propose a hierarchical system of goals to really benefit from goal pursuit. Latham and Seijts (1999) examined productivity and found that individuals assigned both a proximal and a distal goal performed better than those who were assigned just a distal goal or those who were told to simply "do your best." Thus, having multiple goals may help provide the most benefits for the person. Yet the hydra that is goal pursuit remains, because multiple goals may render the person vulnerable to goal conflict.

Goal Conflict

Another goal structural variable that shares relations with negative outcomes is goal conflict. Emmons and King (1988) investigated the relation of goal conflict to psychological and physical well-being. Motivational conflict has long been recognized as a source of human mental suffering (e.g., Freud, 1923/1961). Emmons and King found that individuals whose daily goals showed a large degree of conflict among themselves tended to suffer from heightened psychological distress and physical illness. They also found that individuals tended to think more but act less on those conflictful personal goals. Thus, committing oneself to daily goals that conflict with each other seems to have quite negative consequences for the individual.

Avoidance Goals

To preclude the negative effects of failure, individuals might simply try to avoid having things go wrong, yet a large body of research from a variety of sources indicates that an avoidance strategy is most associated with negative outcomes. Although goals typically are thought of as appetitive states, it may well be that many people succeed at attaining their life ambitions by avoiding dreaded outcomes. Although avoidance goals may be common, they may also be detrimental to the individual's goal attainment and psychological and physical well-being. Research has shown the difficulty in motivating oneself to not do something. "Not doing" is clearly more difficult than "doing" in many circumstances. When an individual seeks to avoid failure, the implications of failure itself are certainly more dire than when an individual fails at attaining a hoped-for success. Imagine the individual who has failed at "not failing my classes" versus the individual who has failed at "getting As in my classes."

Higgins (1997) has contrasted a *prevention* focus versus a *promotion* focus. A prevention focus is associated with avoidance strategies that arise from security needs and a sense of guilt and duty. A prevention focus promotes sensitivity to negative outcomes (Shah & Higgins, 2001). One of the by-products of avoidance strategies is that the individual tends to enjoy less positive affect in the pursuit and attainment of a goal (e.g., Higgins, Shah, & Friedman, 1997).

The research literature is rich with evidence that avoidance goals are associated with negative outcomes. For instance, Elliot and Sheldon (1997) found that avoidance goals were associated with fear of failure. Individuals engaged in avoidance goal pursuit have been found to perceive their pursuit as less enjoyable and report decreased self-esteem and a decline in psychological well-being during the pursuit of such goals. Quite simply, the sheer number of avoidance goals was a significant predictor of lower psychological well-being. In addition, avoidance goals are most likely to be adopted by individuals who perceive their skills as low (Elliot, Sheldon, & Church, 1997). For such individuals, the pursuit of avoidance goals leads to even lower levels of self-esteem (Elliot et al., 1997). Elliot and Sheldon (1998) found that participants who espoused avoidance goals also reported lowered competence and autonomy. Thus, the pursuit of avoidance goals robs goal-directed activity of its typically positive properties. In addition to psychological distress, Elliot and Sheldon (1998) found that pursuit of avoidance goals associated with increased reported physical symptoms.

In those studies, the psychological concomitants of avoidance goals (lowered competence, etc.) were also associated with increases in physical symptoms over time.

King et al. (1998) found that pursuing goals that presumably avoided one's worst fears (e.g., pursuing the goal "to meet people" in service of avoiding the fear "to die alone and lonely") were less satisfied with their lives and more psychologically distressed. King and Williams (2001) found that avoiding one's worst fears was associated with increased thoughts about goals, more behaviors directed toward those goals, and lowered levels of psychological well-being. In addition, worst-fear avoidance was associated with increased health center visits for illness in two samples of undergraduates.

Focusing on avoiding failure is also a major theme in the performance or ego goal orientation identified by Dweck and her colleagues (e.g., Dweck & Leggett, 1988; Elliott & Dweck, 1988). Performance goal orientation is associated with maladaptive attributions for failure—especially attributing failure to low ability. This orientation is therefore likely to relate to negative reactions to failure (e.g., learned helplessness, disengagement, and task derogation). Performance orientation has been shown to relate to the desire to avoid appearing stupid and as such is associated with lowered self-efficacy and self-esteem (Skaalvik, 1997; cf. Elliot & Harackiewicz, 1996).

Thus, adopting goals that are either too high or too low in focus or goals that conflict with each other, or framing one's goals in avoidance language are ways of reversing the apparently positive effects of goal pursuit on well-being. Such goals seem to be more likely to become the object of rumination and more likely to lead to psychological distress and physical illness. In addition, avoidance goals, perhaps because of the more severe implications of failure, tend to involve more negative reactions when things do not go well. These results go a long way in revealing the dark underbelly of goal pursuit. Even though goals have typically been portrayed as hopeful aspects of life associated with fulfillment and meaning, they may, in fact, become agents of misery. It is interesting to note that we have yet to broach what goals are specifically about. Surely the content of goals may hold even graver implications for individuals.

HAZARDOUS GOAL CONTENT:
STRIVING FOR ALL THE WRONG REASONS

In general, it is accurate to say that less research has specifically examined the content of goals (and the implications of that content for well-being) than other aspects of goals. Particularly when goals have been idiographically defined, it is difficult to gauge the influence of goal content on well-being. Still, it is worthwhile to note that the research on psychosocial risk factors for physical illness, such as heart disease, or psychological problems, such as anxiety or depression, often discusses the goal content as problematic. Hostile, competitive goals; self-defeating goals; and goals that express concern over imagined disaster are all potential contributors to various aspects of human misery. In terms of actual goal research per se, however, the content of goals has tended to be a less powerful predictor of important outcomes than has other aspects of goals (e.g., Emmons, 1991). Still, some researchers have examined goal content and have found particular classes of goal content to be problematic.

Working from the framework of self-determination theory (Deci & Ryan, 1995), Kasser and Ryan (1993, 1996) have examined how the content of goals influences psychological well-being. In a series of studies, they showed that individuals who rated the goal of financial success above other values were less likely to engage in self-actualizing activities and experience feelings of self-actualization and vitality and more likely to experience depression and physical symptoms. Thus, individuals whose goals are preoccupied with financial gain may suffer the consequences. These results are important because they suggest that goal pursuit per se may not guarantee an individual the salubrious effects of agency.

Additional extensions of self-determination theory have shown that although the content of goals may vary, the underlying motives of which these goals are expressions may determine whether such pursuit is beneficial for the person. For instance, in Sheldon and Elliot's (1999) *self concordance model*, only individuals who pursue goals that are expressions of organismic needs (e.g., autonomy, relatedness, and competence) benefit from goal progress. These individuals also strive more mightily and feel more positively about success. Although other research reviewed thus far indicates cases in which goal investment can be viewed as legitimately problematic, there are also times when goal investment, although not bad, is also not necessarily good.

CONCLUSION:
LIFE IS COMPLICATED

The research we have reviewed in this chapter indicates that a variety of aspects of goal pursuit have negative consequences for the person. In addition, the pursuit of goals per se may foster worry and leave the individual open to disappointment. Each section of this chapter has ended with an unspoken question: "Would we be better off without goals at all?" This question now warrants discussion. Might an individual without goals be better off than a goal striver? One possible, although deeply unsatisfactory, answer to this question would assert that individuals ought to strive in a particular way to maximize psychological well-being. To wit: The optimally striving individual ought to endeavor to achieve and approach goals that only slightly implicate the self; that are only moderately important, fairly easy, and moderately abstract; that do not conflict with each other; and that concern the accomplishment of something other than financial gain. As a prescription for life, this recipe seems likely to maximize boredom and also to ignore some aspects of life that make it worth living. Moderation in goal pursuit may be overrated.

A deeper answer to the question of whether humans would be better off without goals might draw on Eastern philosophies of what makes a life good. From these perspectives, one might not only acknowledge the pull of wants and goals throughout life but also assert that an ultimate goal of life is the attainment of needlessness or lack of preoccupation (cf. Smith, 1991). Still, it is worth noting that even from such a perspective, needlessness is a goal itself, a state of mind to seek. One might then say that goals are worth having but, in general, the content of goals is not optimal to promote the best life possible.

A final answer to this question, the one with which we conclude, embraces not so much contentment and needlessness but rather the very ambivalence that goal pursuit may engender in life. Recognition of the negative aspects of goal pursuit does not mean that pursuing goals is a bad idea; rather, this examination should be taken as just one example of the ultimate ambiguity of many of the goods of life. Love involves pain. Hope involves risk. Goal pursuit involves sacrifice and the risk of failure and even humiliation. Even the distress of Emmons's (1992) high-level goal strivers might better be characterized as experiencing the affective by-products of being human. In life, some unhappiness is inevitable. Perhaps goals simply make the "why" of one's misery more comprehensible. The subtlety with which sacrifice and pain interweave with the highest of human accomplishments may be difficult to capture in empirical research; however, continual acknowledgement and demonstration of the multifaceted nature of even some of the best things in life is certainly a goal for future research.

Our conclusion, then, to paraphrase Dickens, is that it just might be better to have tried and failed than never to have tried at all. Regardless of its impact on daily affect, making life matter, on a daily basis, might allow for an enhanced sense that life is meaningful. Emotionally investing in one's daily life may mean experiencing disappointment when things do not go well, regretting failures, risking betrayal, and rueing one's mistakes. Truly caring about what happens in one's life, from one day to the next, may well prove challenging: Memories of loss, failure, and mistakes can become a source of considerable misery (Gilovich, Medvec, & Kahneman, 1998; Niedenthal, Tangney, & Gavanski, 1994). However, the alternative—to live unencumbered by such investments—is an empty proposition. Only a hopelessly adolescent psychology of mental functioning would assert that it is best to care about nothing to avoid disappointment.

REFERENCES

Adler, A. (1927). *The practice and theory of individual psychology.* New York: Routledge.

Allport, G. (1961). *Pattern and growth in personality.* New York: Holt, Rinehart and Winston.

Bell, C. (1997). *Self-defining memories and the pursuit of a life dream.* Undergraduate honors thesis, Southern Methodist University.

Borkovec, T. D., Ray, W. J., & Stober, J. (1998). Worry: A cognitive phenomenon intimately linked to affective, physiological, and interpersonal behavioral processes. *Cognitive Therapy and Research, 22,* 561–576.

Brunstein, J. C., (1993). Personal goals and subjective well-being: A longitudinal study. *Journal of Personality and Social Psychology, 65,* 1061–1070.

Brunstein, J. C., & Gollwitzer, P. M. (1996). Effects of failure on subsequent performance: The importance of self-defining goals. *Journal of Personality and Social Psychology, 70,* 395–407.

Cantor, N., Norem, J., Langston, C., & Zirkel, S. (1991). Life tasks and daily life experience. *Journal of Personality, 59,* 425–451.

Cantor, N., & Sanderson, C. A. (1999). Life task participation and wellbeing: The importance of taking part in daily life. In D. Kahneman, E. Diener, & N. Schwarz (Eds.), *Well-being: The foundations of hedonic psychology* (pp. 230–243). New York: Russell Sage Foundation.

Carver, C. S., & Scheier, M. F. (1990). Origins and functions of positive and negative affect: A control-process view. *Psychological Bulletin, 97,* 19–35.

Deci, E. L., & Ryan, R. M. (1995). Human autonomy: The basis for true self-esteem. In M. Kernis (Ed.), *Efficiency, agency, and self-esteem* (pp. 31–49). New York: Plenum.

Dweck, C. S., & Legget, E. L. (1988). A social cognitive approach to motivation and personality. *Psychological Review, 95,* 256–273.

Elliot, E. S., & Dweck, C. S. (1988). Goals: An approach to motivation and achievement. *Journal of Personality and Social Psychology, 70,* 5–12.

Elliot, A. J., & Harackiewicz, J. M. (1996). Approach and avoidance achievement goals and intrinsic motivation: A meditational analysis. *Journal of Personality and Social Psychology, 70,* 461–475.

Elliot, A. J., & Sheldon, K. M. (1997). Avoidance achievement motivation: A personal goals analysis. *Journal of Personality and Social Psychology, 73,* 171–185.

Elliot, A. J., & Sheldon, K. M. (1998). Avoidance personal goals and the personality–illness relationship. *Journal of Personality and Social Psychology, 75,* 1282–1299.

Elliot, A. J., Sheldon, K. M., & Church, M. A. (1997). Avoidance personal goals and subjective well-being. *Personality and Social Psychology Bulletin, 23,* 915–927.

Ellis, A. R. (1997). Rational emotive behavior therapy. In C. Feltham (Ed.), *Which psychotherapy? Leading exponents explain their differences* (pp. 51–67). Thousand Oaks, CA: Sage.

Emmons, R. A. (1989). The personal striving approach to personality. In L. A. Pervin (Ed.), *Goal concepts in personality and social psychology* (pp. 87–126). Hillsdale, NJ: Erlbaum.

Emmons, R. A. (1991). Personal strivings, daily life events, and psychological and physical well-being. *Journal of Personality, 59,* 453–472.

Emmons, R. A. (1992). Abstract versus concrete goals: Personal striving level, physical illness, and psychological well-being. *Journal of Personality and Social Psychology, 62,* 292–300.

Emmons, R. A., Colby, P. M., & Kaiser, H. A. (1998). When losses lead to gains: Personal goals and the recovery of meaning. In P. T. P. Wong & P. S. Fry (Eds.), *The human quest for meaning: A handbook of psychological research and clinical applications* (pp. 163–178). Mahwah, NJ: Lawrence Erlbaum.

Emmons, R. A., & King, L. A. (1988). Conflict among personal strivings: Immediate and long-term implications for psychological and physical well-being. *Journal of Personality and Social Psychology, 53,* 1040–1048.

Freud, S. (1923/1961). *The ego and the id.* New York: Norton.

Gilovich, T., Medvec, V. H., & Kahneman, D. (1998). Varieties of regret: A debate and partial resolution. *Psychological Review, 105,* 602–605.

Greenier, K. D., Kernis, M. H., McNamara, C. W., Waschull, S. B., Berry, A. J., Herlocker, C. E., & Abend, T. A. (1999). Individual differences in reactivity to daily events: Examining the roles of stability and level of self-esteem. *Journal of Personality, 67,* 185–208.

Harlow, R. E., & Cantor, N. (1995). Overcoming lack of self-assurance in an achievement domain: Creating agency in daily life. In M. H. Kernis (Ed.), *Efficacy, agency, and self-esteem* (pp. 171–191). New York: Plenum.

Higgins, E. T. (1997). Beyond pleasure and pain. *American Psychologist, 52,* 1280–1300.

Higgins, E. T., Shah, J., Friedman, R. (1997). Emotional responses to goal attainment: Strength of regulatory focus as moderator. *Journal of Personality and Social Psychology, 72,* 515–525.

Ingram, R. E., & Kendall, P. C. (1987). The cognitive side of anxiety. *Cognitive Therapy and Research, 11,* 523–536.

Kasser, T., & Ryan, R. M. (1993). A dark side of the American dream: Correlates of financial success as a central life aspiration. *Journal of Personality and Social Psychology, 65,* 410–422.

Kasser, T., & Ryan, R. M. (1996). Further examining the American dream: Differential correlates of intrinsic and extrinsic goals. *Personality and Social Psychology Bulletin, 22,* 280–287.

Kernis, M. H., Cornell, D. P., Sun, C., Berry, A., & Harlow, T. (1993). There's more to self-esteem than whether it is high or low: The importance of stability of self-esteem. *Journal of Personality and Social Psychology, 65,* 1190–1204.

Kernis, M. H., Grannemann, B. D., & Barclay, L. C. (1989). Stability and level of self-esteem as predictors of anger arousal and hostility. *Journal of Personality and Social Psychology, 56,* 1013–1022.

Kernis, M. H., Paradise, A. W., Whitaker, D. J., Wheatman, S. R., & Goldman, B. N. (2000). Master of one's psychological domain? Not likely if one's self-esteem is unstable. *Personality and Social Psychology Bulletin, 26,* 1297–1305.

Kernis, M. H., Whisenhunt, C. R., Waschull, S. B., Greenier, K. D., Berry, A. J., Herlocker, C. E., & Anderson, C. A. (1998). Multiple facets of self-esteem and their relations to depressive symptoms. *Personality and Social Psychology Bulletin, 24,* 657–668.

King, L. A. (1996). Who is regulating what and why? The motivational context of self-regulation. *Psychological Inquiry, 7,* 57–61.

King, L. A. (1998). Personal goals and personal agency: Linking everyday goals to future images of the self. In M. Kofta, G. Weary, & G. Sedek (Eds.), *Personal control in action: Cognitive and motivational mechanisms* (pp. 109–128). New York: Plenum.

King, L. A. (in press). The health benefits of writing about life goals. *Personality and Social Psychology Bulletin.*

King, L. A., & Pennebaker, J. W. (1997). *Thinking about goals, glue, and the meaning of life.* In R. S. Wyer Jr. (Ed.), Advances in social cognition (pp. 97–105). Mahwah, NJ: Erlbaum.

King, L. A., Richards, J. H., & Stemmerich, E. (1998). Daily goals, life goals, and worst fears: Means, ends, and subjective well-being. *Journal of Personality, 66,* 713–744.

King, L. A., & Williams, T. (2001). *Enacting a life dream: Implications for daily experience, and psychological and physical well-being.* Unpublished manuscript. University of Missouri, Columbia.

Klinger, E. (1975). Consequences of commitment to and disengagement from incentives. *Psychological Review, 82,* 1–25.

Klinger, E. (1977). *Meaning and void: Inner experience and the incentives in people's lives.* Minneapolis: University of Minnesota Press.

Kuhl, J., & Helle, P. (1986). Motivational and volitional determinants of depression: The degenerated intention hypothesis. *Journal of Abnormal Psychology, 95,* 247–251.

Latham, G. P., & Seijts, G. H. (1999). The effects of proximal and distal goals on a moderately complex task. *Journal of Organizational Behavior, 20,* 421–429.

Locke, E. A. (2001). Motivation by goal setting. In R. T. Golembiewski (Ed.), *Handbook of organizational behavior* (2nd ed., pp. 43–56). New York: Marcel Dekker.

Marsh, H. W. (1993). Relations between global and specific domains of self: The importance of individual importance, certainty, and ideals. *Journal of Personality and Social Psychology, 65,* 975–992.

Marsh, H. W. (1995). A Jamesian model of self-investment and self-esteem: Comment on Pelham (1995). *Journal of Personality and Social Psychology, 69,* 1151–1160.

Martin, L. L., & Tesser, A. (1996). Some ruminative thoughts. In R. S. Wyer Jr. (Ed.), *Advances in social cognition: Ruminative thoughts* (pp. 1–47). Mahwah, NJ: Lawrence Erlbaum.

McIntosh, W. D., Harlow, T. F., & Martin, L. L. (1995). Linkers and nonlinkers: Goal beliefs as a moderator of the effects of everyday hassles on rumination, depression, and physical complaints. *Journal of Applied Social Psychology, 25,* 1231–1244.

McIntosh, W. D., Martin, L. L., & Jones III, J. B. (2001). Goal orientations and the search for confirmatory affect. *Journal of Psychology, 135,* 5–16.

Niedenthal, P. M., Setterlund, M. B., & Wherry, M. B. (1992). Possible self-complexity and affective reactions to goal-relevant evaluation. *Journal of Personality and Social Psychology, 63,* 5–16.

Niedenthal, P. M., Tangney, J. P., & Gavanski, I. (1994). "If only I weren't" versus "If only I hadn't": Distinguishing shame and guilt in counterfactual thinking. *Journal of Personality and Social Psychology, 67,* 585–595.

Nolen-Hoeksema, S. (1996). Chewing the cud and other ruminations. In R. S. Wyer Jr. (Ed.), *Advances in social cognition: Ruminative thoughts* (pp. 135–144). Mahwah, NJ: Lawrence Erlbaum.

Omodei, M. M., & Wearing, A. J. (1990). Need satisfaction and involvement in personal projects: Toward an integrative model of subjective well-being. *Journal of Personality and Social Psychology, 59,* 762–769.

Pelham, B. W. (1991). On confidence and consequence: The certainty and importance of self-knowledge. *Journal of Personality and Social Psychology, 60,* 518–530.

Pomerantz, E. M., Saxon, J. L., & Oishi, S. (2000). The psychological trade-offs of goal investment. *Journal of Personality and Social Psychology, 79,* 617–630.

Ryan, R. M., Rigby, S., & King, K. (1993). Two types of religious internalization and their relations to religious orientations and mental health. *Journal of Personality and Social Psychology, 65,* 586–596.

Rogers, C. R. (1961). *On becoming a person.* Boston: Houghton Mifflin.

Rosenberg, M. (1979). *Conceiving the self.* New York: Basic Books.

Ryff, C. D. (1991). Possible selves in adulthood and old age: A tale of shifting horizons. *Psychology and Aging, 6,* 286–295.

Shah, J. & Higgins, E. T. (2001). Regulatory concerns and appraisal efficiency: The general impact of promotion and prevention. *Journal of Personality and Social Psychology, 80,* 693–705.

Sheldon, K. M., & Elliot, A. J. (1999). Goal striving, need satisfaction, and longitudinal well-being: The self-concordance model. *Journal of Personality and Social Psychology, 76,* 482–497.

Sheldon, K. M., & Kasser, T. (1995). Coherence and congruence: Two aspects of personality integration. *Journal of Personality and Social Psychology, 68,* 531–543.

Skaalvik, E. M. (1997). Self-enhancing and self-defeating ego orientation: Relations with task and avoidance orientation, achievement, self-perceptions, and anxiety. *Journal of Educational Psychology, 89,* 71–81.

Smith, H. (1991). *Religions of man.* San Francisco: Harper.

Tangney, J. P., & Salovey, P. (1999). Problematic social emotions: Shame, guilt, jealousy, and envy. In R. Kowalski & M. R. Leary (Eds.), *The social psychology of emotional and behavioral problems: Interfaces of social and clinical psychology* (pp. 167–195). Washington, DC: American Psychological Association.

Vallacher, R. R., & Wegner, D. M. (2000). What do people think they are doing? In E. T. Higgins & A. Kruglanski (Eds.), *Motivational science: Social and personality perspectives* (pp. 215–228). Philadelphia: Psychology Press. (Original work published 1987)

Waschull, S. B., & Kernis, M. H. (1996). Level and stability of self-esteem as predictors of children's intrinsic motivation and reasons for anger. *Personality and Social Psychology Bulletin, 22,* 4–13.

Zeigarnik, B. (1938). On finished and unfinished tasks. In W. D. Ellis (Ed.), *A sourcebook of Gestalt psychology* (pp. 300–314). New York: Harcourt.

5

THE VIRTUES AND VICES OF PERSONAL CONTROL

MICHAEL J STRUBE, J. SCOTT HANSON, AND LAUREL NEWMAN

Among the many human motives and desires, personal control exerts an especially important influence on human affect, cognition, and behavior. Humans actively seek control and respond to its loss in a wide variety of ways, implicating it as a central concern and prominent problem to solve in everyday life. It is not surprising, then, that the control concept has been a central feature in theory and research. For example, the desire to explain, predict, and control the social world has long been held to underlie the attribution process (e.g., Heider, 1958; Jones & Davis, 1965; Kelley, 1967). Similarly, personal control has been described as a key element of achievement motivation (Dweck & Elliott, 1983), power motivation (Dépret & Fiske, 1993), territoriality (Altman, 1975), and curiosity (Berlyne, 1960). Other theorists have proposed basic human strivings for competence (White, 1959), causation (deCharms, 1968), superiority (Adler, 1930), and survival (Hendrick, 1943), with each having control as a central element. More recently, a basic desire for control has been proposed and validated (Burger, 1992, 1999; Burger & Cooper, 1979) as a specific individual difference.

Some of the most compelling demonstrations of control's importance come from research that has shown the consequences of its loss. Work on learned helplessness, for example, has shown the negative motivational, cognitive, and affective consequences of prolonged loss of control (Seligman,

1975; see also Abramson, Metalsky, & Alloy, 1989; Abramson, Seligman, & Teasdale, 1978; Kofta, 1993). Similarly, some researchers have argued that the debilitating effects of common environmental stressors (e.g., noise and crowding) arise fundamentally from a perceived lack of control (Glass & Singer, 1972; Schmidt & Keating, 1979). Additional research indicates that humans are acutely sensitive to less chronic infringements on their control (e.g., Glass & Singer, 1972; Rodin, Solomon, & Metcalf, 1978; Sherrod, 1974) and strive in the short run to regain lost freedom and choice (Brehm, 1966, 1993).

The aforementioned "loss" research clearly demonstrates the virtues of control by underscoring the negative consequences of its absence. Other research findings amply demonstrate the "gains" that accrue from control as well. For example, in many "loss" studies, conditions are included in which control is provided or restored. These studies usually show benefits of having control on affect and performance (e.g., Glass & Singer, 1972; Sherrod, 1974). Perhaps especially supportive of the view that control is desirable is the substantial amount of research showing how pervasively people harbor positive illusions of control (e.g., Taylor & Brown, 1988) and how readily they perceive control even when it is actually absent (e.g., Langer, 1975; Langer & Roth, 1975; Wortman, 1975). Indeed, positive-control illusions seem to convey some mental health benefits (Taylor & Brown, 1988; but see Baumeister, 1993), whereas accurate (and perhaps lower) control perceptions may be related to depression (e.g., Weary, Marsh, Gleicher, & Edwards, 1993).

One might conclude from this brief overview that control is a virtue, a universal goal, and that people with more control are uniformly better off than those with less control. In this chapter, however, we emphasize that control also has its costs (cf. Burger, 1989; Thompson, Cheek, & Graham, 1988) and that a full understanding of how people seek and manage control can benefit from considering control as both virtue and vice. We begin with a simple definition of control and then describe two control-related personality variables that provide good models of how control strivings can involve a complex interplay of goals and outcomes. We end with a more general discussion of personal control as a strategy that is fraught with pleasure and peril.

PERSONAL CONTROL: A DEFINITION

The term *personal control* is used to describe quite a number of things, and the control construct overlaps with quite a number of other constructs. To keep matters simple, and to be consistent with most major theoretical treatments (e.g., Brehm, 1993; Burger, 1989), we consider personal control to be the *perception* that a person can alter events. According to this view, the key element of control is not the actual enactment of a strategy for producing desired outcomes or preventing undesired outcomes (cf. Thompson, 1981). Rather, we view as sufficient the *perception* that such a strategy is available. Indeed, as Burger (1989) pointed out, the perception of control is all that is often measured or manipulated in most research, and even when actual control is possible, it need not be enacted—just perceived to be possible—in order for its effects to emerge. These control perceptions can include many event-modifying strategies that map onto the varieties of control described by others. For example, Averill (1973) suggested that control can be produced *behaviorally* (e.g., by preventing a stressful event), *cognitively* (e.g., by reinterpreting the meaning of an event), and *decisionally* (e.g., by choosing between two different courses of action). Rothbaum, Weisz, and Snyder (1982) argued that control can be attained not only by acting on the environment directly (i.e., *primary control*) but also by bringing oneself in line with the environment (e.g., by aligning with powerful others, called *secondary control*). All of these forms of control can exist perceptually. Our broad definition means that we will necessarily ignore some subtle and important nuances; these have been described well elsewhere (e.g., Rothbaum et al., 1982; Thompson, 1981). We recognize the complexity of the construct but must take a broader view here.

INDIVIDUAL DIFFERENCES AS A MODEL FOR CONTROL STRIVING STRATEGIES

A personality or individual-difference approach to understanding how striving for personal control can be both adaptive and maladaptive is especially productive. A personality perspective focuses on the proper unit of interpretation—the individual—and makes clear that control strivings necessarily exist in the context of other competing motives and desires that can shift in importance over time and setting. The potential conflicts and their resolution can be an especially telling way to determine the premium placed on control and the maladaptive consequences that it may have. In the discussion that follows, we focus on two extensive lines of research that have mapped the consequences of individual differences in control motivation: (a) Type A behavior and (b) desire for control. Although other related constructs could clearly be included here as well (e.g., locus of control; Rotter, 1966), these two chosen areas have been especially focused and productive.

THE TYPE A BEHAVIOR PATTERN

During the 1970s and 1980s, few individual-difference variables generated as much research interest by psychologists and health scientists as the Type A behavior pattern. That work represented a concerted attempt to identify the underlying motivation behind a constellation of behaviors that had been found to be related to coronary risk. Earlier, in the 1950s, Meyer Friedman and Ray Rosenman, two cardiologists, noted that coronary patients seemed to possess behaviors that distinguished them from noncoronary patients (Friedman & Rosenman, 1974). Systematic observation identified the now-familiar components of the Type A pattern: (a) hard-driving competitiveness, (b) impatience and a sense of time urgency, and (c) easily aroused anger. By contrast, Type B individuals are relatively relaxed and easygoing.

One early and dominant view held that Type A behavior represents the manifestation of a high need for control. According to this control theory explanation (e.g., Glass, 1977), Type A individuals are hard driving and competitive in an attempt to master their worlds; are impatient and time urgent in an attempt to achieve as much as they can in as little time as possible; and are easily aroused to anger, primarily in situations that thwart their control attempts. Research directly testing the control motivation view has been generally supportive. Type A individuals have been found to desire control more than do Type B individuals (Burger, 1985; Dembroski, MacDougall, & Musante, 1984), to exhibit psychological reactance in response to initial control loss or threatened freedom (Rhodewalt & Comer, 1982; Rhodewalt & Davison, 1983), and to exhibit learned helplessness in response to prolonged exposure to loss of control (e.g., Brunson & Matthews, 1981; Krantz, Glass, & Snyder, 1974). Although alternative explanations for some of these findings exist (e.g., see Strube, 1987), collectively they suggest that Type A individuals have a strong desire for control and respond quickly and aggressively when control is lost.

The virtues of this pattern are quite clear. Type A behavior is consistent with the work ethic of Western society, and so it is not surprising that, compared with Type B individuals, Type A individuals achieve greater academic success (Keltikangas-Jaervinen, 1992; Lee, 1992; Ovcharchyn, Johnson, & Petzel, 1981) and have been found to achieve more professional distinction (e.g., Marmot, 1994; K. A. Matthews, Helmreich, Beane, & Lucker, 1980). Other research has examined how well Type A individuals and Type B individuals learn contingencies about their own outcomes and how well they judge the control that others have. Here, too, Type A individuals seem to have an advantage. Compared with Type B individuals, Type A individuals learn contingencies better (Strube, Lott, Heilizer, & Gregg, 1986), seem more motivated to achieve accurate appraisals of their abilities (Strube & Yost, 1993), and are more accurate in their appraisals of the control exhibited by others (Strube & Lott, 1985). It is presumed that these contingency judgments, ability appraisals, and control perceptions allow Type A individuals to strategically plan their interactions and performances in ways that maximize control and success.

However, the vices of Type A behavior are just as easy to find. The most obvious, of course, is the elevated coronary risk that accompanies

Type A behavior, although that risk is now known to be more circumscribed than previously thought (e.g., Booth-Kewley & Friedman, 1987; K. A. Matthews, 1988; Siegman, 1994), residing primarily in the hostility component (e.g., T. Q. Miller, Smith, Turner, Guijarro, & Hallet, 1996). Perhaps more important, some researchers have argued that Type A behavior is a general stress-engendering lifestyle (e.g., Smith & Anderson, 1986; Smith & Rhodewalt, 1986) that can place Type A individuals at risk for health problems other than cardiovascular disease (e.g., Schafer & Mckenna, 1985; Stout & Bloom, 1982; Woods & Burns, 1984). The stress-engendering nature of the Type A pattern has been demonstrated, for example, in the work habits and attitudes of Type A individuals. Type A individuals' desire for control often prevents them from relinquishing control to a more able partner in a cooperative problem-solving situation (e.g., Strube, Berry, & Moergen, 1985; Strube & Werner, 1985) and to prefer working alone (Dembroski & MacDougall, 1978). These work preferences ensure high personal control, but they also fail to take advantage of important resources and may create unnecessary pressure and stress. Indeed, Type A managers report more dissatisfaction with conflicting job demands, heavy responsibilities, and supervision of others (e.g., Howard, Cunningham, & Rechnitzer, 1977). Compared with Type B individuals, Type A individuals also report more hours worked, greater workloads, and more work-related stressful life events (e.g., Burke & Weir, 1980; Chesney & Rosenman, 1980; Jamal, 1985). Because of their investment in the work domain, Type A individuals invest less time in leisure pursuits (Kirkcaldy, Shephard, & Cooper, 1993) and, in fact, seem to have negative attitudes about leisure (Mudrack, 1997). In their attempt to master and control the work environment, Type A individuals clearly may subject themselves to considerable stress. It is not surprising that some research indicates that Type A individuals may be more susceptible than Type B individuals to burnout (Burke & Greenglass, 1995; Lavanco, 1997).

Other facets of the Type A pattern are also problematic. For example, the anger and hostility than can cause health problems for Type A individuals have social consequences as well. In particular, the aggression exhibited by Type A individuals is more likely to be hostile and emotional rather than calculated and instrumental (Strube, Turner, Cerro, Stevens, & Hinchey, 1984). When faced with problems, people with the Type A behavior pattern report being more likely to become angry, to plunge into their work, and to be less likely to forget their problems (Vroege & Aaronson, 1994; see also Baron, Neuman, & Geddes, 1999). The problems may extend beyond work as well. Some studies have shown that Type A behavior, especially when exhibited by women, may be disruptive in romantic relationships (e.g., Rosenberger & Strube, 1986).

Perhaps most interesting is that many of the features exhibited by Type A individuals can operate as both virtue and vice, depending on the circumstances. For example, Type A individuals demonstrate focused attention that, while enhancing task performance by reducing the impact of distractions (cf. Frei, Racicot, & Travagline, 1999; Perry & Laurie, 1992; Pittman & D'Agostino, 1985), can lead to suppression of symptoms that might either warn of impending health problems (e.g., Carver, Coleman, & Glass, 1976; K. A. Matthews et al., 1983; Weidner & Matthews, 1978) or prevent an acute problem from becoming chronic (Rhodewalt & Strube, 1985). Likewise, the time-urgent nature of Type A behavior can lead to impressive productivity but seems to also carry with it a poor ability to estimate time spent as a resource. Consequently, Type A individuals may be more likely than Type B individuals to experience psychological entrapment and so to sometimes invest time poorly (e.g., Strube, Deichmann, & Kickham, 1989; Strube & Lott, 1984).

Consider also the attributions made by Type A individuals and Type B individuals for their own performances. Past work has shown that people with the Type A behavior pattern are more self-serving than those with the Type B pattern (e.g., Strube, 1985; Strube & Boland, 1986), showing considerable flexibility in the way they construe causality (Rhodewalt, Strube, Hill, & Sansone, 1988; Strube, 1988). Although this might appear to allow Type A individuals a measure of self-esteem enhancement that is not taken by Type B individuals, this bias may also produce overconfidence and overgeneralization by Type A individuals regarding the performance arenas in which their skills apply. These self-views might be reinforced by views of Type A individuals and Type B individuals held by others. Strube et al. (1986) found that Type A participants, compared with Type B participants, were rated by observers to have more control over a task despite equivalent amounts of actual control. Similarly, Strube, Keller, Oxenberg, and Lapidot (1989) found that Type A leaders were rated as more competent than Type B leaders by their respective group members, despite the absence of better performance by Type A-led groups. These perceptions by others, in combination with biased self-attributions, may promote unrealistic expectations that Type A individuals cannot meet.

Together, the vast literature on Type A behavior clearly shows the behavioral, cognitive, and affective consequences of a strong control motive. Those consequences are often desirable, but they can produce negative consequences as well. Additional support for the view that personal control can be both a virtue and a vice comes from more recent work on a closely related variable, the desire for control.

DESIRE FOR CONTROL

At first blush, the desire-for-control (DC) variable introduced by Burger and Cooper (1979; for a review, see Burger, 1992) might seem to be a relabeling of the Type A behavior pattern. After all, both are assumed to have a need for control at their core. Furthermore, research that has attempted to validate the DC construct has produced results that resemble in many ways the evidence presented in support of a control basis for Type A behavior. For example, individuals with high DC perform well in achievement-related settings (Burger, 1985), especially under challenge. In these settings, individuals with high DC have higher and more accurate aspirations, and they persist longer than do individuals with low DC when a task appears difficult but controllable. It is not surprising that individuals with high DC earn higher grades in college than do individuals with low DC. Also reminiscent of the findings for Type A individuals are results indicating that individuals with high DC are more likely to gravitate toward positions of leadership and social control (Burger, 1992; Reed, 1989; Zimmerman, 1990; Zimmerman & Rappaport, 1988). Also, Type A individuals and those with high DC share many of the same voice stylists in conversation (e.g., rapid and accelerated speech, response latency, verbal competitiveness, potential for hostility) that are interpreted as control-seeking tactics (Dembroski et al., 1984). Burger (1992) reported, however, that researchers usually find only a modest positive correlation between measures of Type A behavior and DC. Across nine samples that he reviewed, the correlations ranged from .22 to .68, clearly suggesting substantial unshared variability. Other research offers additional and compelling support for a control motivation underlying the DC variable (for a review, see Burger, 1992). For example, individuals with high DC, compared with individuals with low DC, attend to and seek out attributionally relevant information about others, apparently in an attempt to understand better and possibly control their social worlds (e.g., Burger & Hemans, 1988). Indeed, Schönbach (1990) found that individuals with high DC reacted more strongly than did those with low DC when others acted contrary to expectations. Apparently, the violated expectations were more upsetting to individuals with high DC because they challenged the predictability and controllability of the social environment. Consistent with this line of argument, individuals with high DC also remember more control-relevant information about another person whom they expect to meet (Burger, Hillberry, Huffman, & Kelley, 1991, cited in Burger, 1993).

More pertinent to the present discussion are features of the high DC personality that appear to be decidedly negative in their consequences. Other people, for example, reported liking to interact with individuals with high DC less than with those with low DC in a getting-acquainted conversation (Burger, 1990), presumably because of the more domineering conversation tactics of individuals with high DC. Individuals with high DC have also been found to respond with greater physiological reactivity and to report being more upset by acute stress and control loss (although the normal levels of anxiety reported by individuals with high DC are lower than those reported by individuals with low DC; Burger, 1992, 1995). In other words, individuals with high DC may respond more reactively to isolated incidents of threat but perhaps cope better or encounter less stress overall. One example of a temporary control-threatening setting is a confined environment; individuals with high DC report more crowding in such settings (Burger, Oakman, & Bullard, 1983). Finally, Burger (1984) found that individuals with high DC who felt they had little control over events in their lives reported more suicidal thoughts than did those with low DC, or individuals with high DC who believed that their lives were under their control. These data, too, suggest that individuals with high DC may not handle well the occasional episodes of control loss that most people experience. Indeed, as Burger (1992) suggested, individuals with high DC may bring on some of the stress they experience, reminiscent of the argument that Type A behavior may be a stress-engendering style.

Especially interesting are behavioral differences between individuals with high DC and those with low DC that might be viewed as either virtue or vice, depending on the circumstances. For example, compared with individuals with low DC, those with high DC conform less to the stated opinions of others (Burger, 1987). Although such independence might be hailed as a virtue at first glance, such resistance to the views of others might also hinder taking advantage of others' expertise and knowledge when it would be beneficial to do so. Indeed, individuals with high DC are more threatened than those with low DC by help from another person (Daubman, 1990, cited in Burger, 1992) suggesting an element of reactance that goes beyond simply failing to be influenced by another's opinion or input. Allowing "control issues" to thwart the honest and potentially productive offers of help by others can be self-defeating. Both of the aforementioned findings are reminiscent of Type A individuals' reluctance to relinquish control to more capable partners in cooperative problem-solving settings and suggest that an overreliance on primary control over secondary control might preserve immediate perceptions of control but at the expense of long-term task performance (i.e., actual control). Still other research indicates that individuals with high DC are more likely than those with low DC to have a high belief in a just world (Feinberg, Powell, & Miller, 1982). Although a belief that "people get what they deserve and deserve what they get" preserves the perception of an orderly, predictable, and potentially controllable world (Lerner, 1980), it can have some unfortunate by-products. Individuals with high just-world beliefs are more likely to blame victims for their plight (e.g., Borgida & Brekke, 1985; Summers & Feldman, 1984).

Taken together, the pattern of findings for the DC variable clearly shows that a high control motivation has its benefits. However, like the findings from the Type A literature, the DC research also makes quite clear that striving for control does not produce uniformly positive experiences. Instead, it seems that striving for control requires striking a balance between the readily apparent benefits and the often-unappreciated costs. Indeed, the fact that control striving is an individual difference and not a universal preference suggests that for some people the costs of control quite often outweigh the benefits. Perhaps the costs are more widespread and important than previously thought. It is to a broader discussion of those costs that we now turn.

VIRTUE AND VICE IN
THE STRATEGIC SEEKING OF CONTROL

In this final section, we elaborate on the wide variety of control-related costs that may play a key role in the strategic seeking of control. This discussion will necessarily be more speculative and will build on the excellent earlier treatments by Burger (1989) and Thompson et al. (1988). Our goal is to suggest the different types of costs and their possible interplay that may accompany a striving for control. Along the way, some fruitful avenues for future research will be identified.

We consider first the initial decision to seek control. As previously noted, control can be enacted in many ways; choosing among them can be daunting. The decision may be between substantially different forms of control, such as the decision to directly influence the environment versus the decision to give up control and to place one's fate in the hands of a more capable other (e.g., S. M. Miller, 1979, 1980; Rothbaum et al., 1982). Or, the decision may be more subtle, such as between two different forms of cognitive control (e.g., distraction vs. information seeking) that might be exerted over a stressor. In each case, the decision maker must weigh the likelihood of success for each tactic, and the likely positive consequences, against the potential costs that each option may have. This decision process is likely to be cognitively demanding, especially when the stakes are high, and to carry with it considerable opportunity for worry and rumination, especially as more opportunities for control and possible failure are entertained. Indeed, as Burger (1989) pointed out, confronting the possibility of control can focus a person's attention on possible aversive features of the control setting. Furthermore, having control may carry with it an increased predictability, including the predictable onset of negative aspects of a control setting. Although this predictability may allow one to prepare for the negative side effects of control, it may produce anxiety as well (S. M. Miller, 1981).

Once control is sought and attained, there are likely to be additional cognitive costs. Having and maintaining control necessarily require monitoring and vigilance. Rarely is the contingency landscape static and cooperative; instead, the features of the social and physical environment that facilitate or hinder control may shift unexpectedly. The cues signaling such shifts must be monitored, because a quick and timely response may be the difference between control maintained and control irrevocably lost.

The costs here are of two types. Cognitive resources devoted to monitoring control cues detract from the limited resources that can be applied to other cognitive demands (cf. Burger, 1989; Cohen, 1978). Furthermore, such monitoring itself may be fatiguing, potentially hampering the performance of other tasks (cf. Kofta & Sedek 1998). Indeed, monitoring control cues while also attending to other cognitive demands is akin to a divided-attention task, which may hamper task performance (e.g., Lundberg, 1993; G. Matthews, Davies, Westerman, & Stammers, 2000; Sanders, 1998). Although with time and practice this vigilance may become relatively automatic, it still will presumably require some cognitive resources that cannot be allocated to other demands.

Having and maintaining control also produces skill maintenance costs. Having control usually means that having to do something behaviorally or cognitively may require that certain skills be attained and maintained through practice or periodic use. Indeed, threats to control often may appear in the form of declines in the skills that are used to sustain control. This seems especially to be a problem with control-related skills that may decline with age, that are affected by physical illness, or that compare unfavorably to increasingly more able competitors. Here too the costs are of two types. It seems likely that detecting a skill deficit will be an aversive affective experience, signaling as it does potential control loss and the loss of benefits that control provides. The skill deficit signals as well the need for remedial action either in the form of practice, acquisition of additional control-related skills, or a shift to a completely different control strategy that may include relinquishing control altogether. All undoubtedly are costly in terms of time and resources that must be taken away from other demands in an attempt to keep control or regain it when lost.

An especially large class of control-related costs is likely to be affective in nature. People often attempt to control things about which they care deeply. Indeed, many control strivings are elements of self-definition as one seeks to set oneself apart from others through mastery or dominance in one performance arena or another. Control loss then can go well beyond the mere loss of a physical resource or social opportunity and represent a loss of identification as well. Having control carries with it then quite a number of potential affective outcomes: fear and anxiety about one's uncertain ability to maintain control, disappointment if control and valuable outcomes are lost, shame and embarrassment if others' expectations are not met. The social and self-presentational element seems especially important (Burger, 1989). Having control quite often means having the fate of others linked to one's own (S. M. Miller, 1980), or having the opinions of others ride on the success of one's control attempts. Simply put, having control creates a substantial burden of expectations and the potential for blame and ridicule if control attempts fail. Accordingly, anticipated control loss likely creates considerable anxiety and, depending on the stakes, actual control loss may be devastating emotionally as skill deficits are confirmed (cf. Thompson et al., 1988). Some of the emotional consequences of control have been verified by past research showing that having control is sometimes accompanied by higher anxiety and lower self-esteem than is not having control (e.g., Burger, Brown, & Allen, 1983; Rodin, Rennert, & Solomon, 1980; see also Folkman, 1984; S. M. Miller, 1980). Increases in anxiety may in turn harm task performance and lead to the paradoxical consequence that the people in control may produce less desirable task outcomes than those not in control (Burger, 1989).

Finally, control and its loss can have physiological consequences. Having control means having to confront and overcome control threats and challenges. These threats can produce physiological reactivity as a function of their appearance or anticipation, the active coping with them, and in the aftermath of control attempts. Indeed, much of the stress and control literature deals with the physiological consequences of coping with stressors that can be conceptualized as control threats.

Of course, many of these costs are linked. Decisional uncertainty no doubt creates anxiety, behavioral control attempts inform cognitions about the control strategies that might best maintain control in the future, and some of the cognitions we entertain about control are about the affective consequences that may occur. Exploring these linkages will be an important task for future research. Perhaps most challenging will be the need to understand better the *process* of control striving and maintenance. To date, most research has focused on the isolated consequences of single episodes of control loss in single domains. However, control striving occurs in multiple domains of varying importance, over time, and while one considers the multiple other demands and sometimes-conflicting goals of everyday life. Understanding how people manage this process is an especially important area for future research. It will help shed light on the "rationality" of control striving and help place the consequences of control in a broader context.

That people strive for control in general—and some people especially—despite the numerous costs speaks to the powerful nature of this construct in guiding everyday behavior. However, in light of the numerous costs it is perhaps not at all surprising that people will sometimes forgo control with little regret or angst. Even when control is sought, it is not surprising that the path taken and the eventual outcomes are sometimes less than optimal. As should now be clear, there is a bewildering array of factors to consider. Understanding better how people creatively strike a balance among the costs and benefits of control will help reveal adaptive strategies of potentially considerable importance. Indeed, we venture to suggest that the ultimate measure of control lies not in the absolute amount of control that one can achieve but in the ability to recognize and sensibly manage the multitude of costs and benefits that control tactics can produce.

REFERENCES

Abramson, L. Y., Metalsky, G. I., & Alloy, L. B. (1989). Hopelessness depression: A theory-based subtype of depression. *Psychological Review, 96,* 358–372.

Abramson, L. Y., Seligman, M. E. P., & Teasdale, J. D. (1978). Learned helplessness in humans: Critique and reformulation. *Journal of Abnormal Psychology, 87,* 49–74.

Adler, A. (1930). Individual psychology. In C. Murchison (Ed.), *Psychologies of 1930.* Worcester, MA: Clark University Press.

Altman, I. (1975). *The environment and social behavior: Privacy, personal space, territory, crowding.* Monterey, CA: Brooks/Cole.

Averill, J. R. (1973). Personal control over aversive stimuli and its relationship to stress. *Psychological Bulletin, 80,* 286–303.

Baron, R. A., Neuman, J. H., & Geddes, D. (1999). Social and personal determinants of workplace aggression: Evidence for the impact of perceived injustice and the Type A behavior pattern. *Aggressive Behavior, 25,* 281–296.

Baumeister, R. F. (1993). The optimal margin of illusion. *Journal of Social and Clinical Psychology, 8,* 176–189.

Berlyne, D. D. (1960). *Conflict, arousal, and curiosity.* New York: McGraw-Hill.

Booth-Kewley, S., & Friedman, H. S. (1987). Psychological predictors of heart disease: A quantitative review. *Psychological Bulletin, 101,* 343–362.

Borgida, E., & Brekke, N. (1985). Psycholegal research on rape trials. In A. W. Burgess (Ed.), *Rape and sexual assault: A research handbook* (pp. 313–324). New York: Garland.

Brehm, J. W. (1966). *A theory of psychological reactance.* New York: Academic Press.

Brehm, J. W. (1993). Control, its loss, and psychological reactance. In G. Weary, F. Gleicher, & K. L. Marsh (Eds.), *Control motivation and social cognition* (pp. 3–30). New York: Springer-Verlag.

Brunson, B. I., & Matthews, K. A. (1981). The Type A behavior pattern and reactions to uncontrollable stress: An analysis of performance strategies, affect, and attributions during failure. *Journal of Personality and Social Psychology, 40,* 906–918.

Burger, J. M. (1984). Desire for control, locus of control, and proneness to depression. *Journal of Personality, 52,* 71–89.

Burger, J. M. (1985). Desire for control and achievement-related behaviors. *Journal of Personality and Social Psychology, 48,* 1520–1533.

Burger, J. M. (1987). Desire for control and conformity to a perceived norm. *Journal of Personality and Social Psychology, 53,* 355–360.

Burger, J. M. (1989). Negative reactions to increases in perceived personal control. *Journal of Personality and Social Psychology, 56,* 246–256.

Burger, J. M. (1990). Desire for control and interpersonal interaction style. *Journal of Research in Personality, 24,* 32–44.

Burger, J. M. (1992). *The desire for control: Personality, social, and clinical perspectives.* New York: Plenum.

Burger, J. M. (1993). Individual differences in control motivation and social information processing. In G. Weary, F. Gleicher, & K. L. Marsh (Eds.), *Control motivation and social cognition* (pp. 203–219). New York: Springer-Verlag.

Burger, J. M. (1995). Need for control and self-esteem: Two routes to a high desire for control. In M. H. Kernis (Ed.), *Efficacy, agency, and self-esteem* (pp. 217–233). New York: Plenum.

Burger, J. M. (1999). Personality and control. In V. J. Derlega, B. A. Winstead, & W. H. Jones (Eds.), *Personality: Contemporary theory and research* (pp. 282–306). Chicago: Nelson-Hall.

Burger, J. M., Brown, R., & Allen, C. A. (1983). Negative reactions to personal control. *Journal of Social and Clinical Psychology, 1,* 322–342.

Burger, J. M., & Cooper, H. (1979). The desirability of control. *Motivation & Emotion, 3,* 381–393.

Burger, J. M., & Hemans, L. T. (1988). Desire for control and the use of attribution processes. *Journal of Personality, 56,* 531–546.

Burger, J. M., Oakman, J. A., & Bullard, N. G. (1983). Desire for control and the perception of crowding. *Personality and Social Psychology Bulletin, 9,* 475–479.

Burke, R. J., & Greenglass, E. R. (1995). Job stressors, Type A behavior, coping responses, and psychological burnout among teachers. *International Journal of Stress Management, 2,* 45–57.

Burke, R. J., & Weir, T. (1980). The Type A experience: Occupational and life demands, satisfaction, and well-being. *Journal of Human Stress, 6,* 28–38.

Carver, C. S., Coleman, A. E., & Glass, D. C. (1976). The coronary-prone behavior pattern and suppression of fatigue on a treadmill test. *Journal of Personality and Social Psychology, 33,* 460–466.

Chesney, M. A., & Rosenman, R. H. (1980). Type A behavior in the work setting. In C. L. Cooper & R. Payne (Eds.), *Current concerns in occupational stress* (pp. 187–212). London: Wiley.

Cohen, S. (1978). Environmental load and the allocation of attention. In A. Baum, J. E. Singer, & S. Valins (Eds.), *Advances in environmental psychology: Volume 1. The urban environment* (pp. 1–29). Hillsdale, NJ: Erlbaum.

deCharms, R. (1968). *Personal causation: The internal affective determinants of behavior.* New York: Academic Press.

Dembroski, T. M., & MacDougall, J. M. (1978). Stress effects on affiliation preferences among subjects possessing the Type A coronary-prone behavior pattern. *Journal of Personality and Social Psychology, 36,* 23–33.

Dembroski, T. M., MacDougall, J. M., & Musante, L. (1984). Desirability of control versus locus of control: Relationship to paralinguistics in the Type A interview. *Health Psychology, 3,* 15–26.

Dépret, E., & Fiske, S. T. (1993). Social cognition and power: Some cognitive consequences of social structure as a source of control deprivation. In G. Weary,

F. Gleicher, & K. L. Marsh (Eds.), *Control motivation and social cognition* (pp. 176–202). New York: Springer-Verlag.

Dweck, C. S., & Elliott, E. S. (1983). Achievement motivation. In E. M. Hetherington (Ed.), *Handbook of child psychology: Volume 4. Socialization, personality, and social development* (pp. 643–691). New York: Wiley.

Feinberg, R. A., Powell, A., & Miller, F. G. (1982). Control and belief in the just world: What's good also can be bad. *Social Behavior and Personality, 10,* 57–61.

Folkman, S. (1984). Personal control and stress and coping processes: A theoretical analysis. *Journal of Personality and Social Psychology, 46,* 839–852.

Frei, R. L., Racicot, B., & Travagline, A. (1999). The impact of monochronic and Type A behavior patterns on research productivity and stress. *Journal of Managerial Psychology, 14,* 374–387.

Friedman, M., & Rosenman, R. H. (1974). *Type A behavior and your heart.* New York: Knopf.

Glass, D. C. (1977). *Behavior patterns, stress, and coronary disease.* Hillsdale, NJ: Erlbaum.

Glass, D. C., & Singer, J. E. (1972). *Urban stress: Experiments on noise and social stressors.* New York: Academic Press.

Heider, F. (1958). *The psychology of interpersonal relations.* New York: Wiley.

Hendrick, I. (1943). The discussion of the instinct to master. *Psychoanalytic Quarterly, 12,* 561–565.

Howard, J. H., Cunningham, D. A., & Rechnitzer, P. A. (1977). Work patterns associated with Type A behavior: A managerial population. *Human Relations, 30,* 825–836.

Jamal, M. (1985). Type A behavior and job performance. *Journal of Human Stress, 11,* 60–68.

Jones, E. E., & Davis, K. E. (1965). From acts to dispositions: The attribution process in person perception. In L. Berkowitz (Ed.), *Advances in experimental social psychology* (Vol. 2, pp. 219–266). New York: Academic Press.

Kelley, H. H. (1967). Attribution theory in social psychology. In D. Levine (Ed.), *Nebraska Symposium on Motivation* (Vol. 15, pp. 192–238). Lincoln: University of Nebraska Press.

Keltikangas-Jaervinen, L. (1992). Type A behaviour and school achievement. *European Journal of Personality, 6,* 71–81.

Kirkcaldy, B. D., Shephard, R. J., & Cooper, C. L. (1993). Relationships between Type A behaviour, work and leisure. *Personality and Individual Differences, 15,* 69–74.

Kofta, M. (1993). Uncertainty, mental models, and learned helplessness: An anatomy of control loss. In G. Weary, F. Gleicher, & K. L. Marsh (Eds.), *Control motivation and social cognition* (pp. 122–153). New York: Springer-Verlag.

Kofta, M., Weary, G., & Sedek, G. (1998). Uncontrollability as a source of cognitive exhaustion: Implications for helplessness and depression. In M. Kofta et al. (Eds.), *Personal control in action: Cognitive and motivational mechanisms* (pp. 391–418). New York: Plenum.

Krantz, D. S., Glass, D. C., & Snyder, M. L. (1974). Helplessness, stress level, and the coronary-prone behavior pattern. *Journal of Experimental Social Psychology, 10*, 284–300.

Langer, E. J. (1975). The illusion of control. *Journal of Personality and Social Psychology, 32*, 311–328.

Langer, E. J., & Roth, J. (1975). Heads I win, tails it's chance: The illusion of control as a function of the sequence of outcomes in a purely chance task. *Journal of Personality and Social Psychology, 32*, 951–955.

Lavanco, G. (1997). Burnout syndrome and Type A behavior in nurses and teachers in Sicily. *Psychological Reports, 81*, 523–528.

Lee, C. (1992). The relations of personality and cognitive styles on job and class performance. *Journal of Organizational Behavior, 13*, 175–185.

Lerner, M. J. (1980). *The belief in a just world: A fundamental delusion.* New York: Plenum.

Lundberg, U. (1993). On the psychobiology of stress and health. In O. Svenson & A. J. Maule (Eds.), *Time pressure and stress in human judgment and decision making* (pp. 41–53). New York: Plenum.

Marmot, M. (1994). Work and other factors influencing coronary health and sickness absence. *Work and Stress, 8*, 191–201.

Matthews, G., Davies, D. R., Westerman, S., & Stammers, R. B. (2000). *Human performance: Cognition, stress and individual differences.* Hove, England: Psychology Press/Taylor & Francis.

Matthews, K. A. (1988). Coronary heart disease and Type A behaviors: Update on and alternative to the Booth-Kewley and Friedman (1987) quantitative review. *Psychological Bulletin, 104*, 373–380.

Matthews, K. A., Helmreich, R. L., Beane, W. E., & Lucker, G. W. (1980). Pattern A, achievement striving, and scientific merit: Does pattern A help or hinder? *Journal of Personality and Social Psychology, 39*, 962–967.

Matthews, K. A., Siegel, J. M., Kuller, L. H., Thompson, M., & Varat, M. (1983). Determinants of decisions to seek medical treatment by patients with acute myocardial infarction symptoms. *Journal of Personality and Social Psychology, 44*, 1144–1156.

Miller, S. M. (1979). Controllability and human stress: Method, evidence and theory. *Behavior Research and Therapy, 17*, 287–304.

Miller, S. M. (1980). Why having control reduces stress: "If I can stop the roller coaster, I don't want to get off." In J. Garber & M. E. P. Seligman (Eds.), *Human helplessness: Theory and application* (pp. 71–95). New York: Academic Press.

Miller, S. M. (1981). Predictability and human stress: Toward a clarification of evidence and theory. In L. Berkowitz (Ed.), *Advances in experimental social psychology* (pp. 203–256). New York: Academic Press.

Miller, T. Q., Smith, T. W., Turner, C. W., Guijarro, M., & Hallet, A. J. (1996). Meta-analytic review of research on hostility and physical health. *Psychological Bulletin, 119*, 322–348.

Mudrack, P. E. (1997). Protestant work-ethic dimensions and work orientations. *Personality and Individual Differences, 23*, 217–225.

Ovcharchyn, C. A., Johnson, H. H., & Petzel, T. P. (1981). Type A behavior, academic aspirations, and academic success. *Journal of Personality, 49*, 248–256.

Perry, A. R., & Laurie, C. A. (1992). Sustained attention and the Type A behavior pattern: The effect of daydreaming on performance. *Journal of General Psychology, 119*, 217–228.

Pittman, T. S., & D'Agostino, P. R. (1985). Motivation and attribution: The effects of control deprivation on subsequent information processing. In J. H. Harvey & G. Weary (Eds.), *Attribution: Basic issues and applications* (pp. 117–141). Orlando, FL: Academic Press.

Reed, T. F. (1989). Do union organizers matter? Individual differences, campaign practices, and representation election outcomes. *Industrial and Labor Relations Review, 43*, 103–119.

Rhodewalt, F., & Comer, R. (1982). Coronary-prone behavior: The attractiveness of an eliminated choice. *Personality and Social Psychology Bulletin, 8*, 152–158.

Rhodewalt, F., & Davison, J. Jr. (1983). Reactance and the coronary-prone behavior pattern: The role of self-attribution in response to reduced behavioral freedom. *Journal of Personality and Social Psychology, 44*, 220–228.

Rhodewalt, F., & Strube, M. J. (1985). A self-attribution-reactance model of recovery from injury in Type A individuals. *Journal of Applied Social Psychology, 15*, 330–344.

Rhodewalt, F., Strube, M. J., Hill, C. A., & Sansone, C. (1988). Strategic self-attribution and Type A behavior. *Journal of Research in Personality, 22*, 60–74.

Rodin, J., Rennert, K., & Solomon, S. K. (1980). Intrinsic motivation for control: Fact or fiction. In A. Baum & J. E. Singer (Eds.), *Advances in environmental psychology: Volume 2. Applications of personal control* (pp. 131–148). Mahwah, NJ: Erlbaum.

Rodin, J., Solomon, S. K., & Metcalf, J. (1978). Role of control in mediating perceptions of density. *Journal of Personality and Social Psychology, 36*, 988–999.

Rosenberger, L. M., & Strube, M. J. (1986). The influence of Type A and B behavior patterns on the perceived quality of dating relationships. *Journal of Applied Social Psychology, 16*, 277–286.

Rothbaum, F., Weisz, J. R., & Snyder, S. S. (1982). Changing the world and changing the self: A two-process model of perceived control. *Journal of Personality and Social Psychology, 42*, 5–37.

Rotter, J. B. (1966). Generalized expectancies for internal versus external control of reinforcement. *Psychological Monographs, 80*(1, Whole No. 609).

Sanders, A. F. (1998). *Elements of human performance: Reaction processes and attention in human skill.* Mahwah, NJ: Erlbaum.

Schafer, W. E., & Mckenna, J. F. (1985). Type A behavior, stress, injury and illness in adult runners. *Stress Medicine, 1*, 245–254.

Schmidt, D. E., & Keating, J. P. (1979). Human crowding and personal control: An integration of the research. *Psychological Bulletin, 86*, 680–700.

Schönbach, P. (1990). *Account episodes: The management of escalation of conflict.* Cambridge, England: Cambridge University Press.

Seligman, M. E. P. (1975). *Helplessness: On depression, development, and death.* San Francisco: Freeman.

Sherrod, D. (1974). Crowding, perceived control, and behavioral aftereffects. *Journal of Applied Social Psychology, 4,* 171–186.

Siegman, A. W. (1994). From Type A to hostility to anger: Reflections on the history of coronary-prone behavior. In A. W. Siegman & T. W. Smith (Eds.), *Anger, hostility, and the heart* (pp. 1–21). Hillsdale, NJ: Erlbaum.

Smith, T. W., & Anderson, N. B. (1986). Models of personality and disease: An interactional approach to Type A behavior and cardiovascular risk. *Journal of Personality and Social Psychology, 50,* 1166–1173.

Smith, T. W., & Rhodewalt, F. (1986). On states, traits, and processes: An alternative to the individual difference assumptions in Type A behavior and physiological reactivity. *Journal of Research in Personality, 20,* 229–251.

Stout, C. W., & Bloom, L. J. (1982). Type A behavior and upper respiratory infections. *Journal of Human Stress, 8,* 4–7.

Strube, M. J. (1985). Attributional style and the Type A coronary-prone behavior pattern. *Journal of Personality and Social Psychology, 49,* 500–509.

Strube, M. J. (1987). A self-appraisal model of the Type A behavior pattern. In R. Hogan & W. H. Jones (Eds.), *Perspectives in personality* (Vol. 2, pp. 201–250). Greenwich, CT: JAI Press.

Strube, M. J. (1988). Performance attributions and the Type A behavior pattern: Causal sources versus causal dimensions. *Personality and Social Psychology Bulletin, 14,* 709–721.

Strube, M. J., Berry, J. M., & Moergen, S. (1985). Relinquishment of control and the Type A behavior pattern: The role of performance evaluation. *Journal of Personality and Social Psychology, 49,* 831–842.

Strube, M. J., & Boland, S. M. (1986). Post-performance attributions and task persistence among Type A and B individuals: A clarification. *Journal of Personality and Social Psychology, 50,* 413–420.

Strube, M. J., Deichmann, A. K., & Kickham, T. (1989). Time urgency and the Type A behavior pattern: Time investment as a function of cue salience. *Journal of Research in Personality, 23,* 287–301.

Strube, M. J., Keller, N. R., Oxenberg, J., & Lapidot, D. (1989). Actual and perceived group performance as a function of group composition: The moderating role of the Type A and B behavior patterns. *Journal of Applied Social Psychology, 19,* 140–158.

Strube, M. J., & Lott, C. L. (1984). Time urgency and Type A behavior: Implications for time investment and psychological entrapment. *Journal of Research in Personality, 18,* 395–409.

Strube, M. J., & Lott, C. L. (1985). Type A behavior pattern and the judgment of noncontingency: Mediating roles of mood and perspective. *Journal of Personality and Social Psychology, 49,* 510–519.

Strube, M. J., Lott, C. L., Heilizer, R., & Gregg, B. (1986). Type A behavior pattern and the judgment of control. *Journal of Personality and Social Psychology, 50,* 403–412.

Strube, M. J., Turner, C. W., Cerro, D., Stevens, J., & Hinchey, F. (1984). Interpersonal aggression and the Type A coronary-prone behavior pattern: A theoretical distinction and practical implications. *Journal of Personality and Social Psychology, 47,* 839–847.

Strube, M. J., & Werner, C. (1985). Relinquishment of control and the Type A behavior pattern. *Journal of Personality and Social Psychology, 48,* 688–701.

Strube, M. J., & Yost, J. H. (1993). Control motivation and self-appraisal. In G. Weary, F. Gleicher, & K. L. Marsh (Eds.), *Control motivation and social cognition* (pp. 220–254). New York: Springer-Verlag.

Summers, G., & Feldman, N. S. (1984). Blaming the victim versus blaming the perpetrator: An attributional analysis of spouse abuse. *Journal of Social and Clinical Psychology, 2,* 339–347.

Taylor, S. E., & Brown, J. D. (1988). Illusion and well-being: A social psychological perspective on mental health. *Psychological Bulletin, 103,* 193–210.

Thompson, S. C. (1981). Will it hurt less if I can control it? A complex answer to a simple question. *Psychological Bulletin, 90,* 89–101.

Thompson, S. C., Cheek, P., & Graham, M. (1988). The other side of perceived control: Disadvantages and negative effects. In S. Spacapan & S. Oskamp (Eds.), *The social psychology of health* (pp. 69–93). Newbury Park, CA: Sage.

Vroege, J. A., & Aaronson, N. K. (1994). Type A behavior and social support among employed women. *Behavioral Medicine, 19,* 169–173.

Weary, G., Marsh, K. L., Gleicher, F., & Edwards, J. A. (1993). Depression, control motivation, and the processing of information about others. In G. Weary, F. Gleicher, & K. L. Marsh (Eds.), *Control motivation and social cognition* (pp. 255–287). New York: Springer-Verlag.

Weidner, G., & Matthews, K. A. (1978). Reported physical symptoms elicited by unpredictable events and the Type A coronary-prone behavior pattern. *Journal of Personality and Social Psychology, 36,* 1213–1220.

White, R. W. (1959). Motivation reconsidered: The concept of competence. *Psychological Review, 66,* 297–333.

Woods, P. J., & Burns, J. (1984). Type A behavior and illness in general. *Journal of Behavioral Medicine, 7,* 411–415.

Wortman, C. B. (1975). Some determinants of perceived control. *Journal of Personality and Social Psychology, 31,* 282–294.

Zimmerman, M. A. (1990). Toward a theory of learned hopefulness: A structural model analysis of participation and empowerment. *Journal of Research in Personality, 24,* 71–86.

Zimmerman, M. A., & Rappaport, J. (1988). Citizen participation, perceived control, and psychological empowerment. *American Journal of Community Psychology, 16,* 725–750.

II

NEGATIVE PERSONALITIES: WHEN VICE CAN BECOME VIRTUE

6

PESSIMISM: ACCENTUATING THE POSITIVE POSSIBILITIES

JULIE K. NOREM

To present a balanced view of pessimism assumes—at least provisionally—that there might be *something* positive to say about pessimism. Pessimism, however, runs with some pretty negative company: Even when it does not instigate trouble, its reputation suffers by association, just as optimism basks in the halo of positive mood and other rosy companions. It even has historical burdens: Pessimism has been conceived of as sinful because it demonstrates a lack of faith in the benevolence of the universe (e.g., Pope, 1733–1734/1994) or as representing a lack of faith in humans' ability to decipher and control the universe (e.g., Descartes, 1649/1985).

Hundreds of studies relate optimism of various sorts to positive outcomes, and one has to look carefully to find empirical results that do not fall neatly into the "optimism is good" category. Yet careful review of this research reveals the complexity of the issues involved in trying to weigh the evidence on pessimism. Many different ideas hover underneath that broad appellation, and to make sense of how pessimism works one needs to know what is meant when the term is used. Fortunately for the purposes of this chapter, the vast majority of published research focuses on two constructs—attributional pessimism and dispositional pessimism—and I can begin with them.

ATTRIBUTIONAL PESSIMISM

A pessimistic attributional style, as defined in the research programs of Seligman and his colleagues (e.g., Seligman, 1998), is the tendency to explain negative events in terms of internal, stable, and global causes and to explain positive events in terms of external, unstable, and specific causes. Revised learned helplessness theory (Abramson, Seligman, & Teasdale, 1978) proposes that when confronted with negative events, individuals who tend to attribute those events to internal, stable, and global causes are more likely to become depressed because they believe they are to blame for bad events, which they also believe are due to factors that will influence everything in their life and will not change over time; for example, "I was fired because I am stupid and incompetent." These attributions, in addition to exacerbating the immediate negative affect one feels when something bad happens, are thought to lead to continued negative affect over time, the expectation that bad things will continue to happen (hopelessness), and to helplessness based on lack of perceived control over future outcomes.

As reviewed by Gillham, Shatte, Reivich, and Seligman (2001), the evidence on attributional style shows impressively consistent patterns of relations between pessimistic attributions and a host of negative constructs: negative affect, depressive symptoms, lower academic achievement, poorer physical health, poorer athletic performance, lower marital satisfaction, and political losses. Direct evidence that a pessimistic attributional style is a risk factor for depression is somewhat less consistent, and there is less of it; only a few studies have shown a direct link between changes in pessimistic attributions and subsequent prevention or alleviation of depression, or improvement on other outcome variables besides mood.

A couple of studies have found a pessimistic attributional style to be related to better outcomes: Isaacowitz and Seligman (2001), for example, found that attributional pessimism interacted with negative life events to predict fewer depressive symptoms in a sample of elderly individuals (see also Follette & Jacobson, 1987; Satterfield, Monahan, & Seligman, 1997).

The assumption, of course, is that the way one explains events that have already happened will influence one's expectations about future events. Thus, explanations that suggest that past negative events have causes that are likely to persist unchanged and to have widespread influence across many life domains should lead one to have negative—that is, pessimistic—expectations for the future. Negative attributions should lead to more negative affect, to feeling less in control, and to hopelessness about future events. This should lead to decreases in motivation and effort, generally ineffective coping, and thus an increased probability of negative outcomes in the future.

Although this sequence sounds plausible, the evidence that "pessimistic'" attributions about the past lead directly to pessimistic expectations about the future is both sparse and inconsistent (Gillham et al., 2001). It is not clear that researchers should even expect a particularly strong or definitive relationship between pessimistic attributions and subsequent expectations; both particular explanations and general attributional trends often leave room for multiple future expectations that are influenced by other variables. Researchers have reported correlations between attributional style and expectations that range from weak to moderate (Hjelle, Belongia, & Nesser, 1996; Scheier & Carver, 1992), and few studies have prospectively examined the proposed causal sequence. Specific connections between pessimistic attributions and coping are similarly scarce, and one of the few studies that examined that relationship found that students with a pessimistic attributional style who performed poorly had better coping plans than students with a more optimistic attributional style (Follette & Jacobson, 1987). As Gillham et al. (2001) also noted, it is surprising, given the central role that perceptions of control play in theorizing about attributional styles, that those perceptions are usually inferred, as opposed to directly measured (see Peterson, 1991).

With the exception of the three studies noted above, little evidence suggests that a pessimistic attributional style is typically beneficial and considerable evidence indicates that it is associated with a host of negative outcomes. The relatively weak links between attributional style and expectations, however, also suggest that researchers be cautious about assuming that any particular attributional style is synonymous with pessimism.

DISPOSITIONAL OPTIMISM AND PESSIMISM

Dispositional optimism and pessimism, as psychological constructs, correspond most closely to lay usage of the terms. Pessimism, as a disposition, is the generalized tendency to expect negative outcomes (Scheier & Carver, 1992). In Scheier and Carver's self-regulatory model, pessimistic expectations and perceptions of lack of control should lead to disengagement from goals, that is, giving up. Empirically speaking, pessimism is related to more negative affect and depressive symptoms, greater perceptions of stress, reports of more physical symptoms, slower recovery from stressors, lower life satisfaction, a more external locus of control, and more reliance on emotion-focused coping. Consistent with this list, Affleck, Tennen, and Apter (2001) concurred with the conclusion of a previous meta-analysis (Andersson, 1996) that "emotional states are the most reliable consequence of optimism and pessimism" (p. 163).

Most researchers have assumed that pessimism is the opposite of whatever they think optimism is. If this bipolar conception of optimism were universally true, then there would be little need for separate chapters on both optimism and pessimism in this volume. Recent efforts, however, show that optimism and pessimism are not necessarily opposite ends of the same dimension (Chang, Maydeu Olivares, & D' Zurilla, 1997; Dember & Brooks, 1989; Marshall, Wortman, Kusulas, Herrig, & Vickers, 1992) but instead are separate dimensions, with divergent correlates. Dember and his colleagues (Dember, 1989; Dember & Brooks, 1989) have found that optimism was correlated with the extent to which people were committed to a religious or political ideology, but pessimism was uncorrelated with ideological commitment. Räikkönen, Matthews, Flory, Owens, and Gump (1999) found that pessimism, but not optimism, was associated with higher ambulatory blood pressure. Schulz, Bookwala, Knapp, Scheier, and Williamson (1996) found that pessimism was correlated with earlier death in cancer patients but that optimism was unrelated to survival.

Affleck et al. (2001) found in experience-sampling studies that pessimism predicted daily sadness and that optimism predicted daily happiness. Pessimism also predicted venting and seeking emotional support, whereas optimism predicted seeking spiritual comfort. Chang (1996) found that lack of optimism is a strong predictor of poor adjustment among Asian Americans but not among White Americans; in contrast, pessimism was a predictor of poor adjustment among White Americans (see also Robinson-Whelen, Kim, MacCallum, & Kiecolt Glaser, 1997). In examining the relations between pessimism and coping, Chang (1996) also found that pessimism was negatively associated with expressing emotions and problem solving for White Americans but positively associated with those coping mechanisms for Asian Americans.

PESSIMISM AND NEGATIVE AFFECT

Research shows that optimism tends to be related to extraversion, positive affectivity, and susceptibility to cues for reward—all of which tend to be related to each other. Pessimism, in contrast, is related to neuroticism, negative affectivity, and susceptibility to cues for punishment (Ball & Zuckerman, 1990; Gray, 1982; Zuckerman, 2001). Twin research has revealed small to moderate heritabilities for optimism and pessimism. These converging lines of research suggest that biological substrates may contribute to variations in individual tendencies to respond to environmental stimuli with wariness, negative emotions, and pessimism (Zuckerman, 2001).

Across constructs and methodologies, one resoundingly clear and robust finding is that pessimism is associated with negative affect. Pessimism and negative affect may both be influenced by other variables, such as negative affectivity or susceptibility to cues for punishment, as described above. Pessimism can lead to negative affect, as when thinking about possible negative outcomes makes one feel anxious or dejected. It may also be a consequence of negative affect, as when, in the midst of a depressive episode, one cannot believe in the possibility of future good outcomes.

Negative affect—one's beliefs about it and reactions to it—is also key to understanding the interpersonal and social consequences of pessimism. Put simply, pessimism does not make a good impression on others. Helweg-Larsen, Sadeghian, and Webb (2002) showed that people, at least in the dominant cultural contexts of the United States, do not like to be around people who express pessimism, in part because they assume that pessimism indicates depression. The stigma of mental illness may be off-putting, and one may also avoid people one thinks are depressed (whether that depression is a clinical diagnosis or a brief state) because negative affect is contagious: Seeing others glum can make one feel glum, too (Coyne, 1976). Moreover, if one believes that someone else feels bad, then one is unlikely to expect social support from them, which makes them less socially desirable (Peterson & Bossio, 2001). Indeed, one may not expect much of them at all: People tend to believe that confident people are justifiably so (despite some evidence to the contrary; Kruger & Dunning, 1999), and expressions of anxiety and pessimism are easily seen as expressions of a lack of confidence that stems from a lack of competence (Leary, Kowalski, & Bergen, 1988).

One should be careful, however, about too readily assuming that negative affect is always bad. Even if negative moods and emotions are hedonically unpleasant, they serve important functions. They warn of potential dangers, or that something is wrong, and can motivate a person to change the conditions that create them. Mood functions as input or information (Martin, Ward, Achee, & Wyer, 1993) that helps one to decide where to direct one's attention and how to deploy one's efforts.

Mood also influences cognitive processing: Negative mood leads to more detail-oriented, locally biased processing; a deliberative mind set; and rule-based problem-solving approaches, in contrast to the globally biased processing, implemental mind set, and heuristic-based problem-solving induced by positive mood (Basso, Schefft, Ris, & Dember, 1996; Gollwitzer, Heckhausen, & Steller, 1990; Isen, 1990). Whether these influences are negative or positive depends on how they fit with particular tasks, goals, and contexts. Vosberg (1998) found, for example, that positive mood led to more creativity, if creativity was measured in terms of the frequency and diversity of responses on a creativity task. If, however, creativity was measured in terms of the usefulness and originality of the responses, negative mood was associated with greater creativity. Particular tasks or situations may better accommodate different modes of thinking. The virtues of these processes lie in process–task fit rather than being inherent to the processes themselves.

Although these results may seem far removed from discussions of pessimism, they highlight the importance of considering the context of pessimism when evaluating its effects. Cheerfulness, independence, and self-confidence, for example, are highly valued characteristics in American culture. Pessimism, which is associated with negative mood and expressions of anxiety and doubt, may make one especially vulnerable in that cultural context. In contrast, as Chang (2001) suggested, the social and personal costs of pessimism may be much less in different cultural contexts; indeed, there may even be benefits to pessimism in those contexts, as his findings on Asian Americans suggest.

PESSIMISM AS AN AFFECT MANAGEMENT STRATEGY: DEFENSIVE PESSIMISM

In much of the research mentioned above, negative affect is considered to be evidence of poor coping. For example, greater anxiety and less satisfaction among pessimists means that they are not adapting as successfully as optimists. There are, however, alternate ways of framing such negative affect. Anxiety can be viewed as part of the problem, situation, or task individuals face. Some people may be more likely to feel anxious across many situations because of stronger tendencies to experience negative affect generally or greater sensitivity to punishment cues (which create anxiety). Some people may feel more anxious in particular situations because they face conflicts or difficulties that others do not; for example, women in leadership positions often face a conflict between professional role and gender role expectations that men may not have to confront. In both of these cases, considering anxiety as indicative of poor coping may miss the point that for those people, anxiety itself is woven into the psychological situation with which they need to cope.

This perspective on negative affect gives an entrée into seeing how pessimism can function as a strategy—as something people do rather than something they are victims of or simply "have" (Cantor, 1990). Research on the construct of defensive pessimism does just that (Norem, 2001b). *Defensive pessimism* refers to two processes conjoined to form a strategy that plays out over time as individuals work toward their goals (Cantor & Kihlstrom, 1987; Norem, 1989; Norem & Cantor, 1986). The first process is setting negative expectations for an upcoming situation, event, or performance— that is, pessimism. The second is playing through a worst-case analysis of what might go wrong in that situation: imagining in specific and vivid detail how the expected negative outcomes could eventuate. The counterintuitive findings from research on defensive pessimism are that people who use it typically perform quite well on objective indicators—at least as well as the optimists with whom they are usually compared (for reviews, see Norem, 2001a; Norem & Chang, 2001). People who use defensive pessimism typically perform better when they are using their strategy than when they are trying to be optimistic.

People who use defensive pessimism are anxious and feel out of control, but they want to persevere. They use defensive pessimism to manage their anxiety so that they do not feel compelled to avoid the situations that elicit that anxiety, and they are able to perform well in those situations. Setting low expectations allows them to feel more prepared for negative outcomes, and mentally simulating specific negative possibilities helps them to plan ways to avoid them. This, in turn, allows them to feel more in control, less anxious, less self-focused, and more task focused. Defensive pessimists do not always feel in control, but their attributions and other self-reports suggest that they believe it is possible for them to *take* control, if not over everything, then at least over their own behavior. One of the mechanisms—feeling a sense of control—by which both dispositional and attributional optimism are thought to lead to positive outcomes seems to be operative in defensive pessimism too.

Much of the research on defensive pessimism has contrasted that strategy with *strategic optimism* (so called to differentiate it from dispositional and attributional optimism). Strategic optimists are not anxious to begin with, have positive expectations, and actively distract themselves from playing through possible outcomes. People who use this strategy typically use the self-enhancing positive illusions that Taylor and Brown (1988) argued are adaptive, they are moderate to high in dispositional optimism, and they exhibit an optimistic attributional style.

Defensive pessimists typically do as well on objective measures of performance as strategic optimists. Both groups show impaired performance when their strategies are interfered with (e.g., under positive mood conditions for defensive pessimists or negative mood conditions for strategic optimists; Norem & Illingworth, in press; Sanna, 1998), or when they use the other group's strategy (e.g., pessimism and worst-case analyses for the strategic optimists, or optimism and distraction for the defensive pessimists; Norem, 1986; Norem & Illingworth, 1993; Spencer & Norem, 1996).

Defensive pessimists often, however, score higher on negative affect, both before and after a performance: Their strategy "fails" to the extent that it does not erase their negative feelings or necessarily make them feel good. (Even in this comparison, of course, it is important to remember that defensive pessimists do better with their own strategy than with strategic optimism.) It is arguable, though, that defensive pessimists are coping with a different situation than strategic optimists are, even when the external or objective context is the same; that is, they have to manage their already manifest anxiety in addition to whatever situational demands there may be, whereas the strategic optimists focus instead on remaining unanxious.

This suggests that comparing defensive pessimists to strategic optimists (or other kinds of pessimism only to optimism) may not always be the most relevant or informative comparison, because it does not take into account the intrapsychological context of expectations, including what people are trying to do (Norem & Chang, 2001). Defensive pessimists do better, both in terms of objective achievement and in terms of subjective satisfaction, self-esteem, and psychological symptoms, than chronic self-handicappers, impostors, overachievers, and other groups who are anxious but use strategies other than defensive pessimism (Norem, 2001b; Norem & Chang, 2002; Oleson, Poehlmann, Yost, Lynch, & Arkin, 2000). In those comparisons, the virtues of defensive pessimism seem clear, while its vices recede.

NURTURING POSITIVE PESSIMISM

Studies of defensive pessimism (along with scattered other results) point to the positive possibilities of pessimism within particular circumstances, as used in particular ways by particular people. Yet despite this research, pessimism's vices would still appear to outweigh its virtues in any overall reckoning or summary judgment.

People often seem to look for summary judgments such as this; certainly researchers, practitioners, and teachers are often asked "Which is better: optimism or pessimism?" It is not clear that such summaries are useful; indeed, they may be misleading. If psychologists were to conclude that optimism is often better than pessimism, what follows? Should they, in whatever venue they work, try to increase optimism? Could they, if they tried? Should they try to decrease pessimism? Räikkönen et al. (1999) found that optimism was unrelated to ambulatory blood pressure, whereas pessimism was positively related. If lowering blood pressure is the goal, then it makes little sense to try to increase optimism, on the basis of those data. It is not clear, however, that attempts to decrease dispositional pessimism would be successful. To my knowledge, there is little evidence that either dispositional optimism or pessimism can be readily changed through known interventions. Psychologists might do just as well to use standard treatments to lower blood pressure and see whether that helps decrease pessimism over time.

Although this example is slightly facetious, it does remind us of the cardinal rule that one cannot infer causation from correlation. More important, one needs to be cautious about trying to change expectations in the absence of knowledge about the effects of that change in particular contexts. Bohart and Tallman (1999) noted that it is crucial to be sensitive to and respectful of the reality of the individual in a therapeutic context, and I would argue that that is the case in any context in which one might think of applying optimism and pessimism research. The point itself risks the triteness of truisms in the abstract but gains poignancy and relevance in specific situations.

As Chang (2001) argued, among Asian Americans pessimism may provide motivation for effective coping in the context of a particular cultural sensibility. Therapeutic attempts to change pessimism under those circumstances may be misguided at best and destructive at worst. Similarly, Norem's work (2001b) suggests that the same may be true for people who use defensive pessimism. Defensive pessimism is an effective tool for those individuals; even though it is possible to make their expectations more optimistic, efforts to do so risk leaving them without a strategy for managing their anxiety and the likelihood of worse rather than improved life outcomes.

I was completing this chapter in the weeks after the September 11, 2001, terrorist attacks in the United States. In that context it seems both disrespectful and absurd to try to convince people that bad things will not happen to them or that they have control over their worlds. Even if "objective" computation of the odds (always, a pessimist might note, based on what *has* happened, not on what could happen) suggests that there is little discernable increased risk for any particular individual, that point does little to touch on the shaken worldviews and increased anxiety of the people affected by these events.

On a less dramatic but much more chronic level, groups within a society who have less power and are relatively disadvantaged may frequently encounter situations in which their anxiety and their pessimism is based on realistic appraisal of their relative lack of control or increased risk. Minority members driving through neighborhoods in which the police use racial profiling as the basis for harassment seem unlikely to benefit from the optimistic illusion that "it won't happen to me" or the generally optimistic assumption that "everything will work out fine." They might be well served, however, by learning to use defensive pessimism to expect the worst so that they can use mental rehearsal to prepare their reactions should the worst happen. In this context, defensive pessimism is a strategy that fits the reality that there is much in the larger world that cannot be controlled but that one can control one's own behavior.

A QUESTION OF BALANCE

This last point—that defensive pessimism can help people take control of their own preparations when they are anxious—is the key to that strategy's value and to understanding more generally when pessimism may be positive and how one can maximize its virtue and minimize its vice. Optimism makes people feel good, more in control, and thus more motivated. They then try harder and typically do better, leading to a virtuous cycle that encompasses several discrete positive outcomes: feeling better, feeling in control, taking effective action, and accomplishing more. Along the way, they reap the benefits—in American society, at least—of others' positive reactions to their optimism and good mood.

Pessimism is unlikely to create positive affect (in oneself or others) and is thus unlikely to kick off this precise cycle, even in its most positive manifestations. Nevertheless, there are other starting points that can lead to the other positive outcomes in this cycle, and there are times when it is unrealistic or even inappropriate to assume that the presence of positive affect is the most important outcome to achieve. For anxious defensive pessimists, for example, feeling good is not the paramount goal—controlling anxiety is. They gain control by focusing on negative possibilities in very concrete, specific steps—a style of thinking facilitated by negative affect and a very effective problem-solving approach. This process, in turn, leads to increased effort and positive outcomes. In limited forms, pessimism may be a useful adjunct strategy even for die-hard optimists, who may be able to use pessimism to induce deliberative, detail-oriented thinking in situations where unrealistic optimism has important negative consequences or where one wants to avoid the consequences of threatened egotism or overconfidence (e.g., when evaluating the risk of sexual behavior or how one's behavior will affect others).

For people who are dispositionally inclined to experience negative affect, or whose social roles or life situations present considerable conflict or difficulty, learning to manage that affect to promote effective action (without the costs of denial or repression) can be a powerful intervention—and one that is potentially more to the point than a focus on changing the affect itself. Indeed, few people can hope to banish anxiety and other negative emotions from their lives (neither is it clear that they should try to do so). Thus, all people need to develop ways to tolerate negative emotion and break the connection between negative affect and lack of motivation.

The key to positive pessimism would seem to lie in awareness of its potential as a strategy, coupled with the ability to regulate when and how much one uses it. Knowing, for example, that other people typically infer depression from and respond negatively to pessimism, can one inhibit public expression of one's pessimism when appropriate? Alternatively, can one be explicit about the functions pessimism serves in ways that mitigate negative inferences (e.g., "I like to think first of how things might go wrong so I'm prepared—then I can get enthusiastic")? Perhaps most important, can one move from abstract pessimistic rumination ("we're doomed") to specific pessimistic scenarios that can lead to well-planned action ("we're doomed because global warming will destroy the planet unless we are able to reverse it, which would involve . . . ")?

For teachers, therapists, and others, the implication of this perspective on pessimism is that no one size fits all. Encouraging optimism may be helpful to some people, some of the time (or even most of the time). However, there are individuals (and situations) for whom pessimism—in a limited, focused way—may be a more appropriate prescription. For researchers, this implies that they need to turn their attention to further exploration of the ways in which people can turn debilitating, depressing, global pessimism into effective, motivating strategic pessimism. Researchers know that this variety of pessimism exists, but they know relatively little about how it develops and how it can be cultivated. The overall picture is gradually taking shape, but there is a great deal of crucial work to be done on the details.

REFERENCES

Abramson, L. Y., Seligman, M. E. P., & Teasdale, J. D. (1978). Learned helplessness in humans: Critique and reformulation. *Journal of Abnormal and Social Psychology*, *87*, 49–74.

Affleck, G., Tennen, H., & Apter, A. (2001). Optimism, pessimism, and daily life with chronic illness. In E. C. Chang (Ed.), *Optimism and pessimism: Implications for theory, research and practice* (pp. 147–168). Washington, DC: American Psychological Association.

Andersson, G. (1996). The benefits of optimism: A meta-analytic review of the Life Orientation Test. *Personality and Individual Differences*, *21*, 719–725.

Ball, S. A., & Zuckerman, M. (1990). Sensation seeking, Eysenck's personality dimensions and reinforcement sensitivity in concept formation. *Personality and Individual Differences*, *11*, 343–353.

Basso, M. R., Schefft, B. K., Ris, M. D., & Dember, W. N. (1996). Mood and global–local visual processing. *Journal of the International Neuropsychological Society*, *2*, 249–255.

Bohart, A. C., & Tallman, K. (1999). *How clients make therapy work: The process of active self-healing*. Washington, DC: American Psychological Association.

Cantor, N. (1990). From thought to behavior: "Having" and "doing" in the study of personality and cognition. *American Psychologist*, *45*, 735–750.

Cantor, N., & Kihlstrom, J. F. (1987). *Personality and social intelligence*. Englewood Cliffs, NJ: Erlbaum.

Chang, E. C. (1996). Cultural differences in optimism, pessimism, and coping: Predictors of subsequent adjustment in Asian American and Caucasian American college students. *Journal of Counseling Psychology*, *43*, 113–123.

Chang, E. C. (2001). Cultural influences on optimism and pessimism: Differences in Western and Eastern construals of the self. In E. C. Chang (Ed.), Optimism and pessimism: Implications for theory, research, and practice (pp. 257–280). Washington, DC: American Psychological Association.

Chang, E. C., Maydeu Olivares, A., & D' Zurilla, T. J. (1997). Optimism and pessimism as partially independent constructs: Relationship to positive and negative affectivity and psychological well-being. *Personality and Individual Differences*, *23*, 433–440.

Coyne, J. (1976). Depression and the response of others. *Journal of Abnormal and Social Psychology*, *85*, 29–45.

Dember, W. N. (1989). Cognition, motivation, and emotion: Ideology revisited. In R. R. Hoffman & D. S. Palermo (Eds.), *Cognition and symbolic processes: Applied and ecological perspectives* (pp. 153–162). Hillsdale, NJ: Erlbaum.

Dember, W. N., & Brooks, J. (1989). A new instrument for measuring optimism and pessimism: Test–retest reliability and relations with happiness and religious commitment. *Bulletin of the Psychonomic Society, 27,* 365–366.

Descartes, R. (1985). The passions of the soul. In J. Cottingham, R. Stoothoff, & D. Murdoch (Eds.), *The philosophical writings of Descartes* (Vol. 1, pp. 326–404). New York: Cambridge University Press. (Original work published 1649)

Follette, V. M., & Jacobson, N. S. (1987). Importance of attributions as a predictor of how people cope with failure. *Journal of Personality and Social Psychology, 52,* 1205–1211.

Gillham, J. E., Shatte, A. J., Reivich, K. J., & Seligman, M. E. P. (2001). Optimism, pessimism, and explanatory style. In E. C. Chang (Ed.), *Optimism and pessimism: Implications for theory, research and practice* (pp. 53–75). Washington, DC: American Psychological Association.

Gollwitzer, P. M., Heckhausen, H., & Steller, B. (1990). Deliberative and implemental mind-sets: Cognitive tuning toward congruous thoughts and information. *Journal of Personality and Social Psychology, 59,* 1119–1127.

Gray, J. A. (1982). *The neuropsychology of anxiety: An enquiry into the functions of the septohippocampal system.* New York: Oxford University Press.

Helweg-Larsen, M., Sadeghian, P., & Webb, M. S. (2002). The stigma of being pessimistically biased. *Journal of Social and Clinical Psychology, 21,* 92–107.

Hjelle, L., Belongia, C., & Nesser, J. (1996). Psychometric properties of the Life Orientation Test and Attributional Style Questionnaire. *Psychological Reports, 78,* 507–515.

Isaacowitz, D. M., & Seligman, M. E. P. (2001). Is pessimism a risk factor for depressive mood among community-dwelling older adults? *Behaviour Research and Therapy, 39,* 255–272.

Isen, A. M. (1990). The influence of positive and negative affect on cognitive organization: Some implications for development. In N. L. Stein (Ed.), *Psychological and biological approaches to emotion* (pp. 75–94). Hillsdale, NJ: Erlbaum.

Kruger, J., & Dunning, D. (1999). Unskilled and unaware of it: How difficulties in recognizing one's own incompetence lead to inflated self-assessments. *Journal of Personality and Social Psychology, 77,* 1121–1134.

Leary, M. R., Kowalski, R. M., & Bergen, D. J. (1988). Interpersonal information acquisition and confidence in first encounters. *Personality and Social Psychology Bulletin, 14,* 68–77.

Marshall, G. N., Wortman, C. B., Kusulas, J. W., Hervig, L. K., & Vickers, R. R., Jr. (1992). Distinguishing optimism from pessimism: Relations to fundamental dimensions of mood and personality. *Journal of Personality and Social Psychology, 62,* 1067–1074.

Martin, L. L., Ward, D. W., Achee, J. W., & Wyer, R. S. (1993). Mood as input: People have to interpret the motivational implications of their moods. *Journal of Personality and Social Psychology, 64,* 315–326.

Norem, J. K., & Cantor, N. (1986). Defensive pessimism: Harnessing anxiety as motivation. *Journal of Personality and Social Psychology, 51*, 1208–1217.

Norem, J. K. (1989). Cognitive strategies as personality: Effectiveness, specificity, flexibility and change. In D. M. Buss & N. Cantor (Eds.), *Personality psychology: Recent trends and emerging issues* (pp. 45–60). New York: Springer-Verlag.

Norem, J. K. (2001a). Defensive pessimism, optimism, and pessimism. In E. C. Chang (Ed.), *Optimism and pessimism: Implications for theory, research and practice* (pp. 77–100). Washington, DC: American Psychological Association.

Norem, J. K. (2001b). *The positive power of negative thinking.* New York: Basic Books.

Norem, J. K., & Chang, E. C. (2001). A very full glass: Adding complexity to our thinking about the implications and applications of optimism and pessimism research. In E. C. Chang (Ed.), *Optimism and pessimism: Implications for theory, research and practice* (pp. 347–367). Washington, DC: American Psychological Association.

Norem, J. K., & Chang, E. C. (2002). The positive psychology of negative thinking. *Journal of Clinical Psychology, 58*, 993–1001.

Norem, J. K., & Illingworth, K. S. S. (1993). Strategy-dependent effects of reflecting on self and tasks: Some implications of optimism and defensive pessimism. *Journal of Personality and Social Psychology, 65*, 822–835.

Norem, J. K., & Illingworth, K. S. S. (in press). Mood and performance among strategic optimists and defensive pessimists. *Journal of Research in Personality.*

Oleson, K. C., Poehlmann, K. M., Yost, J. H., Lynch, M. E., & Arkin, R. M. (2000). Subjective overachievement: Individual differences in self-doubt and concern with performance. *Journal of Personality, 68*, 491–524.

Peterson, C. (1991). The meaning and measurement of explanatory style. *Psychological Inquiry, 2*, 1–10.

Peterson, C., & Bossio, L. M. (2001). Optimism and physical well-being. In E. C. Chang (Ed.), *Optimism and pessimism: Implications for theory, research and practice* (pp. 127–145). Washington, DC: American Psychological Association.

Pope, A. (1994). *An essay on man.* New York: Dover. (Original work published 1733–1734)

Räikkönen, K., Matthews, K. A., Flory, J. D., Owens, J. F., & Gump, B. B. (1999). Effects of optimism, pessimism, and trait anxiety on ambulatory blood pressure and mood during everyday life. *Journal of Personality and Social Psychology, 76*, 104–113.

Robinson-Whelen, S., Kim, C., MacCallum, R. C., & Kiecolt Glaser, J. K. (1997). Distinguishing optimism from pessimism in older adults: Is it more important to be optimistic or not to be pessimistic? *Journal of Personality and Social Psychology, 73*, 1345–1353.

Sanna, L. J. (1998). Defensive pessimism and optimism: The bitter-sweet influence of mood on performance and prefactual and counterfactual thinking. *Cognition & Emotion, 12*, 635–665.

Satterfield, J. M., Monahan, J., & Seligman, M. E. P. (1997). Law school performance predicted by explanatory style. *Behavioral Sciences and the Law, 15*, 95–105.

Scheier, M. F., & Carver, C. S. (1992). Effects of optimism on psychological and physical well-being: Theoretical overview and empirical update. *Cognitive Therapy and Research, 16*, 201–228.

Schulz, R., Bookwala, J., Knapp, J. E., Scheier, M., & Williamson, G. M. (1996). Pessimism, age, and cancer mortality. *Psychology and Aging, 11*, 304–309.

Seligman, M. E. P. (1998). The prediction and prevention of depression. In D. K. Routh (Ed.), *The science of clinical psychology: Accomplishments and future directions* (pp. 201–214). Washington, DC: American Psychological Association.

Spencer, S. M., & Norem, J. K. (1996). Reflection and distraction: Defensive pessimism, strategic optimism, and performance. *Personality and Social Psychology Bulletin, 22*, 354–365.

Taylor, S. E., & Brown, J. D. (1988). Illusion and well-being: A social psychological perspective on mental health. *Psychological Bulletin, 103*, 193–210.

Vosberg, S. K. (1998). Mood and the quantity and quality of ideas. *Creativity Research Journal, 11*, 315–331.

Zuckerman, M. (2001). Optimism and pessimism: Biological foundations. In E. C. Chang (Ed.), *Optimism and pessimism: Implications for theory, research and practice* (pp. 169–188). Washington, DC: American Psychological Association.

7

RUMINATION, IMAGINATION, AND PERSONALITY: SPECTERS OF THE PAST AND FUTURE IN THE PRESENT

LAWRENCE J. SANNA, SHEVAUN L. STOCKER, AND JENNIFER A. CLARKE

I will live in the Past, the Present, and the Future. The Spirits of all Three shall strive within me. I will not shut out the lessons that they teach.
—Ebenezer Scrooge (*A Christmas Carol* [Dickens, 1843/1984])[1]

Like Scrooge in Dickens's tale, we all are affected by remnants of our pasts, assessments of our present, and forecasts of our futures. For us, however, these ghostly specters more likely take their form in imaginative thoughts about the past and future, which inexorably intertwine and intermingle with those of our present, determining varied reactions such as affect and emotions and future behaviors. Rumination deals with the recurrent or temporal persistence of particular thoughts and is generally viewed as negative; that is, in many cases, ruminations appear maladaptive or, in keeping with the theme of this book, can be considered a vice. When one fans the flames of a

---

[1]All quotations in each section were taken from Dickens (1843/1984).

The writing of this chapter was supported in part by both the Mason and Linda Stephenson Faculty Award and a Junior Faculty Development Award to Lawrence J. Sanna from the University of North Carolina at Chapel Hill. We thank the Imagination, Goals, and Affect (IGoA, or ego) laboratory group members at the University of North Carolina at Chapel Hill for their comments on this chapter.

no-longer-attainable but not forgotten past love, or when one has an interfering preoccupation with thoughts about an upcoming vacation or a walk to the local corner deli for a pastrami on rye, it seems there is little to gain. However, there may be other circumstances under which ruminations appear more positive or adaptive or, in keeping with the theme of this book, can be considered a virtue. In these cases, ruminations may aid problem solving, goal striving, and coping with life events.

Our purpose is to conceptualize ruminations as both virtue and vice. We first describe two predominant views of ruminations. Both emphasize a repetitive or recurrent nature; however, one view defines ruminations as negative thoughts about the past, whereas the other depicts them as thoughts about future goals. After discussing this work, we outline a model of imaginative mental simulations that incorporates these two perspectives and moves beyond them. Viewed within this broader integrative framework, the virtues and vices of engaging in various mental simulations may be seen and evaluated more completely. The model not only may enable a greater understanding of existing findings but also suggests novel and unique predictions for future research. We end the chapter by offering conclusions and by suggesting how this model may inform an understanding of personality processes and strategies, automaticity in mental simulations, and coping with life events.

RUMINATIVE THOUGHTS:
THE GOOD, THE BAD, AND THE UGLY

Ruminations have been described as good or positive, in that they sometimes appear to be functional, and bad or negative, in that they sometimes appear to be dysfunctional. In this section, we provide an overview of research that describes them as being good or bad, including possible individual differences, and we mention a few points of controversy.

The Good

Research on the good aspects of rumination indicates that ruminations can be positive, functional, adaptive, or virtuous. This research suggests they are useful for problem solving. Ruminations, from this view, are future oriented and goal based, whether they are used strategically or result from individual differences (Martin & Tesser, 1989, 1996; Martin, Tesser, & McIntosh, 1993). They result from attempts at goal attainment. This is consistent with general control theory or discrepancy-based models of goal-directed action (Carver & Scheier, 1998; Klinger, 1977; Miller, Galanter, & Pribram, 1960). Ruminations involve mentally simulating, or "looking," for ways to meet a goal (Martin & Tesser, 1989). They persist until a person finds what he or she is looking for (i.e., a route or routes to the desired goal).

Ruminations differ from nonruminative thoughts by the fact that it normally takes longer for people to find what they are looking for, so thoughts have greater persistence.

A person who has a goal will try to attain it. He or she will also assess progress toward the goal along the way. As an example, a young academician who has visions of becoming rich, famous, and adored by all may take specific steps to bring that goal to fruition. He or she may write influential articles and incredibly insightful chapters. If the steps are successful, the person will move on to other goals. If the steps are unsuccessful, the young and budding academic star may attempt to attain the goal in other ways or may pursue alternate goals. Perhaps he or she will begin focusing on writing that grant which allows for a new direction in a program of intriguing research. Mentally simulated routes to goal attainment, as well as simulations of alternate routes when necessary, involve ruminations. If goals are obtained immediately, if substitute goals can be found quickly, or if goals are abandoned instantaneously, then there will be no ruminative thoughts.

Indications of goal progress, however, involve subjective assessments and thus cannot necessarily be objectively defined. In many cases, affect signals goal attainment (Schwarz & Clore, 1996). Movement toward goals elicits positive affect, and movement away from goals elicits negative affect; quicker movement leads to more intense affect (Carver & Scheier, 1990; Hsee & Abelson, 1991). A person's pre-existing affect can also influence goal appraisal (Schwarz & Bless, 1992). People in bad moods infer lack of progress, whereas those in good moods infer progress, toward goals (Martin, Ward, Achee, & Wyer, 1993; Sanna, Turley, & Mark, 1996).

Not all goals instigate ruminations. For example, most people ruminate over a vociferous brawl with a superior or over the loss of a loved one rather than whether to choose a Coke or a Pepsi. The reason lies in goal hierarchies (Martin & Tesser, 1996; see also Carver & Scheier, 1998). People ruminate more over higher level goals that are central to their well-being than over lower level goals that are less central (McIntosh & Martin, 1992). Consistent with this, there may be individual differences in rumination depending on how goals are construed. Some people are "linkers" and are apt to interpret lower level goals (e.g., improving one's swimming speed) as connected to higher level goals (e.g., becoming an accomplished Olympic-caliber swimmer), whereas "nonlinkers" are less apt to make that connection. Linkers will ruminate more than nonlinkers, which can be positive when goal progress is being made but negative with problematic goal progress (see chap. 4, this volume).

The Bad

Research on the bad aspects of rumination indicates that ruminations can be negative, dysfunctional, maladaptive, or vicious. Ruminations are seen as analogous to a cow chewing its cud in that a person goes over the same thought repeatedly, without necessarily having anything to do with goal progress or attainment. The ruminations emphasized by these researchers are past oriented and not goal based, whether resulting from situational features (e.g., negative events) or individual differences (Nolen-Hoeksema, 1996; Nolen-Hoeksema, McBride, & Larson, 1997). The defining characteristic of ruminations from this view is their repetitive or recurrent nature, without further assumptions about progression toward goals, whether they are instrumental, or whether they involve a commitment to solving problems.

Ruminations intensify reactions to negative life events. For example, Nolen-Hoeksema et al. (1997) examined bereavement and adjustment of men who had lost a partner to AIDS. Losing a loved one may be especially devastating, requiring traversing a long and bumpy cognitive, emotional, and physical rollercoaster on the way to adjustment. Men who ruminated about the loss showed increased negative emotions and risk for severe and prolonged periods of depression. For these men, rumination was a slippery slope of negativity whereby those with repetitive thoughts about despair (e.g., sadness, lack of motivation, or hopelessness) showed more psychological and physical distress both 1 month and 1 year after the loss (see also Holman & Silver, 1998). The men were not ruminating about goals, they were not thinking about problems to solve, they did not even so much as attempt to elevate their moods; they simply were thinking repeatedly about their lost loved ones.

People with depression or in bad moods who ruminate exhibit worse moods and display many negative cognitive biases. For example, individuals with depression who ruminated recalled negative memories about the past, interpreted current circumstances harshly, and judged hypothetical events pessimistically (Gold & Wegner, 1995; Lyubomirsky & Nolen-Hoeksema, 1993). People in bad moods also ruminate more (Pyszczynski & Greenberg, 1987; Segerstrom, Tsao, Alden, & Craske, 2000), suggesting a reciprocal relation between negative affect and rumination. Consistent with this, there may be individual differences. Women ruminate more than men about bad moods (Butler & Nolen-Hoeksema, 1994), which perhaps explains why women exhibit greater depression. More broadly, several scales appraising individual differences exist (Just & Alloy, 1997; Nolen-Hoeksema et al., 1997) and are predictive of ruminations in naturalistic settings (Nolen-Hoeksema & Morrow, 1991).

The Ugly

Research on the good or virtuous versus the bad or vicious has been somewhat controversial. If not exactly characterized as "ugly," the area has involved extensive debate (see Wyer, 1996, for discussions). On the positive side, ruminations may be useful for problem solving. This presumes that ruminations are future oriented and goal based. On the negative side, ruminations are more reactive. This presumes that ruminations are past oriented, responsive to negative events or moods.

THE IMAGINATION, GOALS, AND AFFECT MODEL

Our imagination, goals, and affect (IGoA, or "ego") model attempts to resolve some of the controversy. *Ego* also refers to the degree that self-motives or goals are activated. It builds on prior ideas (Sanna, 2000; Sanna, Chang, & Meier, 2001; Sanna, Turley-Ames, & Meier, 1999) and places the views of ruminations—the good and the bad—in a broader context of other imaginative mental simulations. There is a common focus on thought persistence. Our idea follows this shared emphasis on repetitiveness, without using positive or negative as inherent to the definition. All mental simulations can be ruminative if they are recurrent. They all can also be construed as virtue or vice. The IGoA model is depicted in Figure 7.1, and we next describe each aspect in turn.

Dimensions of Imaginative Mental Simulations

Mental simulations are imaginative cognitive constructions of hypothetical events or reconstructions of real events (Sanna, 2000; Taylor, Pham, Rivkin, & Armor, 1998). They include forecasts of the future (e.g., thinking about what might happen on a date later this evening), assessments of the

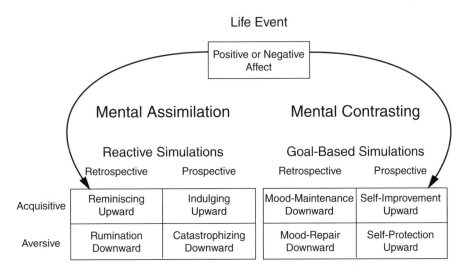

Figure 7.1. The imagination, goals, and affect (IGoA) model.

present (e.g., thinking about how fortunate one is to have such a captivating job), and retrospections of the past (e.g., thinking about a disagreement at yesterday's committee meeting). We propose that simulations can be classified according to three underlying dimensions.

Reactive Versus Goal Based

This refers to whether there is a clear goal underlying the mental simulation or whether it is more reactive and does not have an apparent underlying objective. For instance, Klinger (1975, 1977) has divided thoughts into *respondent* and *operant*. Respondent thoughts occur without premeditation or purpose (see also Rachman, 1981). They are not goal based and may involve shifts away from goal-directed tasks. In contrast, other mental simulations are goal based (Sanna, 2000; Sanna et al., 2001; Taylor & Schneider, 1989). What is meant by *goal based* is a matter of degree. This is not to say that what we have classified as reactive simulations can never be goal based, just that they are normally less so than clear goal-based ones (see also Klinger, 1977).

Retrospective Versus Prospective

Mental simulations can also be distinguished on the basis of temporal perspective. Retrospective simulations emphasize the past or a previously obtained outcome. Counterfactuals (Roese, 1997; Sanna, 2000) exemplify this. One may have had an automobile accident, for example, and later wonder whether things could have been different and whether the crash might have been avoided if only an alternate route home had been taken. Focusing on just the past, however, would be a lot like trying to drive a car while looking only through the rear-view mirror. In contrast, prospective simulations focus on the future or on thinking about what the future might bring. Prefactual thoughts of "what may be" (Sanna, 1996, 1999) exemplify this. One may forecast losing money in a failed real estate investment, or feeling happier after moving to warm and sunny North Carolina (see also Gilbert, Pinel, Wilson, Blumberg, & Wheatley, 1998).

Acquisitive Versus Aversive

Mental simulations can be acquisitive or aversive. *Acquisitive* refers to a focus on obtaining or retaining something good or positive (Arkin & Shepperd, 1989). A person might, for example, reminisce about the glory days of old when he or she was a star high school athlete, or might think about improving that sagacious manuscript that was so wrongfully rejected by obviously inattentive reviewers. In contrast, aversive simulations focus on something negative or are geared toward avoiding or protecting against negatives (Baumeister, Tice, & Hamilton, 1989). A young mother may think repeatedly about the loss of her baby, or a student may think about how an exam score might have been even worse if only he had not looked at the study guide. When it comes to goal-based simulations, acquisitive ones might also be viewed as promotion focused, whereas aversive ones might be viewed as prevention focused (Higgins, 1998).

Reactions to Valenced Life Events

The IGoA model emphasizes reactions to life events and accompanying affect. We do not presume that valenced events are the only thing that influences mental simulations. However, valenced events are unavoidable, and by assessing responses to them researchers can gain insight into coping and well-being. Another reason for our emphasis is that affect or moods are an integral part of descriptions of ruminations, whether viewed as virtue or vice.

Valenced Outcomes and Moods

Outcomes and moods influence mental simulations in an identical fashion. For instance, upward counterfactuals invoke better realities (e.g., "If only I studied harder, I might have been admitted to medical school"); downward counterfactuals invoke worse realities (e.g., "At least I was wearing my seatbelt, or I might have been more seriously injured"). This is similar to social comparison direction (Collins, 1996; Wood, 1989), but it refers to alternatives to reality rather than comparisons with other people. Markman, Gavanski, Sherman, and McMullen (1993) obtained downward counterfactuals most often, particularly after successes, and upward ones after failures, particularly on repeatable tasks. Other research has found this same pattern after failures and successes (Sanna & Turley-Ames, 2000). Moods have similar effects. Sanna et al.'s (1999; Sanna, Meier, & Turley-Ames, 1998) bad and good moods elicited upward and downward counterfactuals, respectively. Outcomes and moods are connected directly, as numerous life events, like failures and successes, exert influences through moods (Brown & Mankowski, 1993).

Mental Contrasting and Assimilation

Mental contrasting and assimilation may provide a mechanism for how life events and moods influence simulations (Oettingen, Pak, & Schnetter, 2001; Sanna, 2000; Schwarz & Bless, 1992). Research on mental simulations emphasizes contrasting. For example, counterfactual research entails contrasting realities with alternatives. Contrast is also a focus for prefactuals (Sanna, 1998, 1999). Oettingen et al. (2001) argued that comparing desired futures with present realities underlies goal setting, a mental contrasting. We extend this idea to include all goal-based simulations, depicted on the right side of Figure 7.1. Each involves a contrast with reality. To the contrary, reactive simulations depicted on the left of Figure 7.1 do not involve a contrast with reality, at least not to the same degree. For example, Oettingen et al. found that people "indulge" in fantasies by focusing only on the future, without regard to reality (see also McMullen, 1997; Oettingen, 1996). We extend this idea to all reactive simulations, by focusing on only the future or the past without contrast with reality, a mental assimilation.

Summary

The IGoA model discusses ruminations in a broader context of imaginative mental simulations. We propose three underlying dimensions and that reactions to life events and accompanying affect cue mental simulations. Positive and negative events elicit downward and upward simulations, respectively. However, mental contrasting and assimilation further determine the nature and direction of the mental simulation and its consequences.

CLASSIFICATION OF MENTAL SIMULATIONS

In this section we describe prototypical mental simulations that may fit our classification scheme. This is not necessarily assumed to be an exhaustive list, but we present examples that may conform to the framework. Simulation direction is also presented within each cell of Figure 7.1.

Retrospective Mental Simulations: Specters of the Past

"I told you these were shadows of the things that have been," said the Ghost. "They are what they are, do not blame me!"

In this section we describe retrospective mental simulations. These simulations can be either goal based or reactive, and they can be either acquisitive or aversive.

Goal-Based Retrospective Simulations

Retrospective goal-based simulations are depicted on the right of Figure 7.1.

Mood Maintenance

People in happy moods, or those who have experienced positive life events or outcomes such as successes, behave in ways that preserve positive affect. The goal or motive underlying this is *mood maintenance* (Isen, 1987). For example, good moods make accessible pleasant self-thoughts (Bower, 1991) or induce people to select only information that propagates their positive affect (Wegener & Petty, 1994). With regard to counterfactuals, evidence for mood maintenance comes from the finding that people in happy moods generate greater numbers of downward counterfactuals, and they report high enjoyment in doing so (Sanna, Meier, & Wegner, 2001). Mood maintenance is retrospective, goal based, and involves a contrast of pleasant reality with an even worse alternative to perpetuate a positive affective state.

Mood Repair

People in bad moods, or those who have experienced negative life events or outcomes such as failures, work slavishly to reinstate more positive affect. The goal or motive underlying this is *mood repair* (Erber & Erber, 1994; Sedikides & Strube, 1997). For example, when confronted with negative outcomes or bad moods, people recall positive information about the self (Parrott & Sabini, 1990), denigrate out-groups (Fein & Spencer, 1997), or perform helpful acts (Schaller & Cialdini, 1990) to make themselves feel better. With regard to counterfactuals, people have been shown to generate downward counterfactuals to repair mood (Sanna et al., 1998; Sanna et al., 1999). Mood repair is retrospective and goal based and involves contrasting a currently negative reality with worse alternatives to reinstate positive affect.

Reactive Retrospective Simulations

Retrospective reactive simulations are depicted on the left of Figure 7.1.

Reminiscing

People reminisce by thinking about positive aspects of their lives with a focus on past accomplishments, achievements, or successes (Fivush, Haden, & Reese, 1996; Strack, Schwarz, & Gschneidinger, 1985). Reminiscing increases life satisfaction, extends cognitive functioning, alleviates depression, and sustains a positive self-image (Rybarczyk, 1995). Self-reported frequency of reminiscing appears to be quite high (Webster, 1993), especially among older adults. People who reminisce about past glories and assimilate these thoughts to their current state experience an increased sense of well-being (Strack et al., 1985; see also McMullen, 1997; Sanna, 1997). We propose that reminiscing is retrospective, reactive, and involves an assimilation of upward, or positive, thoughts with a focus only on the past.

Rumination

This naming is consistent with that which describes rumination as bad or a vice. Rumination involves thoughts about past events and can have an irrevocable quality (Gold & Wegner, 1995). Ruminations may focus on negatives or be associated with bad moods (Nolen-Hoeksema, 1996; Nolen-Hoeksema & Morrow, 1991). They are respondent or intrusive (Klinger, 1977) and may have little to do with goal setting or problem solving in this case. We propose that ruminations are retrospective and aversive and do not entail a contrast with a present state—that is, they involve mental assimilation. The name *rumination* is used here simply to correspond with some past research (that traditionally viewed them as a vice). However, as we described, we define ruminations on the basis of whether thoughts are temporally persistent and not on the basis of inherent negativity per se.

Prospective Mental Simulations: Specters of the Future

> Said Scrooge, "Answer me one question. Are these the shadows of the things that Will be, or are they shadows of the things that May be, only?"

In this section we describe prospective mental simulations. Prospective simulations can also be either goal based or relatively reactive, and they can be either acquisitive or aversive.

Goal-Based Prospective Simulations

Prospective goal-based simulations are depicted on the right side of Figure 7.1.

Self-Improvement

This classification is consistent with that which describes rumination as good or a virtue, in that they are useful for goal attainment. People are motivated to improve their traits, abilities, health status, or well-being (Collins, 1996; Taylor & Lobel, 1989). Feelings of threat, inadequacy, or negative affect often instigate motivations to get better (Sanna, 2000; Taylor & Schneider, 1989; Wood, Taylor, & Lichtman, 1985). For example, cancer patients focus on better alternatives to improve coping (Wood et al., 1985), and people mentally simulate better realities when preparing for the future (Markman et al., 1993; Sanna, 1996). In accordance with our model, self-improvement is prospective, acquisitive, and goal based. It involves a contrast with the present, as does the originally proposed view of mental contrasting (Oettingen et al., 2001).

Self-Protection

People prospectively protect themselves from negative possibilities by "bracing for loss" (Shepperd, Findley-Klein, Kwavnick, Walker, & Perez, 2000; Shepperd, Ouelette, & Fernandez, 1996). Mentally simulating how the worst may transpire can mitigate the sting of failure, should it occur. Self-protection is especially likely when tests of important attributes are close at hand. Defensive pessimism (Norem & Cantor, 1986; Sanna, 2001) is a strategy that, in part, involves self-protection. Self-handicapping (Berglas

& Jones, 1978; Sanna & Mark, 1995), in which people impose or claim impediments, is another strategy. Upward prefactuals have similarly been shown to help people brace for failure (Sanna, 1999; Sanna & Meier, 2000). Self-protection is prospective, aversive, and goal based, involving a contrast with the present.

Reactive Prospective Simulations

Reactive prospective simulations are depicted on the left side of Figure 7.1.

Indulging

Oettingen et al. (2001) argued that people can look toward the future without specific goals in mind, which they called *indulging*. People indulge by thinking about desired futures without a contrast with the present (or only a very weak contrast with the present). Indulging is a free fantasy in which people "enjoy the desired future in the here and now" (Oettingen et al. 2001, p. 737; see also Oettingen, 1996). Evidence comes from work on goal setting (Oettingen et al., 2001) and from that which indicates that people assimilate upward simulations (McMullen, 1997; Sanna, 1997, 2000). For example, a person who is about to buy a lottery ticket may imagine him- or herself vacationing on white sandy beaches while enjoying fancy feasts and fine champagne. We propose that indulging is prospective, acquisitive, reactive, and occurs by means of mental assimilation.

Catastrophizing

Catastrophizing entails simulating negative "what if" scenarios (Kendall & Ingram, 1987). People worry about how bad things may transpire, resulting in progressive gloom. Poor problem-solving confidence is a contributing factor (Davey, Jubb, & Cameron, 1996); depressed moods and chronic worrying (Vasey & Borkovec, 1992) are others. A passenger at an airport gate waiting for her departure might think about all the bad things that may happen (e.g., "what if my plane crashes," "how will my family get along without me"). There is an internal dialogue characterized by problem-specific pessimism, feelings of inadequacy, despair, and hopelessness. Catastrophizing is linked through lifestyles to negative events (Peterson, Seligman, Yurko, Martin, & Friedman, 1998). We view catastrophizing as prospective, aversive, and reactive.

Comparisons With Current States: Specters of the Present

"My life upon this globe is very brief," replied the Ghost.

The present is captured for only a brief moment. We have thus far considered the present only to the extent that it is used as a reference or standard by which comparisons are made with the future or the past. The reason for this emphasis is the transient nature of the present. People move fluidly from thoughts about the future to present states, which then even more quickly become part of the past. This is not to say that the present is unimportant. It most certainly is extraordinarily important; after all, it is where the majority of us spend most of our lives. It is perhaps ironic, however, that mental simulations relating to the present have received the least attention. In part, this may be because the present is "real" to us, so there is little that needs to be "simulated." However, in addition to serving as a comparison, there are mental simulations that focus only on the present without much regard for the past or future: *basking* and *dwelling*.

We discuss basking as present-focused thoughts emphasizing the positive. Basking involves a person's concentration on what he or she is doing (or has just done). It is an absorption in the moment, without regard for the past or future (Martin & Tesser, 1996). A mother may be immersed completely in the interaction with her newborn and the pleasant feel of his or her skin against hers; the weekend athlete may be engrossed in a game of golf and the enthralling company of his buddies; or the experienced cook may be riveted by the praise she is receiving for the lasagna that turned out so perfectly. Basking, a complete absorption in the moment, may be experienced as "flow" (Csikzentmihalyi, 1975). In contrast, dwelling involves present-focused thoughts that emphasize the negative. Here, a person's focus is only on a dismal reality without any particular regard for the future (Oettingen et al., 2001) or past. The author who gets his or her manuscript rejected may dwell on the time spent conducting the research, be absorbed in the anger of the moment or the embarrassment of rejection, or doubt his or her ability and whether academia was the correct career choice. No specific goals are engaged; neither is problem solving.

CONCLUSION

We have proffered the view that ruminative thoughts can be conceived as both virtue and vice. On the one hand, researchers emphasizing the good have argued that ruminations are positive, functional, or adaptive. On the other hand, researchers emphasizing the bad have argued that ruminations are negative, dysfunctional, or maladaptive. These views were incorporated into the IGoA model, which places them in a broader context of mental simulations. We envisioned temporal persistence, and not inherent negativity or positivity per se, as critical to defining ruminations. All simulations can be "ruminative" if they are recurrent (we did also use the term *rumination* in naming aversive, reactive, and retrospective thoughts simply to emphasize a correspondence with some past research). The IGoA model proposes three underlying dimensions, that simulations are induced by reactions to life events and affect and that simulations involve mental contrasting or assimilation. We conclude by discussing other implications of the IGoA model.

Personality Processes and Strategies

Personality characteristics or strategies may be related to mental simulations. Researchers presenting a positive or virtuous view of ruminations proposed an individual difference of linkers versus nonlinkers and argued that linkers ruminate more because they see greater connections between lower and higher order goals (Martin, Tesser, & McIntosh, 1993; McIntosh & Martin, 1992). Research presenting a negative or vicious view of ruminations has also proposed an individual difference (Just & Alloy, 1997; Nolen-Hoeksema et al., 1997), whereby some people ruminate more often. In addition, there are scales measuring things such as chronic worry (Vasey & Borkovec, 1992), reminiscence (Webster, 1993), attributions related to catastrophizing (Peterson et al., 1998), and so on. Each of these may be associated with rumination in one way or another.

Other personality characteristics may be related to mental simulations. Sanna (2000) already connected some individual differences to such thoughts. Within the IGoA model, goal-based and reactive simulations were emphasized. Personality types, traits, or strategies may represent more global macro-goals or macro-reactions within the model. For example, defensive pessimism and optimism (see also chaps. 2 and 6, this volume) present a comparison of how people might use prospective versus retrospective simulations (Sanna, 1996, 1998): Defensive pessimists use upward simulations prospectively, but optimists use downward ones retrospectively. Defensive pessimists' strategy involves a combination of self-improvement and self-protective motives, whereas that of optimists involves a mood repair motive. Both strategies make use of mental contrasting.

Self-esteem, another example, refers to self-worth (Baumeister et al., 1989; Brown & Mankowski, 1993; see also Chapter 1). People with low self-esteem are governed by self-protective motives; those with high self-esteem are governed by acquisitive motives. Similar to optimists, people with high self-esteem use downward counterfactuals to repair moods (Sanna et al., 1999); people with low self-esteem do not. Although both use upward prefactuals, people with low self-esteem contrast them in a self-protective fashion (Sanna & Meier, 2000), similar to defensive pessimists. People with high self-esteem assimilate upward prefactuals. Findings for self-efficacy, naive optimism, true pessimism, and others may also fit (see Sanna, 2000, for detail). It is important to note that the IGoA model may inform myriad additional individual differences, as mental simulations may distinguish the nature of the underlying processes. Other motives (Helgeson & Mickelson, 1995) may also underlie mental simulations.

Automaticity and Coping

Life events, and affect, trigger mental simulations of a particular direction, and this may enlighten coping and well-being. As we described, negative events or bad moods induce upward simulations, whereas positive events or good moods induce downward simulations (Sanna, 2000). Life events exert influences through affect (Brown & Mankowski, 1993). Moods produce an identical pattern, because they inform people's current states (Schwarz & Clore, 1996; Sanna et al., 1998). People interpret their lives negatively in bad moods (e.g., "I am a failure" or "There is a problem") but positively in good moods (e.g., "I am a success" or "Things are fine").

As depicted in Figure 7.1, and as we have described, mental assimilation involves a focus on only the past or the future. We propose that affect here influences simulations in a mood-congruent manner. Just as assimilating upward simulations leads to good moods (McMullen, 1997), good moods lead to upward simulations (Sanna, 2000). Affect influences the simulation directly. Mental contrasting, however, involves a comparison of future (Oettingen et al., 2001) or past with the present. We propose that affect here influences the present directly (Sanna, 2000; Sanna et al., 1999). Goal-based simulations are contrasted with this present. Mood maintenance occurs for positive affect, and self-improvement, self-protection, and mood repair occur for negative affect (Sanna et al., 2001).

When direction activated by affect (upward for negative and downward for positive) matches that depicted in Figure 7.1, the response is automatic. When there is a mismatch, the response is effortful. To date, research has tested this only for goal-based simulations. Sanna et al. (2001) varied moods and the four goal-based simulations. Half of the participants were put under time pressure, getting at automatic responses (Smith & DeCoster, 2000). In bad moods, with no time pressure, quick reactions arose for upward simulations when self-improvement or self-protection was salient (matches); slow reactions arose for downward simulations when mood repair was salient (mismatch). In good moods with no time pressure, quick reactions arose for downward simulations when mood maintenance was salient (match). Under time pressure, however, responses were quick for upward and downward simulations in bad and good moods, consistent with that activated by affect. Future research is needed to test whether the match-versus-mismatch idea extends to reactive simulations.

CODA

In keeping with the theme of this book, we conceptualized ruminations as virtue and vice. The IGoA model proposes a broad framework, and several hypotheses await future research. Among these hypotheses are the degree that goal-based simulations contrast with the present but reactive ones do not; another is the degree that simulations are automatic or effortful. Researchers should not, however, construe spontaneity (Sanna & Turley, 1996) and automaticity (Bargh, 1994) as isomorphic. Spontaneous ones occur without prompting and can be either automatic or effortful. Ruminations may be negative and enduring (Nolen-Hoeksema, 1996) or simply enduring (Martin & Tesser, 1996), including positives. Both views emphasize temporal persistence, as did ours. To duration, we add that ruminations can also vary by their intensity and number (Sanna & Turley-Ames, 2000). With these final thoughts in mind, in the end, like Scrooge, we all must recognize unequivocally that we live with specters of the past and future in the present:

> "I will live in the Past, the Present, and the Future!" Scrooge repeated, as he scrambled out of bed. "The Spirits of all Three shall strive within me . . ."

REFERENCES

Arkin, R. M., & Shepperd, J. A. (1989). Self-presentation styles in organizations. In R. A. Giacalone & P. Rosenfeld (Eds.), *Impression management in the organization* (pp. 125–139). Hillsdale, NJ: Erlbaum.

Bargh, J. (1994). The four horsemen of automaticity: Awareness, intention, efficiency, and control in social cognition. In R. S. Wyer Jr. & T. K. Srull (Eds.), *Handbook of social cognition* (2nd ed., Vol. 1, pp. 1–40). Hillsdale, NJ: Erlbaum.

Baumeister, R. F., Tice, D. M., & Hamilton, D. G. (1989). Self-presentational motivations and personality differences in self-esteem. *Journal of Personality, 57,* 547–579.

Berglas, S., & Jones, E. E. (1978). Drug choice as a self-handicapping strategy in response to noncontingent success. *Journal of Personality and Social Psychology, 36,* 405–417.

Bower, G. H. (1991). Mood congruity of social judgments. In J. P. Forgas (Ed.), *Emotion and social judgments* (pp. 31–53). Elmsford, NY: Pergamon Press.

Brown, J. D., & Mankowski, T. A. (1993). Self-esteem, mood, and self-evaluation: Changes in mood and the way you see you. *Journal of Personality and Social Psychology, 64,* 421–430.

Butler, L. D., & Nolen-Hoeksema, S. (1994). Gender differences in responses to depressed mood in a college sample. *Sex Roles, 30,* 331–346.

Carver, C. S., & Scheier, M. F. (1990). Origins and functions of positive and negative affect: A control-process view. *Psychological Review, 97,* 19–35.

Carver, C. S., & Scheier, M. F. (1998). *On the self-regulation of behavior.* New York: Cambridge University Press.

Collins, R. L. (1996). For better or worse: The impact of upward social comparison on self-evaluations. *Psychological Bulletin, 119,* 51–69.

Csikzentmihalyi, M. (1975). *Beyond boredom and anxiety*. San Francisco: Jossey-Bass.

Davey, G. C. L., Jubb, M., & Cameron, C. (1996). Catastrophic worrying as a function of changes in problem-solving confidence. *Cognitive Therapy and Research, 20*, 333–344.

Dickens, C. (1984). *A Christmas carol*. New York: Penguin Books. (Original work published 1843)

Erber, R., & Erber, M. W. (1994). Beyond mood and social judgment: Mood incongruent recall and regulation. *European Journal of Social Psychology, 24*, 79–88.

Fein, S., & Spencer, S. J. (1997). Prejudice as self-image maintenance: Affirming the self through derogating others. *Journal of Personality and Social Psychology, 73*, 31–44.

Fivush, R., Haden, C., & Reese, E. (1996). Remembering, recounting, and reminiscing: The development of autobiographical memory in social context. In D. Rubin (Ed.), *Remembering our past: Studies in autobiographical memory* (pp. 341–359). New York: Cambridge University Press.

Gilbert, D. T., Pinel, E. C., Wilson, T. D., Blumberg, S. J., & Wheatley, T. P. (1998). Immune neglect: A source of durability bias in affective forecasting. *Journal of Personality and Social Psychology, 59*, 617–638.

Gold, D. B., & Wegner, D. M. (1995). Origins of ruminative thought: Trauma, incompleteness, nondisclosure, and suppression. *Journal of Applied Social Psychology, 25*, 1245–1261.

Helgeson, V. S., & Mickelson, K. D. (1995). Motives for social comparison. *Personality and Social Psychology Bulletin, 21*, 1200–1209.

Higgins, E. T. (1998). Promotion and prevention: Regulatory focus as a motivational principle. In M. P. Zanna (Ed.), *Advances in experimental social psychology* (Vol. 23, pp. 305–331). New York: Academic Press.

Holman, E. A., & Silver, R. C. (1998). Getting "stuck" in the past: Temporal orientation and coping with trauma. *Journal of Personality and Social Psychology, 74*, 1146–1163.

Hsee, C. K., & Abelson, R. P. (1991). Velocity relation: Satisfaction as a function of the first derivative of outcome over time. *Journal of Personality and Social Psychology, 60*, 341–347.

Isen, A. M. (1987). Affect, cognition, and social behavior. In L. Berkowitz (Ed.), *Advances in experimental social psychology* (Vol. 20, pp. 203–253). San Diego, CA: Academic Press.

Just, N., & Alloy, L. B. (1997). The response style theory of depression: Tests and an extension of the theory. *Journal of Abnormal Psychology, 106*, 221–229.

Kendall, P. C., & Ingram, R. E. (1987). The future for cognitive assessment of anxiety: Let's get specific. In L. Michaelson & L. M. Ascher (Eds.), *Anxiety and stress disorders: Cognitive–behavioral assessment and treatment* (pp. 89–104). New York: Guilford Press.

Klinger, E. (1975). Consequences to commitment to and disengagement from incentives. *Psychological Review, 82*, 223–231.

Klinger, E. (1977). *Meaning and void: Inner experience and the incentives in people's lives*. Minneapolis: University of Minnesota Press.

Lyubomirsky, S., & Nolen-Hoeksema, S. (1993). Self-perpetuating properties of depressive rumination. *Journal of Personality and Social Psychology, 65*, 339–349.

Markman, K. D., Gavanski, I., Sherman, S. J., & McMullen, M. N. (1993). The mental simulation of better and worse possible worlds. *Journal of Experimental Social Psychology, 29*, 87–109.

Martin, L. L., & Tesser, A. (1989). Toward a motivational and structural theory of ruminative thought. In J. S. Uleman & J. A. Bargh (Eds.), *Unintended thought* (pp. 306–326). New York: Guilford Press.

Martin, L. L., & Tesser, A. (1996). Some ruminative thoughts. In R. S. Wyer (Ed.), *Ruminative thoughts: Advances in social cognition* (Vol. 9, pp. 1–47). Mahwah, NJ: Erlbaum.

Martin, L. L., Tesser, A., & McIntosh, W. D. (1993). Wanting but not having: The effects of unattained goals on thoughts and feelings. In D. M. Wegner & J. W. Pennebaker (Eds.), *The handbook of mental control* (pp. 552–572). New York: Prentice Hall.

Martin, L. L., Ward, D. W., Achee, J. W., & Wyer, R. S. (1993). Mood as input: People have to interpret the motivational implications of their moods. *Journal of Personality and Social Psychology, 64*, 317–326.

McIntosh, W. D., & Martin, L. L. (1992). The cybernetics of happiness: The relation between goal attainment, rumination, and depression. In M. S. Clark (Ed.), *Review of personality and social psychology* (Vol. 14, pp. 222–246). Newbury Park, CA: Sage.

McMullen, M. N. (1997). Affective assimilation and contrast in counterfactual thinking. *Journal of Experimental Social Psychology, 33*, 77–100.

Miller, G. A., Galanter, E., & Pribram, K. H. (1960). *Plans and the structure of behavior*. New York: Holt, Rhinehart & Winston.

Nolen-Hoeksema, S. (1987). Sex differences in unipolar depression: Evidence and theory. *Psychological Bulletin, 101*, 259–282.

Nolen-Hoeksema, S. (1996). Chewing the cud and other ruminations. In R. S. Wyer (Ed.), *Ruminative thoughts: Advances in social cognition* (Vol. 9, pp. 135–144). Mahwah, NJ: Erlbaum.

Nolen-Hoeksema, S., McBride, A., & Larson, J. (1997). Rumination and psychological distress among bereaved partners. *Journal of Personality and Social Psychology, 72*, 855–862.

Nolen-Hoeksema, S. & Morrow, J. (1991). A prospective study of depression and posttraumatic stress symptoms after a natural disaster: The 1989 Loma Prieta earthquake. *Journal of Personality and Social Psychology, 61*, 155–171.

Norem, J. K., & Cantor, N. (1986). Defensive pessimism: "Harnessing" anxiety as motivation. *Journal of Personality and Social Psychology, 51*, 1208–1217.

Oettingen, G. (1996). Positive fantasy and motivation. In P. M. Gollwitzer & J. A. Bargh (Eds.), *The psychology of action: Linking cognition and motivation to behavior* (pp. 236–259). New York: Guilford Press.

Oettingen, G., Pak, H., & Schnetter, K. (2001). Self-regulation and goal-setting: Turning free fantasies about the future into binding goals. *Journal of Personality and Social Psychology, 80,* 736–753.

Parrott, W. G., & Sabini, J. (1990). Mood and memory under natural conditions: Evidence for mood incongruent recall. *Journal of Personality and Social Psychology, 59,* 321–336.

Peterson, C., Seligman, M. E. P., Yurko, K. H., Martin, L. R., & Friedman, H. S. (1998). Catastrophizing and untimely death. *Psychological Science, 9,* 127–130.

Pyszczynski, T., & Greenberg, J. (1987). Self-regulatory preservation and the depressive self-focusing style: A self-awareness theory of reactive depression. *Psychological Bulletin, 102,* 122–138.

Rachman, S. (1981). Unwanted intrusive cognitions. *Advances in Behavioral Research and Therapy, 3,* 89–99.

Roese, N. J. (1994). The functional basis of counterfactual thinking. *Journal of Personality and Social Psychology, 66,* 805–818.

Roese, N. J. (1997). Counterfactual thinking. *Psychological Bulletin, 121,* 133–148.

Rybarczyk, B. D. (1995). *The reminiscence interview: A new approach to stress intervention in the medical setting.* New York: Springer-Verlag.

Sanna, L. J. (1996). Defensive pessimism, optimism, and simulating alternatives: Some ups and downs of prefactual and counterfactual thinking. *Journal of Personality and Social Psychology, 71,* 1020–1036.

Sanna, L. J. (1997). Self-efficacy and counterfactual thinking: Up a creek with and without a paddle. *Personality and Social Psychology Bulletin, 23,* 654–666.

Sanna, L. J. (1998). Defensive pessimism and optimism: The bitter-sweet influence of mood on performance and prefactual and counterfactual thinking. *Cognition & Emotion, 12,* 635–665.

Sanna, L. J. (1999). Mental simulations, affect, and subjective confidence: Timing is everything. *Psychological Science, 10,* 339–345.

Sanna, L. J. (2000). Mental simulation, affect, and personality: A conceptual framework. *Current Directions in Psychological Science, 9,* 168–173.

Sanna, L. J. (2001). Defensive pessimism. In W. E. Craighead & C. B. Nemerhoff (Eds.), *The Corsini encyclopedia of psychology and behavioral science* (3rd ed., Vol. 1, pp. 430–432). New York: Wiley.

Sanna, L. J., Chang, E. C., & Meier, S. (2001). Counterfactual thinking and self-motives. *Personality and Social Psychology Bulletin, 27,* 1023–1034.

Sanna, L. J., & Mark, M. M. (1995). Self-handicapping, expected evaluation, and performance: Accentuating the positive and attenuating the negative. *Organizational Behavior and Human Decision Processes, 64,* 84–102.

Sanna, L. J., & Meier, S. (2000). Looking for clouds in a silver lining: Self-esteem, mental simulations, and temporal confidence changes. *Journal of Research in Personality, 34,* 236–251.

Sanna, L. J., Meier, S., & Turley-Ames, K. J. (1998). Mood, self-esteem, and counterfactuals: Externally attributed moods limit self-enhancement strategies. *Social Cognition, 16,* 267–286.

Sanna, L. J., Meier, S., & Wegner, E. C. (2001). Counterfactuals and motivation: Mood as input to affective enjoyment and preparation. *British Journal of Social Psychology, 40,* 235–256.

Sanna, L. J., & Turley, K. J. (1996). Antecedents to spontaneous counterfactual thinking: Effects of expectancy violation and outcome valence. *Personality and Social Psychology Bulletin, 22,* 906–919.

Sanna, L. J., & Turley-Ames, K. J. (2000). Counterfactual intensity. *European Journal of Social Psychology, 30,* 273–296.

Sanna, L. J., Turley, K. J., & Mark, M. M. (1996). Expected evaluation, goals, and performance: Mood as input. *Personality and Social Psychology Bulletin, 22,* 323–335.

Sanna, L. J., Turley-Ames, K. J., & Meier, S. (1999). Mood, self-esteem, and simulated alternatives: Thought-provoking affective influences on counterfactual direction. *Journal of Personality and Social Psychology, 76,* 543–558.

Schaller, M., & Cialdini, R. B. (1990). Happiness, sadness, and helping: A motivational integration. In E. T. Higgins & R. M. Sorrentino (Eds.), *Handbook of motivation and cognition: Foundations of social behavior* (Vol. 2, pp. 265–296). New York: Guilford Press.

Schwarz, N., & Bless, H. (1992). Constructing reality and its alternatives: An inclusion/exclusion model of assimilation and contrast in social judgment. In L. L. Martin & A. Tesser (Eds.), *The construction of social judgments* (pp. 217–245). Hillsdale, NJ: Erlbaum.

Schwarz, N., & Clore, G. L. (1996). Feelings as phenomenal experiences. In E. T. Higgins & A. W. Kruglanski (Eds.), *Social psychology: Handbook of basic principles* (pp. 433–465). New York: Guilford Press.

Sedikides, C., & Strube, M. J. (1997). Self-evaluation: To thine own self be good, to thine own self be sure, to thine own self be true, and to thine own self be better. In M. P. Zanna (Ed.), *Advances in experimental social psychology* (Vol. 29, pp. 209–269). San Diego, CA: Academic Press.

Segerstrom, S. C., Tsao, J. C. I., Alden, L. E., & Craske, M. G. (2000). Worry and rumination: Repetitive thought as a concomitant and predictor of negative mood. *Cognitive Therapy and Research, 24,* 671–688.

Shepperd, J. A., Findley-Klein, C., Kwavnick, K. D., Walker, D., & Perez, S. (2000). Bracing for loss. *Journal of Personality and Social Psychology, 78,* 620–634.

Shepperd, J. A., Ouelette, J. A., & Fernandez, J. K. (1996). Abandoning unrealistic optimism: Performance estimates and the temporal proximity of self-relevant feedback. *Journal of Personality and Social Psychology, 70,* 844–855.

Smith, E. R., & DeCoster, J. (2000). Dual-process models in social and cognitive psychology: Conceptual integration and links to underlying memory systems. *Personality and Social Psychology Review, 4,* 108–131.

Strack, F., Schwarz, N., & Gschneidinger, E. (1985). Happiness and reminiscing: The role of time perspective, affect, and mode of thinking. *Journal of Personality and Social Psychology, 49,* 1460–1469.

Taylor, S. E., & Lobel, M. (1989). Social comparison activity under threat: Downward evaluation and upward contact. *Psychological Review, 96,* 569–575.

Taylor, S. E., Pham, L. B., Rivkin, I. D., & Armor, D. A. (1998). Harnessing the imagination: Mental simulation, self-regulation, and coping. *American Psychologist, 53,* 429–439.

Taylor, S. E., & Schneider, S. K. (1989). Coping and the simulation of events. *Social Cognition, 7,* 174–194.

Vasey, M. W., & Borkovec, T. D. (1992). A catastrophizing assessment of worrisome thoughts. *Cognitive Therapy and Research, 16,* 505–520.

Webster, J. D. (1993). Construction and validation of the Reminiscence Functions Scale. *Journal of Gerontology: Psychological Sciences, 48,* 256–262.

Wegener, D. T., & Petty, R. E. (1994). Mood management across affective states: The hedonic contingency hypothesis. *Journal of Personality and Social Psychology, 66,* 1034–1048.

Wood, J. V. (1989). Theory and research concerning social comparison of personal attributes. *Psychological Bulletin, 106,* 231–248.

Wood, J. V., Taylor, S. E., & Lichtman, R. R. (1985). Social comparison in adjustment to breast cancer. *Journal of Personality and Social Psychology, 49,* 1169–1183.

Wyer, R. S. (Ed.). (1996). *Ruminative thoughts: Advances in social cognition* (Vol. 9). Mahwah, NJ: Erlbaum.

8

ON THE PERFECTIBILITY
OF THE INDIVIDUAL:
GOING BEYOND THE DIALECTIC OF
GOOD VERSUS EVIL

EDWARD C. CHANG

> The shades of night were falling fast,
> As through an Alpine village passed
> A youth, who bore, 'mid snow and ice,
> A banner with the strange device,
>   Excelsior!
> —from *Excelsior* (Longfellow, 1890)

In the poem *Excelsior*, Longfellow (1890; work originally composed in 1841) narrates the painful rise and ultimate fall of a young man blindly obsessed with the lofty pursuits of perfectionism. More than 100 years later, psychologists have come to increasingly recognize and appreciate the potential psychological hazards and pitfalls often associated with perfectionistic pursuits (e.g., Blatt, 1995; Hollender, 1965; Pacht, 1984); however, what is less obvious is whether such pursuits always entail negative outcomes or maladjustment. Accordingly, the purpose of this chapter is to examine the personality process of perfectionism. First, I provide a brief review of past literature linking perfectionism to maladjustment; second, I examine a recent study that shows that perfectionistic pursuits need not always be associated

I acknowledge Chang Suk-Choon and Tae Myung-Sook for their encouragement and support throughout this project.

with severe maladjustment; finally, I end by describing a model of perfectionism that may help researchers and theorists understand perfectionism as more than a vice or a virtue.

THE PURSUIT OF PERFECTION: FROM VIRTUE TO VICE

Long before modern views linked perfectionism to potentially hazardous pursuits, a very different notion of perfectionism dominated. During the Middle Kingdom (1991–1778 BC) in Egypt, the perfect individual was defined as one who was "*effective* because his life [was] in harmonious attunement to society and nature, the universal order" (La Rondelle, 1971, p. 8). Thus, the perfect individual lived a life that was in step with the world around him. Although perfection was not linked to any clear moral notions in ancient Egyptian culture, it became a key concept linked to seeking the good life (*summum bonum*) in ancient Greek thought. For example, in Plato's *The Republic* one finds that the good or just life was one attained when the soul was in perfect harmony with itself, and hence the perfect individual was also the just or virtuous individual. Likewise, in the *Nicomachean Ethics*, Aristotle defined the supreme goal of all human activity as *eudaemonia* or happiness linked to the perfection of one's nature. The notion that perfection and the process of trying to perfect oneself was a good is also found in the ancient and classical writings within Mahāyāna Buddhism and Christianity (Aitken, 1994; Milosh, 1966; Ratnayaka, 1978). Yet, over the last 10 years, studies on perfectionism have shown that there may be more reasons to consider this personality process a vice rather than a virtue.

The Conceptualization and Assessment of Perfectionism

Before reviewing the current literature linking perfectionism with maladjustment, we first provide a brief overview of the two conceptualizations and measurements of perfectionism that have become most popular in the current literature (Flett & Hewitt, 2002). First, we have the conceptualization of perfectionism presented by Frost and his colleagues (Frost, Heimberg, Holt, Mattia, & Neubauer, 1993; Frost, Marten, Lahart, & Rosenblate, 1990). According to Frost et al. (1990), perfectionism is conceptualized as an individual-difference variable involving excessive self-criticism associated with high personal standards, doubts about the effectiveness of one's actions, concerns about meeting social expectations (typically those of the parents), and an excessive focus on organization and neatness. To assess for this conceptualization of perfectionism, Frost et al. (1990) developed the Frost Multidimensional Perfectionism Scale (FMPS), a 35-item multidimensional measure of perfectionism consisting of the following six scales: (a) Concern Over Mistakes (e.g., "People will probably think less of me if

I make a mistake"), (b) Personal Standards (e.g., "I set higher goals than most people"), (c) Parental Expectations (e.g., "My parents have expected excellence from me"), (d) Parental Criticism (e.g., "I never felt like I could meet my parent's standards"), (e) Doubts About Actions (e.g., "Even when I do something very carefully, I often feel that it is not quite right"), and (f) Organization (e.g., "Neatness is very important to me"). Respondents are asked to rate items on the FMPS across a 5-point Likert-type scale ranging from 1 (*strongly disagree*) to 5 (*strongly agree*). It is worth noting that in studies of perfectionism that have used the FMPS, both aggregate FMPS scores and separate FMPS subscale scores have been used. In general, higher aggregate FMPS scores and higher FMPS subscale scores reflect greater perfectionism.

A second important conceptualization of perfectionism represented in the current literature is the one presented by Hewitt and Flett (1991b). According to Hewitt and Flett (1991b), *perfectionism* refers to a multidimensional phenomenon that comprises three relatively distinct dimensions: self-oriented, other-oriented, and socially prescribed perfectionism. *Self-oriented perfectionism* refers to the tendency for an individual to set and seek high self-standards of performance. *Other-oriented perfectionism* refers to the tendency for an individual to expect that others should or will be perfect in their performance. *Socially prescribed perfectionism* refers to the tendency for an individual to believe that others expect perfection from him or her. To assess for these dimensions of perfectionism, Hewitt and Flett (1991b) developed the Multidimensional Perfectionism Scale (MPS), a 45-item measure of perfectionism consisting of three theoretically distinct scales. The Self-Oriented Perfectionism (MPS–Self) scale measures high achievement expectations and striving for perfection (e.g., "One of my goals is to be perfect in everything I do"). The Other-Oriented Perfectionism (MPS–Other) scale measures expectations of perfection from others (e.g., "If I ask someone to do something, I expect it to be done flawlessly"). Last, the Socially Prescribed Perfectionism (MPS–Social) scale measures concern over meeting the expectations of others (e.g., "The people around me expect me to succeed at everything I do"). Respondents are asked to rate their agreement to statements based on a 7-point Likert-type scale that ranges from 1 (*disagree*) to 7 (*agree*). Higher scores on each of the scales reflect greater levels of perfectionism. It is worth noting that given some of the obvious conceptual similarities underlying the FMPS and the MPS, scores on the these two scales have been found to correlate with one another (Frost et al., 1993).

Perfectionism and Maladjustment

To date, a considerable number of studies have shown that perfectionism represents a concomitant of psychological maladjustment at best and a liability associated with the development of maladjustment at worst. For example, studies using the FMPS have shown that both higher global or aggregate scores and higher subscale scores on the FMPS are associated with greater psychological symptoms (Frost et al., 1990), greater obsessive–compulsive behaviors (Frost & Steketee, 1997; Norman, Davies, Nicholson, Cortese, & Malla, 1998), greater worry across different life domains (Chang, 2000), greater social anxiety (Juster et al., 1996; Saboonchi, Lundh, & Öst, 1999), less life satisfaction (Chang, 2000), less self-esteem (Rice, Ashby, & Slaney, 1998), greater perceived stress (Chang, 2000), and greater negative affectivity and less positive affectivity (Chang, 2000; Frost et al., 1993). Likewise, studies using the MPS have also shown that higher scores on some of the three dimensions of perfectionism tapped by this instrument are associated with less self-esteem (Flett, Hewitt, Blankstein, & O'Brien, 1991), greater fears and phobias (Blankstein, Flett, Hewitt, & Eng, 1993), greater procrastination (Saddler & Sacks, 1993), greater irrational thinking (Flett, Hewitt, Blankstein, & Koledin, 1991), greater neuroticism (Hewitt, Flett, & Blankstein, 1991), less sexual satisfaction between spouses (Habke, Hewitt, & Flett, 1999), less attitudinal flexibility (Ferrari & Mautz, 1997), greater perceived stress (Chang & Rand, 2000), and less positive affectivity and greater negative affectivity (Frost et al., 1993).

Among the many correlates found using the FMPS and the MPS (as well as those found using other perfectionism measures) linking perfectionism to psychological maladjustment, two findings have appeared with relative consistency in the literature over the last 10 years. First, several studies indicate that perfectionism, or some aspects of perfectionism, is a significant concomitant and possible causal determinant of depressive symptoms. For example, although elevations on each of the three perfectionism dimensions tapped by the MPS are generally thought to be associated with greater maladjustment, self-oriented and socially prescribed perfectionism are believed to be specifically involved in the manifestation of depressive symptoms (Hewitt, Flett, & Ediger, 1996). Unlike other-oriented perfectionism, these two dimensions place the explicit focus of perfectionistic expectations on the individual. As Hewitt and Flett (1991a) argued, feelings of worthlessness and harsh self-criticism often associated with not measuring up to one's ideal expectations are likely to lead to negative emotional states or conditions such as depression or dysphoria. Similar emotional consequences are expected to occur when an individual fails to measure up to the high expectations of others. Indeed, findings from recent studies have tended to support the view that elevations on self-oriented and socially prescribed perfectionism are associated with greater depressive symptoms in both clinical and nonclinical populations (e.g., Chang & Sanna, 2001; Enns & Cox, 1999; Hewitt & Flett, 1991a, 1993; Hewitt et al., 1996; Joiner & Schmidt, 1995; Lynd-Stevenson & Hearne, 1999). In contrast, other findings have shown that other-oriented perfectionism may sometimes be related to fewer depressive symptoms (e.g., Flett, Hewitt, Blankstein, & Mosher, 1995). Nonetheless, it is worth noting that studies using the FMPS have also shown a significant link between perfectionism and depressive experiences (Enns & Cox, 1999; Frost et al., 1993). Moreover, findings based on other measures of perfectionism have further shown that perfectionism may even impede therapeutic progress in the treatment of clinical depression (Blatt, Zuroff, Bondi, Sanislow, & Pilkonis, 1998). Overall, it appears from these findings that perfectionism represents an important concomitant of dysphoria and depression.

Second, several studies also have indicated a significant link between perfectionism and various indexes of suicidal risk. Specifically, recent studies have shown that greater perfectionism is associated with greater suicidal ideation (Chang, 1998; Dean, Range, & Goggin, 1996; Hewitt, Flett, & Weber, 1994), greater suicide intent (Hewitt, Flett, & Turnbull-Donovan, 1992), greater preoccupation with suicide (Adkins & Parker, 1996), and greater hopelessness (Chang, 1998; Dean et al., 1996; Hewitt et al., 1994). This last finding is important to note insofar as hopelessness has been found to be predictive of eventual suicide (Beck, Steer, Kovacs, & Garrison, 1985).

All in all, given these research findings linking perfectionism with psychological maladjustment, it should be of little surprise that there has been a growing trend to look at perfectionism as a destructive and dysfunctional condition (Blatt, 1995) and as a condition that appears to necessitate clinical attention and treatment (e.g., Barnett & McNamara, ca. 1980; Ferguson & Rodway, 1994; Halgin & Leahy, 1989; Hirsh & Hayward, 1998). However, it is not clear if perfectionism is always detrimental and hazardous to one's psychological adjustment, as some of these findings seem to indicate. In the next section I provide a summary of a recent study in which I tried to determine whether some perfectionists may be better able than other perfectionists to manage their perilous pursuits, especially as they relate to the two critical variables noted earlier, namely, depressive experiences and suicidal ideation.

A CLOSER LOOK AT PERFECTIONISM: A STRATEGY THAT IS SOMETIMES HARMFUL AND SOMETIMES BENIGN

As I noted (Chang, 2002), although numerous studies have found a significant link between perfectionism and maladjustment, it is important to realize that the magnitude of such associations have been far from robust. For example, associations between different measures of perfectionism and depressive symptoms in normal adult populations have averaged around .15, with average associations around .26 between perfectionism scales found to be significantly associated with depressive symptoms (see Table 2 of Frost et al., 1993). In clinically depressed adult populations, the associations between different measures of perfectionism and depressive symptoms have been slightly higher, averaging about .31 (see Table 3 of Enns & Cox, 1999).

Thus, if perfectionism is taken as a strategy, reflective of what people intentionally do, then it may be that perfectionism may not always be harmful for some people in the context of other personal factors.

Specifically, according to findings from one recent study, one possible explanation for these weaker-than-anticipated associations between perfectionism and psychological maladjustment may involve the role of certain types of moderators that may buffer the negative influence of perfectionism on adjustment (Chang, 2002). Just as some moderators, such as negative life stress and procrastination, have been hypothesized and sometimes found to exacerbate the link between perfectionism and poor psychological adjustment (e.g., Adkins & Parker, 1996; Chang & Rand, 2000; Hewitt & Flett, 1993; Hewitt et al., 1996), other moderators may actually help mitigate the negative influences of perfectionism on adjustment. Thus, some individuals may use perfectionism as a personality strategy because it is not harmful or maladaptive for them. For reasons I describe shortly, social problem solving was identified as one variable that may lessen the presumed emotional spillovers of the relentless pursuit of perfection.

What Makes One Perfectionist Different From Another? Considering Differences in Social Problem Solving

In recent years, studies on social problem solving have shown that it is a significant predictor of psychological maladjustment (e.g., D'Zurilla & Sheedy, 1991; Elliott, Godshall, Shrout, & Witty, 1990; Heppner, Kampa, & Brunning, 1987; Nezu & Ronan, 1988). Indeed, similar to what was noted earlier in this chapter about studies on perfectionism, problem-solving deficits also have been linked to experiences of greater depressive symptoms (e.g., Haaga, Fine, Terrill, Stewart, & Beck, 1995; Marx, Williams, & Claridge, 1992; Priester & Clum, 1993) and greater suicide risk (e.g., Bonner & Rich, 1988; Chang, 1998; Dixon, Heppner, & Anderson, 1991; Priester & Clum, 1993).

According to D'Zurilla and his associates (D'Zurilla, 1986; D'Zurilla & Goldfried, 1971; D'Zurilla & Nezu; 1990; D'Zurilla, Nezu, & Maydeu-Olivares, 2002), *social problem solving* refers to problem solving as it occurs in the real world and is defined as the self-generated cognitive–affective–behavioral process by which a person attempts to discover effective ways of coping with problematic situations encountered in everyday living. Social problem solving is conceptualized as both a global construct as well as a construct composed of multiple components (e.g., D'Zurilla & Maydeu-Olivares, 1995; Heppner, 1988). For example, social problem solving as measured by the Social Problem Solving Inventory—Revised (D'Zurilla et al., 2002; Maydeu-Olivares & D'Zurilla, 1996) provides both a global social problem-solving score and separate subscales scores reflecting the five different problem-solving components (viz., Positive Problem Orientation, Negative

Problem Orientation, Rational Problem Solving, Impulsivity/Carelessness Style, and Avoidance Style) believed to underlie the general construct.

Recently, I (Chang, 2002) hypothesized that social problem solving would interact with perfectionism in predicting psychological maladjustment. Consider previous studies, for example, that have examined the potential moderating role of social problem solving in the link between life stress and depressive symptoms. Studies conducted by Nezu and his associates (Nezu, 1987; Nezu, Nezu, Saraydarian, Kalmar, & Ronan, 1986; Nezu & Ronan, 1985, 1988) have found that the positive association between life stress and depressive symptoms is often weaker for individuals with high problem-solving abilities compared with those with low problem-solving abilities. In that vein, social problem solving should also act as a buffer against the negative influence of perfectionism on adjustment; that is, for people who are highly perfectionistic, those who possess strong social problem-solving abilities (e.g., viewing problems as challenges, not avoiding problems) should experience less psychological maladjustment than those who possess poor or low problem-solving abilities (e.g., viewing problems as unsolvable or as a threat, avoiding problems). Put another way, possessing high social problem-solving abilities should help some perfectionists better manage the expected psychological spillovers of being driven by high standards and high self-criticism compared with perfectionists who lack such adaptive coping resources (Lazarus & Folkman, 1984). Therefore, using perfectionism as a personality strategy may not always be associated with maladaptive outcomes, as the extant literature would suggest.

To test this possibility, I conducted a study of 371 college students to see whether perfectionism and social problem solving interacted in predicting psychological maladjustment (Chang, 2002). To assess for perfectionism, participants were administered the FMPS. Social problem solving was assessed by the 25-item short form of the Social Problem-Solving Inventory—Revised (D'Zurilla et al., 2002), with higher scores on the global index indicating better social problem-solving skills and abilities and lower scores indicating problem-solving deficiencies. Finally, psychological maladjustment was assessed by the Beck Depression Inventory (Beck, Ward, Mendelson, Mock, & Erbaugh, 1961) and the Adult Suicide Ideation Questionnaire (Reynolds, 1991).

With respect to the key question I posed (Chang, 2002), the results from a set of regression analyses indicated that the Perfectionism × Social Problem Solving interaction was significant for predicting additional variance in both depressive symptoms ($R = 1\%$) and suicidal ideation ($R = 9\%$), even after partialing out the variances accounted for by both perfectionism and social problem solving. For predicting depressive symptoms, the full regression model was found to account for 33% of the variance in Beck Depression Inventory scores, $F(3, 367) = 59.78, p < .001$. For predicting suicidal ideation, the full regression model was found to account for 34% of the variance in Adult Suicide Ideation Questionnaire scores, $F(3, 367) = 63.33$, $p < .001$.

To examine the Perfectionism × Social Problem Solving interaction for depressive symptoms, the regression of depressive symptoms on perfectionism at low and high levels of social problem solving was plotted (see Figure 8.1). As shown in Figure 8.1, a significant positive relation was found between perfectionism and depressive symptoms at low levels of social problem solving ($b = .20$), $t(367) = 2.66$, $p < .01$ (two-tailed). Similarly, for individuals with high problem-solving abilities, perfectionism was also found to have a positive, albeit weaker influence on depressive symptoms ($b = .12$), $t(367) = 2.10$, $p < .05$. Likewise, the regression of suicidal ideation on perfectionism at low and high levels of social problem solving to examine the Perfectionism × Social Problem Solving interaction was plotted (see Figure 8.2). As shown in Figure 8.2, a significant positive relation was found between perfectionism and suicidal ideation at low levels of social problem-

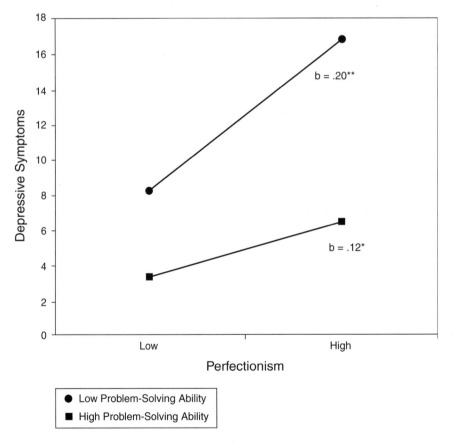

Figure 8.1. Relationship of perfectionism with depressive symptoms at high and low levels of social problem solving ($N = 371$). *$p < .05$. **$p < .01$.

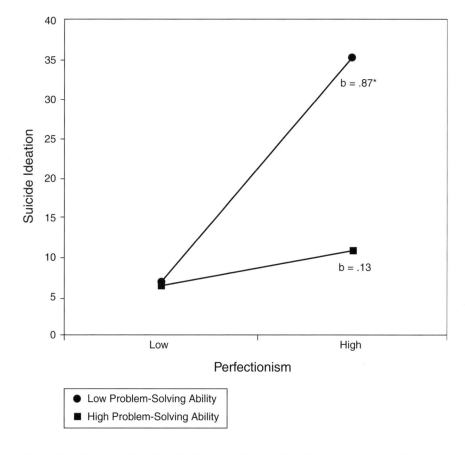

Figure 8.2. Relationship of perfectionism with suicide ideation at high and low levels of social problem solving ($N = 371$). *$p < .01$.

solving abilities ($b = .87$), $t(367) = 10.12$, $p < .01$. At high levels of social problem solving, the relation between perfectionism and suicidal ideation was not significant ($b = .13$), $t(367) = 1.82$, *ns*. Hence, for individuals with low social problem-solving abilities, but not for those with high social problem-solving abilities, perfectionism was found to be a significant determinant of suicidal ideation. It is not surprising that the slope for individuals with low social problem-solving abilities was found to be significantly steeper compared with the slope for those with higher problem-solving abilities, $t(367) = -6.94$, $p < .01$.

Thus, these recent findings provide some illumination on the notion of perfectionism as a vice. The consistent finding that social problem solving buffered the negative influence of perfectionism on maladjustment (as was especially the case for suicidal ideation) raises an important issue for understanding perfectionism in adults. Specifically, my findings (Chang, 2002) suggest that not all perfectionists will necessarily get caught up in a vicious cycle involving unrealistic standards and high self-criticism resulting in poor psychological adjustment; that is, some perfectionistic adults will undoubtedly have greater resources for coping with their perfectionism than others. In turn, and consistent with the reviewed findings, differences in coping resources and effectiveness are likely to influence adjustment (Lazarus & Folkman, 1984). Accordingly, not all perfectionists will act in the same manner or incur the same consequences. Therefore, as a general caution to researchers and practitioners who may have developed a proclivity to view perfectionism as always unhealthy or maladaptive, it may be useful to appreciate the conditions around which perfectionism may have "good" effects (or at least benign effects) on psychological adjustment.

PERFECTIONISM AS BOTH GOOD AND BAD: GOING BEYOND THE DIALECTIC OF VIRTUE AND VICE

In the previous section, I reviewed the results of a recently conducted study that suggest the value of a more contextualized view of perfectionism, that is, one in which perfectionists may vary across other important psychological processes. In this final section, I briefly look at some recent efforts that attempt to represent perfectionism as neither a vice nor a virtue, but as both virtue and vice.

Adaptive Versus Maladaptive Perfectionism

Decades before researchers conducted numerous empirical studies linking perfectionism to maladjustment, Hamachek (1978) made an important distinction between neurotic and normal perfectionism:

> Persons who might fit under the label "normal perfectionists" (whom we could just as easily refer to as skilled artists or careful workers or masters of their craft) are those who derive a very real sense of pleasure from the labors of a painstaking effort and *who feel free to be less precise as the situation permits.* (p. 27)

> This is not, however, apt to be true for neurotic perfectionists. Here we have the sort of people whose efforts—even their best ones—never seem quite good enough, at least in their own eyes. It always seems to these persons that they could—and should—do better. Of course, what this does is to rob them of the satisfaction which might ordinarily accompany a superior achievement or at least a well-done job. And this is also why neurotic perfectionists are neurotic. They are unable to feel satisfaction because in their own eyes they *never seem to do things good enough to warrant that feeling.* (p. 27)

Hamachek's (1978) distinction is useful for many reasons, but maybe it is especially important because the distinction helps one reconcile a key conundrum faced by researchers and scholars alike: How can perfectionism always be bad when it is also obvious that perfectionism within society is often sought and desired? After all, it seems quite obvious that in a meritorious society one prizes the painstaking efforts of the perfectionist who is able to do things at a level of unparalleled excellence. It also seems clear from the writings of modern psychologists such as Rogers (1961) and Maslow (1962) that, following in the traditions of Plato and Aristotle, the process of striving for excellence is something that should be valued and be seen as a virtue. Indeed, in recent years, educators have tended to write about the desirability of nurturing, rather than eliminating, perfectionistic tendencies in students (e.g., Kottman & Ashby, 2000; Schuler, 2000; Silverman, 1999). The answer to the conundrum may be that we have failed to realize that not all perfectionists look or act alike and, perhaps more important, that we have failed to also consider the coexistence of two kinds of perfectionism strategies, one adaptive (desirable) and the other maladaptive (undesirable). With regard to the latter, several recent studies appear to increasingly support a conceptual distinction between adaptive and maladaptive perfectionism.

What Does the FMPS Really Measure?

In a recent study based on a large national sample of academically talented sixth graders (students who scored at least at the 97th percentile on the Secondary School Admission Test; Educational Testing Service, 1991), Parker (1997) was able to distinguish adaptive perfectionists from maladaptive perfectionists on the basis of a cluster analysis of scores on the FMPS. In general, maladaptive perfectionists had higher global FMPS scores and higher Concerns Over Mistakes scores, but lower Organization scores, compared with adaptive perfectionists. Again, in a more recent study, Stumpf and Parker (2000) looked at perfectionism as measured by the FMPS in a large national sample of academically talented sixth graders. This time, however, the investigators used factor-analytic procedures to identify a higher order factor structure in which the FMPS appeared to tap an adaptive perfectionism factor as measured by Personal Standards and Organization, and to tap a maladaptive perfectionism factor as measured by Concern Over Mistakes, Parental Expectations, Parental Criticism, and Doubts about Actions. Accordingly, Stumpf and Parker concluded that adaptive and maladaptive perfectionism represented not opposite poles on a single continuum but rather two largely independent constructs. Thus, obtaining high scores on adaptive perfectionism was different from obtaining low scores on maladaptive perfectionism.

It is worth noting that using very similar procedures but on a less selective population than Parker and his colleague, Rice and his colleagues have obtained very similar results using the FMPS in samples of general college students. In one study, Rice et al. (1998) showed that scales on the FMPS reflected adaptive or maladaptive dimensions. On the basis of a factor analysis of responses on the FMPS provided by college students, Rice et al. identified the Personal Standards and Organization subscales of the FMPS to map onto adaptive perfectionism, whereas the remaining FMPS subscales (viz., Concerns Over Mistakes, Parental Expectations, Parental Criticism, and Doubts about Actions) were identified to map onto maladaptive perfectionism. Hence, these results were identical to those obtained by Stumpf and Parker (2000). In a more recent study, Rice and Dellwo (2002) were able to support the distinction made previously by Rice et al. between adaptive and maladaptive perfectionism using cluster analytic procedures in another sample of college students. Taken together, these findings show that past measures of perfectionism, rather than getting at a single global perfectionism dimension or getting at several maladaptive perfectionism dimensions, in fact tapped adaptive and maladaptive dimensions of perfectionism.

Measuring for Adaptive and Maladaptive Perfectionism

Recognizing the need to get beyond past approaches that have tended to largely emphasize the maladaptive aspects of perfectionism as reflected in measures such as the FMPS and the MPS (Slaney et al., 2001), Slaney and his colleagues (Slaney & Johnson, 1992; Slaney et al., 2001) have developed measures of perfectionism that attempted to more directly mirror both the adaptive and maladaptive processes involved in perfectionism. Slaney and Johnson's (1992) original Almost Perfect Scale (APS) comprised four perfectionism dimensions, namely, Standards and Order (e.g., "I have high standards for my performance at work or at school"), Difficulty in Relationships (e.g., "I wish I had closer relationships with my friends"), Procrastination (e.g., "I tend to procrastinate so long that I never have enough time to do things right"), and Anxiety (e.g., "I have trouble relaxing"). Only the first dimension was considered to reflect adaptive perfectionism; the other three dimensions were considered to reflect maladaptive perfectionism. More recently, Slaney et al. (2001) attempted to improve on the conceptual distinctiveness of the APS to get at the distinction between adaptive and maladaptive perfectionism, resulting the in the Almost Perfect Scale—Revised (APS–R). In contrast to the APS, the APS–R is a briefer instrument composed of three scales, namely, High Standards (e.g., "I have high standards for performance at work or at school"), Order (e.g., "I am an orderly person"), and Discrepancy (e.g., "I often feel frustrated because I can't meet my goals"). The High Standards scale appears to tap an adaptive dimension of perfectionism. For example, scores on this scale have been found to correlate positively with a measure of self-esteem (Slaney et al., 2001). In contrast, the Discrepancy scale appears to tap a maladaptive dimension of perfectionism.

For example, scores on this scale have been found to correlate negatively with a measure of self-esteem (Slaney et al., 2001). Also, although orderliness has often been considered a key attribution of perfectionism, results for the Order scale were less clear, leading Slaney et al. (2001) to note a need for future studies to determine the importance, or lack thereof, of this variable for understanding perfectionism. Notwithstanding this, scores on the High Standards and Discrepancy scales have been found to differ significantly between a group of academically talented middle school students and a control group of middle school students (LoCicero & Ashby, 2000). Specifically, academically talented students, compared with their peers, had significantly higher scores on High Standards and significantly lower scores on Discrepancy. Thus, the APS–R appears to be a useful measure that is, unlike past measures, driven by a model of perfectionism that reflects distinct adaptive and maladaptive processes.

These new (or renewed) considerations of perfectionism as both adaptive and maladaptive are not only important in their own right but can also have very important implications for intervention. As Kottman and Ashby (2000) argued, little intervention or treatment may be needed for people who embody predominantly adaptive aspects of perfectionism, whereas some degree of intervention or treatment may be necessary for those who express predominantly maladaptive aspects of perfectionism. Hence, in contrast to earlier trends pointing to the need to treat perfectionism as if it represented only a liable personality dimension, this conceptualization of perfectionism points to the need to be more careful in identifying and treating only those aspects of perfectionism that may be dysfunctional and maladaptive for the individual. This conceptualization also points indirectly to the value of possibly nurturing those aspects of perfectionism that are functional and adaptive.

The recent works of Slaney and his colleagues are promising, to say the least, and they offer researchers and practitioners a balanced conceptualization of perfectionism that did not exist in any concrete form in the past. It is worth noting that, in addition to their efforts, other researchers, also dissatisfied with the predominant negative view of perfectionism, have attempted to develop more balanced conceptualizations and assessments of perfectionism that tap adaptive and maladaptive processes (e.g., Terry-Short, Owens, Slade, & Dewey, 1995).

CONCLUSION: PERFECTIONISM AS BOTH A VIRTUE AND A VICE

It seems that in many ways researchers have come full circle. Although perfectionism, like any personality process, does not inherently refer to a virtue or a vice, it is clear that our understanding of perfectionism through the ages has tended to portray it as more one or the other. Also, as the review of the literature in this chapter has shown, there has clearly been a trend to base perfectionism on a predominantly negative foundation over the last 10 years or so. Only recently have researchers come to recognize what may be obvious to many laypeople: namely, that perfectionism can engender both adaptive and maladaptive processes. However, it may also be worth considering how for some groups the potential effects of using maladaptive perfectionism may not only be benign but also in some cases quite adaptive. For example, in a study I conducted using the FMPS (Chang, 1998), Asian American college students, compared with European American college students, had significantly higher scores on maladaptive perfectionism and significantly lower scores on adaptive perfectionism. Yet, in considering the notion that Asian Americans tend to be high academic achievers, my (Chang, 1998) findings suggest that even the heightened presence of presumed maladaptive aspects of perfectionism in some groups compared with others may not necessarily be associated with poor performance or outcomes. Although this possibility remains nothing more than mere speculation at this point, it is an interesting possibility worthy of future examination. At the very least, my (Chang, 1998) findings do make one point clear, namely, how little is known about perfectionism across different ethnic or cultural groups. In some cultural groups, some aspects of perfectionism that may be presumed to be maladaptive may actually be valued and associated with positive outcomes. For example, among Asian Americans, being overly concerned about not being able to meet the high expectations of others may help Asian Americans strive for and reach levels of excellence they may otherwise not have sought to obtain for themselves (Chang, 1998). Consequentially, some maladaptive aspects of perfectionism may become highly valued and reinforced over time for Asian Americans. Thus, among some groups, even the heightened expression of maladaptive aspects of perfectionism may not or should not necessitate intervention or treatment. Moreover, insofar that there is often considerable variation among individuals even within a given ethnic or cultural group, the same can be said for identifying and treating maladaptive aspects of perfectionism across individuals. Unfortunately, it remains difficult to clearly distinguish between items that engender positive outcomes versus negative outcomes in current measures of perfectionism, including in the APS–R. Most recently, findings from a series of studies indicate some promise in a novel conception of *performance perfectionism*, based on high standards of performance and outcome expectancies, for considering different aspects of perfectionism as virtue and as vice (Chang, 2003).

In sum, rather than see the world as a place where we need to perfectly rid ourselves of people who strive for the impossible, it may be worth considering what the world would look like if we did not have perfectionists who attempted to, and who sometimes did, reach standards and marks that most people may have considered illusory, unobtainable, or impractical. Some who use perfectionism to help them reach previously unimaginable goals will clearly likely meet up with failure and disappointment, but should we not applaud their efforts nonetheless? Indeed, what a dull place the world would be without perfectionists who strove for and who were driven to excellence.

REFERENCES

Adkins, K. K., & Parker, W. (1996). Perfectionism and suicidal preoccupation. *Journal of Personality, 64,* 529–543.

Aitken, R. (1994). *The practice of perfection: The Pāramitās from a Zen Buddhist perspective.* New York: Pantheon Books.

Aristotle. (1908). Nichomachean ethics (W. D. Ross, Trans.). Oxford: Clarendon Press. (Original work published 350 BC)

Barnett, D., & McNamara, K. (ca. 1980). *Perfectionism: The double-edged sword.* Clearinghouse for Structured/Thematic Groups and Innovative Programs, University of Texas at Austin.[Au: Is this an unpublished manuscript?]

Beck, A. T., Steer, R. A., Kovacs, M., & Garrison, B. (1985). Hopelessness and eventual suicide: A 10-year prospective study of patients hospitalized with suicidal ideation. *American Journal of Psychiatry, 142,* 559–563.

Beck, A. T., Ward, C. H., Mendelson, M., Mock, L., & Erbaugh, J. (1961). An inventory for measuring depression. *Archives of General Psychiatry, 4,* 561–571.

Blankstein, K. R., Flett, G. L., Hewitt, P. L., & Eng, A. (1993). Dimensions of perfectionism and irrational fears: An examination with the Fear Survey Schedule. *Personality and Individual Differences, 15,* 323–328.

Blatt, S. J. (1995). The destructiveness of perfectionism: Implications for the treatment of depression. *American Psychologist, 50,* 1003–1020.

Blatt, S. J., Zuroff, D. C., Bondi, C. M., Sanislow, C. A. III, & Pilkonis, P. A. (1998). When and how perfectionism impedes the brief treatment of depression: Further analyses of the National Institute of Mental Health Treatment of Depression Collaborative Research Program. *Journal of Consulting and Clinical Psychology, 66,* 423–428.

Bonner, R. L., & Rich, A. (1988). Negative life stress, social problem-solving self-appraisal, and hopelessness: Implications for suicide research. *Cognitive Therapy and Research, 12,* 549–556.

Chang, E. C. (1998). Cultural differences, perfectionism, and suicidal risk: Does social problem solving still matter? *Cognitive Therapy and Research, 22,* 237–254.

Chang, E. C. (2000). Perfectionism as a predictor of positive and negative psychological outcomes: Examining a mediation model in younger and older adults. *Journal of Counseling Psychology, 47,* 18–26.

Chang, E. C. (2002). Examining the link between perfectionism and psychological maladjustment: Social problem solving as a buffer. *Cognitive Therapy and Research, 26,* 581–595.

Chang, E. C. (2003). *Performance perfectionism theory: An application of outcome expectancy theory to high standards of performance*. Manuscript in preparation.

Chang, E. C., & Rand, K. L. (2000). Perfectionism as a predictor of subsequent adjustment: Evidence for a specific diathesis–stress mechanism among college students. *Journal of Counseling Psychology, 47*, 129–137.

Chang, E. C., & Sanna, L. J. (2001). Negative attributional style as a moderator of the link between perfectionism and depressive symptoms: Preliminary evidence for an integrative model. *Journal of Counseling Psychology, 48*, 490–495.

Dean, P. J., Range, L. M., & Goggin, W. C. (1996). The escape theory of suicide in college students: Testing a model that includes perfectionism. *Suicide and Life-Threatening Behavior, 26*, 181–186.

Dixon, W. A., Heppner, P. P., & Anderson, W. P. (1991). Problem-solving appraisal, stress, hopelessness, and suicide ideation in a college population. *Journal of Counseling Psychology, 38*, 51–56.

D'Zurilla, T. J. (1986). *Problem-solving therapy: A social competence approach to clinical intervention*. New York: Springer.

D'Zurilla, T. J., & Goldfried, M. R. (1971). Problem solving and behavior modification. *Journal of Abnormal Psychology, 78*, 107–126.

D'Zurilla, T. J., & Maydeu-Olivares, A. (1995). Conceptual and methodological issues in social problem-solving assessment. *Behavior Therapy, 26*, 409–432.

D'Zurilla, T. J., & Nezu, A. M. (1990). Development and preliminary evaluation of the Social Problem-Solving Inventory (SPSI). *Psychological Assessment, 2*, 156–163.

D'Zurilla, T. J., Nezu, A. M., & Maydeu-Olivares, A. (2002). *Manual for the Social Problem-Solving Inventory—Revised (SPSI–R): Technical manual*. North Tonawanda, NY: Multi-Health Systems.

D'Zurilla, T. J., & Sheedy, C. F. (1991). The relation between social problem-solving ability and subsequent level of psychological stress in college students. *Journal of Personality and Social Psychology, 61*, 841–846.

Educational Testing Service. (1991). *Secondary School Admission Test interpretive guide*. Princeton, NJ: Educational Testing Service.

Elliott, T. R., Godshall, F., Shrout, J. R., & Witty, T. E. (1990). Problem-solving appraisal, self-reported study habits, and performance of academically at-risk college students. *Journal of Counseling Psychology, 37*, 203–207.

Enns, M. W., & Cox, B. J. (1999). Perfectionism and depressive symptom severity in major depressive disorder. *Behaviour Research and Therapy, 37*, 783–794.

Ferguson, K. L., & Rodway, M. R. (1994). Cognitive behavioral treatment of perfectionism: Initial evaluation studies. *Research on Social Work Practice, 4*, 283–308.

Ferrari, J. R., & Mautz, W. T. (1997). Predicting perfectionism: Applying tests of rigidity. *Journal of Clinical Psychology, 53*, 1–6.

Flett, G. L., & Hewitt, P. L. (Eds.). (2002). *Perfectionism: Theory, research, and treatment*. Washington, DC: American Psychological Association.

Flett, G. L., Hewitt, P. L., Blankstein, K. R., & Koledin, S. (1991). Dimensions of perfectionism and irrational thinking. *Journal of Rational–Emotive and Cognitive–Behavior Therapy, 9*, 185–201.

Flett, G. L., Hewitt, P. L., Blankstein, K. R., & Mosher, S. W. (1995). Perfectionism, life events, and depressive symptoms: A test of a diathesis-stress model. *Current Psychology, 14*, 112–137.

Flett, G. L., Hewitt, P. L., Blankstein, K. R., & O'Brien, S. (1991). Perfectionism and learned resourcefulness in depression and self-esteem. *Personality and Individual Differences, 12*, 61–68.

Frost, R. O., Heimberg, R. G., Holt, C. S., Mattia, J. I., & Neubauer, A. L. (1993). A comparison of two measures of perfectionism. *Personality and Individual Differences, 14*, 119–126.

Frost, R. O., Marten, P., Lahart, C., & Rosenblate, R. (1990). The dimensions of perfectionism. *Cognitive Therapy and Research, 14*, 449–468.

Frost, R. O., & Steketee, G. (1997). Perfectionism in obsessive–compulsive disorder patients. *Behaviour Research and Therapy, 35*, 291–296.

Haaga, D. A. F., Fine, J. A., Terrill, D. R., Stewart, B. L., & Beck, A. T. (1995). Social problem-solving deficits, dependency, and depressive symptoms. *Cognitive Therapy and Research, 19*, 147–158.

Habke, A. M., Hewitt, P. L., & Flett, G. L. (1999). Perfectionism and sexual satisfaction in intimate relationships. *Journal of Psychopathology and Behavioral Assessment, 21*, 307–322.

Halgin, R. P., & Leahy, P. M. (1989). Understanding and treating perfectionistic college students. *Journal of Counseling and Development, 68*, 222–225.

Hamachek, D. E. (1978). Psychodynamics of normal and neurotic perfectionism. *Psychology, 15*, 27–33.

Heppner, P. P. (1988). *The Problem-Solving Inventory.* Palo Alto, CA: Consulting Psychologist Press.

Heppner, P. P., Kampa, M., & Brunning, L. (1987). The relationship between problem-solving self-appraisal and indices of physical and psychological health. *Cognitive Therapy and Research, 11*, 155–168.

Hewitt, P. L., & Flett, G. L. (1991a). Dimensions of perfectionism in unipolar depression. *Journal of Abnormal Psychology, 100*, 98–101.

Hewitt, P. L., & Flett, G. L. (1991b). Perfectionism in the self and social contexts: Conceptualization, assessment, and association with psychopathology. *Journal of Personality and Social Psychology, 60*, 456–470.

Hewitt, P. L., & Flett, G. L. (1993). Dimensions of perfectionism, daily stress, and depression: A test of the specific vulnerability hypothesis. *Journal of Abnormal Psychology, 102*, 58–65.

Hewitt, P. L., Flett, G. L., & Blankstein, K. R. (1991). Perfectionism and neuroticism in psychiatric patients and college students. *Personality and Individual Differences, 12*, 273–279.

Hewitt, P. L., Flett, G. L., & Ediger, E. (1996). Perfectionism and depression: Longitudinal assessment of a specific vulnerability hypothesis. *Journal of Abnormal Psychology, 105,* 276–280.

Hewitt, P. L., Flett, G. L., & Turnbull-Donovan, W. (1992). Perfectionism and suicide potential. *British Journal of Clinical Psychology, 31,* 181–190.

Hewitt, P. L., Flett, G. L., & Weber, C. (1994). Dimensions of perfectionism and suicide ideation. *Cognitive Therapy and Research, 18,* 439–460.

Hirsh, C. R., & Hayward, P. (1998). The perfect patient: Cognitive–behavioural therapy for perfectionism. *Behavioural and Cognitive Psychotherapy, 26,* 359–364.

Hollender, M. H. (1965). Perfectionism. *Comprehensive Psychiatry, 6,* 94–103.

Joiner, T. E. Jr., & Schmidt, N. B. (1995). Dimensions of perfectionism, life stress, and depressed and anxious symptoms: Prospective support for diathesis–stress but not specific vulnerability among male undergraduates. *Journal of Social and Clinical Psychology, 14,* 165–183.

Juster, H. R., Heimberg, R. G., Frost, R. O., Holt, C. S., Mattia, J. I., & Faccenda, K. (1996). Social phobia and perfectionism. *Personality and Individual Differences, 21,* 403–410.

Kottman, T., & Ashby, J. (2000). Perfectionistic children and adolescents: Implications for school counselors. *Professional School Counseling, 3,* 182–188.

La Rondelle, H. K. (1971). *Perfection and perfectionism: A dogmatic–ethical study of biblical perfection and phenomenal perfectionism.* Berrien Spring, MI: Andrews University Press.

Lazarus, R. S., & Folkman, S. (1984). *Stress, appraisal, and coping.* New York: Springer.

LoCicero, K. A., & Ashby, J. S. (2000). Multidimensional perfectionism in middle school age gifted students: A comparison to peers from the general cohort. *Roeper Review, 22,* 182–185.

Longfellow, H. W. (1890). *The poetical works of Henry Wadsworth Longfellow* (Riverside ed.). New York: Houghton Mifflin.

Lynd-Stevenson, R. M., & Hearne, C. M. (1999). Perfectionism and depressive affect: The pros and cons of being a perfectionist. *Personality and Individual Differences, 26,* 549–562.

Marx, E. M., Williams, J. M. G., & Claridge, G. C. (1992). Depression and social problem solving. *Journal of Abnormal Psychology, 101,* 78–86.

Maslow, A. (1962). *Toward a psychology of being.* New York: Van Nostrand.

Maydeu-Olivares, A., & D'Zurilla, T. J. (1996). A factor-analytic study of the Social Problem-Solving Inventory: An integration of theory and data. *Cognitive Therapy and Research, 20,* 115–133.

Milosh, J. E. (1966). *The scale of perfection and the English mystical tradition.* Madison: University of Wisconsin Press.

Nezu, A. M. (1987). A problem-solving formulation of depression: A literature review and proposal of a pluralistic model. *Clinical Psychology Review, 7,* 121–144.

Nezu, A. M., Nezu, C. M., Saraydarian, L., Kalmar, K., & Ronan, G. F. (1986). Social problem solving as a moderating variable between life stress and depressive symptoms. *Cognitive Therapy and Research, 10,* 489–498.

Nezu, A. M., & Ronan, G. F. (1985). Life stress, current problems, problem solving, and depressive symptoms: An integrative model. *Journal of Consulting and Clinical Psychology, 53,* 696–697.

Nezu, A. M., & Ronan, G. F. (1988). Social problem solving as a moderator of stress-related depressive symptoms: A prospective analysis. *Journal of Counseling Psychology, 35,* 134–138.

Norman, R. M. G., Davies, F., Nicholson, I. R., Cortese, L., & Malla, A. K. (1998). The relationship of two aspects of perfectionism with symptoms in a psychiatric outpatient population. *Journal of Social and Clinical Psychology, 17,* 50–68.

Pacht, A. R. (1984). Reflections on perfectionism. *American Psychologist, 39,* 386–390.

Parker, W. D. (1997). An empirical typology of perfectionism in academically talented children. *American Educational Research Journal, 34,* 545–562.

Plato. (1908). The *republic of Plato* (B. Jowett, Trans.). Oxford: Clarendon Press. (Original work published 390 BC)

Priester, M. J., & Clum, G. A. (1993). Perceived problem-solving ability as a predictor of depression, hopelessness, and suicide ideation in a college population. *Journal of Counseling Psychology, 40,* 79–85.

Ratnayaka, S. (1978). *Two ways of perfection: Buddhist and Christian.* Sri Lanka, India: Lake House.

Reynolds, W. M. (1991). *Adult Suicidal Ideation Questionnaire: Professional manual.* Odessa, FL: Psychological Assessment Resources.

Rice, K. G., Ashby, J. S., & Slaney, R. B. (1998). Self-esteem as a mediator between perfectionism and depression: A structural equations analysis. *Journal of Counseling Psychology, 45,* 304–314.

Rice, K. G., & Dellwo, J. P. (2002). Perfectionism and self-development: Implications for college adjustment. *Journal of Counseling and Development, 80,* 188–196.

Rogers, C. (1961). *On becoming a person.* Boston: Houghton Mifflin.

Saboonchi, F., Lundh, L.-G., & Öst, L.-G. (1999). Perfectionism and self-consciousness in social phobia and panic disorder with agoraphobia. *Behaviour Research and Therapy, 37,* 799–808.

Saddler, C. D., & Sacks, L. A. (1993). Multidimensional perfectionism and academic procrastination: Relationships with depression in university students. *Psychological Reports, 73,* 863–871.

Schuler, P. A. (2000). Perfectionism and gifted adolescents. *Journal of Secondary Gifted Education, 11,* 183–196.

Silverman, L. K. (1999). Perfectionism. *Gifted Education International, 13,* 216–225.

Slaney, R. B., & Johnson, D. G. (1992). *The Almost Perfect Scale.* Unpublished manuscript, Pennsylvania State University.

Slaney, R. B., Rice, K. G., Mobley, M., Trippi, J., & Ashby, J. S. (2001). The Revised Almost Perfect Scale. *Measurement and Evaluation in Counseling and Development, 34,* 130–145.

Stumpf, H., & Parker, W. D. (2000). A hierarchical structural analysis of perfectionism and its relation to other personality characteristics. *Personality and Individual Differences, 28,* 837–852.

Terry-Short, L. A., Owens, R. G., Slade, P. D., & Dewey, M. E. (1995). Positive and negative perfectionism. *Personality and Individual Differences, 18,* 663–668.

9

NEUROTICISM: ADAPTIVE AND MALADAPTIVE FEATURES

DAVID WATSON AND ALEX CASILLAS

Neuroticism is a broad dimension of personality representing individual differences in the extent to which a person experiences the world as threatening, problematic, and distressing (Watson, Clark, & Harkness, 1994). It is an old concept that can be traced back to ancient Greece and the Hippocratic notion of the four basic temperaments (i.e., choleric, melancholic, sanguine, phlegmatic). Serious scientific investigation of this dimension originated in the 19th century, when investigators began to conduct systematic research on individual differences in personality and emotionality (Eysenck & Eysenck, 1985). As this research progressed, it became clear that individual differences in negative emotionality represented an essential dimension of personality. Indeed, a neuroticism-like dimension was included in virtually every prominent trait model developed during the 20th century (see Watson, 2001; Watson & Clark, 1984). However, it is noteworthy that the trait was given many different names by personality researchers, including *psychasthenia*, *trait anxiety*, *repression–sensitization*, *ego resiliency*, *emotional control*, and *emotional stability* (Watson, 2001; Watson & Clark, 1984). The term *neuroticism* began to be used early in the 20th century by researchers in Holland and London; however, this research was not disseminated very widely. Thus, it was not until the 1950s that Hans Eysenck popularized the term by including a scale with that name in the Maudsley Personality Inventory (Watson, 2001).

As one can imagine, this diversity of labels led to considerable confusion in the field, as it was unclear whether concepts such as "repression–sensitization," "emotional stability," and "neuroticism" actually were measuring the same construct. However, integrative research in the 1980s (e.g., Mc-Crae & Costa, 1985; Watson & Clark, 1984) clearly established that the same basic dimension was being assessed in all of these models. This integration, in turn, stimulated an explosion of research on the trait during the 1980s and 1990s; during this time, *neuroticism* emerged as the pre-eminent label for the dimension, due in large part to a growing awareness of its prominent correlates. Research on such correlates has increased knowledge about the adaptive and maladaptive features of the dimension.

BASIC FEATURES OF NEUROTICISM

Facets of Neuroticism

Personality traits can be ordered hierarchically, ranging from narrow, lower order characteristics to broad, higher order dimensions. Neuroticism is one of a small number of general traits (thought to range between two and five) that comprise the apex of this hierarchy. Although there is no consensus regarding its lower order subcomponents, Watson et al. (1994) presented a multifaceted model that captures most of its essential features (see their Table 3). As articulated in this model, individuals who score high on measures of neuroticism are prone to frequent and intense episodes of negative emotionality (e.g., anxiety, depression, anger, guilt). Neurotic individuals report that they worry a great deal and, as a result, tend to have difficulty concentrating and sleeping. They are more likely to report minor health problems and to feel discomfort in a wide range of situations. In addition, these individuals express dissatisfaction with themselves and their lives, often portraying the world in a very negative light. In contrast, low scorers on this dimension are self-satisfied and view the world as essentially benign. They report few physical or psychological problems, low levels of negative emotionality, and little stress (Watson, 2001; Watson et al., 1994).

Biological Basis of Neuroticism

The genetic basis of neuroticism has been extensively investigated, and it now is clear that it is strongly heritable (see Clark & Watson, 1999, for a review). Heritability estimates based on twin studies generally fall in the .40 to .60 range (e.g., Finkel & McGue, 1997; Loehlin, 1992). Adoption studies tend to yield somewhat lower heritability estimates, but this may be largely due to their failure to assess nonadditive genetic variance (Plomin, Corley, Caspi, Fulker, & DeFries, 1998). The remaining variance can be attributed entirely to the unshared environment; indeed, the evidence overwhelmingly suggests that the common rearing environment (i.e., the effects of living together in the same household) exerts virtually no effect on the development of neuroticism.

How do these genotypic differences manifest themselves phenotypically? The evidence suggests that neuroticism reflects individual differences in the *behavioral inhibition system* (BIS; Clark & Watson, 1999; Tellegen, 1985). The BIS is a warning system, activated under conditions of uncertainty, that produces a diffuse state of negative affect; this, in turn, motivates the organism to scan the environment for danger. Gray (1987) called the BIS a "stop, look, and listen system" to emphasize how it focuses maximum attention on analyzing environmental stimuli, especially novel stimuli that may signal danger. The BIS also has a strongly anticipatory quality; it promotes a vigilant scanning of the environment for potential threats and motivates the organism to move cautiously until safety is indicated. If safety is signaled, then negative affect decreases and behavioral inhibition is lifted. Individuals high in neuroticism appear to have an overactive BIS so that they are hypervigilant, constantly scanning their environment for signs of trouble (Clark & Watson, 1999; Tellegen, 1985). This overactive BIS also makes these individuals highly sensitive to aversive stimuli; that is, high scorers on the trait are innately disposed to show stronger adverse reactions to noxious and threatening stimuli.

In light of these findings, high neuroticism is often assumed to be inherently maladaptive (i.e., a vice), whereas low neuroticism is thought to be innately adaptive (i.e., a virtue). We show, however, that this simplified view is inaccurate and misleading. Thus, our aim in the following sections is to present a more balanced view of this dimension. To do that, it is useful to conceptualize neuroticism not only as a *trait* (i.e., how one is) but also as a *strategy* (i.e., what one does). We then provide a more balanced perspective of this trait by illustrating the maladaptive and adaptive properties of scores falling at both extremes of the dimension.

NEUROTICISM AS A STRATEGY

Introspection, Rumination, and Sensitization

Byrne (1961) viewed the ends of neuroticism (which he labeled *repression–sensitization*) as reflecting fundamentally different defensive styles. Specifically, Byrne argued that neurotic individuals ("sensitizers") characteristically approach and confront threatening stimuli, whereas those low on the dimension ("repressors") try to avoid or deny threat. In support of this view, research has shown that high scorers on this dimension are more willing to confront internal psychological stimuli; to analyze their own thoughts, feelings, and emotions; and to discuss them with other people. In a related vein, neurotic individuals are more introspective and ruminative; moreover, it is noteworthy that this association has been demonstrated in both self-ratings (e.g., Roberts, Gilboa, & Gotlib, 1998) and in clinicians' ratings (Block, 1965).

These data establish that neuroticism scores reflect fundamentally different strategies in dealing with stress and distress. Furthermore, these differing strategies are at least partly motivated and intentional. For instance, Lefcourt (1966) asked participants to judge the construct assessed by the items comprising Byrne's (1961) Repression–Sensitization Scale: Low scorers interpreted the items as pertaining to mental health and adjustment, whereas high scorers interpreted the scale as assessing emotionality, seriousness, and honesty with oneself. Individuals high in neuroticism clearly place a particularly high value on emotional honesty and self-awareness, and they see themselves as exemplifying these characteristics.

Neuroticism and Coping

Neurotic individuals report that they cope poorly with stress. A number of studies have corroborated this self-assessment by examining the specific cognitive and behavioral strategies adopted by high- versus low-neuroticism individuals. The data are quite consistent and indicate that high levels of neuroticism are broadly related to passive and ineffective forms of coping (e.g., Costa & McCrae, 1989; Watson, David, & Suls, 1999; Watson & Hubbard, 1996); that is, neuroticism is associated with the increased use of wishful thinking, self-blame, escape–avoidance, and emotion-focused coping as well as, to a lesser extent, with the decreased use of problem-focused coping, positive reappraisal and support seeking (Bolger, 1990; Smith, Pope, Rhodewalt, & Poulton, 1989; Watson & Hubbard, 1996).

McCrae and Costa (1986) reported the results of two studies that provide an especially informative view of this trait. Consistent with the findings discussed previously, neuroticism had significant, replicable correlations with several different coping mechanisms across the two studies; specifically, neuroticism was associated with an increased frequency of indecisiveness, hostile reaction, wishful thinking, escapist fantasy, self-blame, withdrawal, passivity, and sedation. Moreover, factor analyses of the coping mechanisms identified two replicable dimensions, one of which—labeled Neurotic Coping—was defined by these same neuroticism-related variables. Finally, McCrae and Costa had their respondents rate the extent to which these various coping mechanisms had been helpful in (a) solving the problem and (b) reducing distress. These ratings then were used to rank order the coping mechanisms from most to least effective. Analyses of these data revealed that neurotic individuals tended to use the least effective coping mechanisms (i.e., hostile reaction, indecisiveness, wishful thinking, self-blame, and passivity).

NEUROTICISM AS A VICE: THE COST OF HIGH NEUROTICISM

Neuroticism and Psychopathology

Neuroticism is widely regarded as the single most important dimension of human personality. Its prominence stems from having important corre-lates across a broad range of human functioning. Most notably, neuroticism has stronger, clearer, and broader associations with psychopathology than does any other personality trait (Clark & Watson, 1999; Mineka, Watson, & Clark, 1998; Widiger, Verheul, & van den Brink, 1999). Significant eleva-tions in neuroticism are associated with a wide array of clinical syndromes, including the anxiety disorders, mood disorders, substance use disorders, so-matoform disorders, eating disorders, personality and conduct disorders, and schizophrenia (see Krueger, Caspi, Moffitt, Silva, & McGee, 1996; Mineka et al., 1998; Trull & Sher, 1994; Watson, 2000). In fact, Widiger and Costa (1994) concluded that "neuroticism is an almost ubiquitously elevated trait within clinical populations" (p. 81). This pervasive association is unsurpris-ing, given that emotional distress is a defining feature of both neuroticism and psychological disorder (American Psychiatric Association, 1994).

Thus, neuroticism shows particularly strong associations with disorders that contain a prominent component of subjective distress, such as major depression, dysthymic disorder, generalized anxiety disorder, and borderline personality disorder (Clark & Watson, 1999; Watson, 2000). Its association with generalized anxiety disorder is so strong that some researchers have sug-gested that this syndrome essentially represents an extreme form of the trait (see Brown, Chorpita, & Barlow, 1998; Watson, 1999). It is interesting that several investigators have reached the same conclusion regarding borderline personality disorder, arguing that it simply may be "an extreme variant of Neuroticism" (Widiger & Trull, 1992, p. 369). These arguments are further supported by twin-study data demonstrating that (a) major depression and generalized anxiety disorder reflect a single, common genetic diathesis and (b) this shared genetic diathesis is strongly linked to neuroticism (Kendler, 1996; Mineka et al., 1998). High levels of neuroticism clearly represent an extremely important risk factor for psychopathology, thereby exacting a high cost from the individuals who suffer from these disorders.

Neuroticism and Dissatisfaction

Neurotic individuals report a pervasive dissatisfaction with themselves and the world around them. This dissatisfaction touches almost every aspect of their lives. For instance, studies consistently have shown that neuroticism is negatively correlated with overall ratings of life satisfaction (e.g., Brief, Butcher, George, & Link, 1993; DeNeve & Cooper, 1998; Judge, Locke, Durham, & Kluger, 1998). Moreover, neurotic individuals report greater marital dissatisfaction and show greater instability in their relationships (Karney & Bradbury, 1995; Watson, 2000; Watson, Hubbard, & Wiese, 2000). It is noteworthy that much of this evidence is longitudinal, establishing that neuroticism scores obtained early in a relationship predict its subsequent course. Kelly and Conley (1987) reported particularly striking evidence in a sample of 278 couples over a time span of more than 40 years. The participants initially were assessed (Time 1) on measures of neuroticism and marital satisfaction between 1936 and 1941; their marital satisfaction subsequently was retested in 1954–1955 (Time 2) and 1980–1981 (Time 3). Respondents who were high in neuroticism at Time 1 were more likely to become divorced over the course of the study. Moreover, Time 1 neuroticism was significantly correlated with marital dissatisfaction among the husbands at Times 1 and 2 and among the wives at Times 1 and 3.

In a related vein, neurotic individuals report greater dissatisfaction with their jobs and work environments (e.g., Connolly & Viswesvaran, 2000; Judge et al., 1998; Watson, 2000). Again, much of the evidence is longitudinal. For instance, Watson and Slack (1993) found that initial neuroticism scores predicted various aspects of job dissatisfaction measured more than 2 years later. Similarly, Staw, Bell, and Clausen (1986) reported that neuroticism assessed in adolescence was a significant predictor of job dissatisfaction nearly 50 years later, even after controlling for objective differences in work conditions.

Thus, we again see striking evidence of the high cost of neuroticism. Individuals with elevated scores on this dimension experience marked distress and pervasive dissatisfaction across diverse aspects of their lives. Moreover, this cost is borne not only by neurotics themselves but also by those close to them; this is well illustrated by the robust link between neuroticism and divorce (Karney & Bradbury, 1995).

NEUROTICISM AS A VIRTUE: THE COST OF LOW NEUROTICISM

The Adaptive Value of Neuroticism

Because of its pervasive associations with stress, distress, and dissatisfaction, neuroticism invariably—and not surprisingly—is seen as an extremely undesirable trait. To be sure, high levels of neuroticism are broadly associated with a wide range of unfavorable outcomes; thus, it seems that the substantial costs associated with these high scores far outweigh any benefits.

Nevertheless, this should not be overgeneralized into the conclusion (which is implicit in much of the research in this area) that neuroticism itself is an inherently undesirable characteristic. Indeed, although it is traditionally viewed in an extremely negative light, neuroticism is not invariably associated with unfavorable outcomes.

In this context, it is important to recall that neuroticism scores are strongly heritable. As with other aspects of our ancient genetic heritage, neuroticism is a characteristic that gradually evolved through the process of natural selection; as a successful product of evolution, it emerged because it facilitated the survival of the individual (Fowles, 1994; Nesse, 1991; Watson, 2000). Indeed, as discussed previously, neuroticism is strongly linked to the BIS. In behavioral terms, the essential purpose of the BIS is to keep organisms out of trouble—that is, it inhibits behavior that might lead to pain, punishment, and other aversive consequences. It does so by (a) promoting vigilant scanning of the environment and (b) motivating the organism to proceed cautiously until safety is indicated.

Viewed in this light, it becomes clear that the negative emotions associated with neuroticism evolved to promote this vigilant apprehensiveness. They seize the attention of the organism and force it to scan the environment carefully; moreover, their strongly aversive nature motivates behavioral responses that have evolved to protect the organism from various types of threat. Feelings of fear and panic motivate organisms to escape from situations of potential threat or danger. Similarly, anticipatory states of apprehension and worry encourage individuals to avoid settings that previously were associated with pain and punishment. Feelings of anger and hostility help organisms to protect themselves and their resources. Finally, feelings of disgust and revulsion protect organisms by keeping them away from noxious and toxic substances (Fowles, 1994; Nesse, 1991; Watson, 2000). Therefore, although emotions such as fear and disgust may be unpleasant to experience, they are absolutely essential for our survival. Any organism that lacked these emotions would have little hope of survival. In parallel fashion, extremely low levels of neuroticism—which reflect a hypoactive BIS and a deficit in vigilant apprehensiveness—can be expected to expose the individual to various types of threat. In the following sections, we discuss several costs that may result from very low scores on this dimension.

Neuroticism and Health

Throughout much of the 20th century, the *psychosomatic hypothesis*— the idea that chronically elevated levels of negative emotion eventually will lead to illness—was a dominant theoretical paradigm in behavioral medicine (see Watson, 2000; Watson & Pennebaker, 1989). Given that neurotic individuals report more frequent and intense episodes of negative emotion, it was widely assumed that neuroticism was a significant vulnerability factor for physical illness. Consistent with this assumption, neuroticism scales show significant, moderate correlations with measures of physical symptoms and health complaints. Moreover, this association is quite broad, with neurotic individuals reporting more frequent headaches, chest pain, dizziness, nausea, coughing, sneezing, congestion, and various other problems (Watson & Pennebaker, 1989).

However, research conducted during the 1970s and 1980s indicated that neuroticism was neither strongly nor consistently related to objective indicators of health status, such as health-related behaviors (e.g., number of physician visits for illness), biological markers (e.g., immune system functioning), and health outcomes (e.g., mortality rates). In other words, neuroticism is a much better predictor of subjective health complaints than it is of objective health status (Watson, 2000; Watson & Pennebaker, 1989).

Likewise, the results of the Terman Life-Cycle Study (Terman & Oden, 1947)—a longitudinal study of roughly 1,200 individuals over a period of 66 years—suggest that neuroticism does not play a substantial role in longevity (Friedman et al., 1993). Indeed, on the basis of their results, Friedman et al. concluded that "simple models that propose that a neurotic constitution is a major factor in adult health are probably inadequate" (p. 181). Somewhat paradoxically, Friedman et al. also found that cheerfulness (i.e., optimism and a sense of humor) was *negatively* associated with longevity. In discussing this surprising finding, Friedman et al. suggested that cheerful and optimistic people may "underestimate the danger of certain risks to their health and thereby fail to take precautions or to follow medical advice" (p. 181). These results therefore support our earlier argument that hypovigilance and a lack of proper caution (i.e., low neuroticism) can be expected to increase the individual's vulnerability to various types of threat.

Similarly, research by Eysenck (1994) suggests that low levels of neuroticism may increase an individual's vulnerability to cancer, particularly among those who tend to suppress their negative emotions. On the basis of a review of the literature, Eysenck (1994) argued for the existence of a "cancer-prone personality" that is characterized by (a) an inability to cope with stress effectively and (b) a tendency to suppress negative emotions, such as anxiety and anger. Eysenck's model has been supported by both longitudinal and cross-sectional studies reporting that cancer patients have significantly lower neuroticism scores than controls (Watson, 2000). Thus, it seems that low levels of neuroticism may have deleterious health consequences, at least for those individuals who tend to repress their negative feelings or ignore possible health threats.

Neuroticism and Antisocial Behavior

Neuroticism also appears to exert protective effects against the manifestation of recurrent antisocial behaviors. In this section, we provide a brief introduction to this area of research along with an exposition of the relevant findings.

Psychophysiological studies (i.e., those using heart rate and skin conductance response [SCR]) indicate that antisocial individuals show less autonomic and cortical arousal and responsivity than controls (e.g., Hare, 1978). Moreover, this lack of psychophysiological arousal has been consistently associated with a range of antisocial behaviors, most notably with psychopathy (e.g., Raine & Venables, 1992). Conversely, increased physiological arousal has been linked to anxiety, both in patient populations (e.g., Zahn, Nurnberger, Berrettini, & Robinson, 1991) and in children (Fowles & Kochanska, 2000).

However, until recently, studies had not specifically examined whether physiological arousal (i.e., anxiety) might actually protect individuals against antisocial activities. To fill this void, Raine, Venables, and Williams (1995) evaluated the hypothesis that antisocial adolescents exhibiting greater physiological arousal would be less likely to become adult criminals than antisocial adolescents showing lower levels of arousal. The rationale behind this hypothesis stemmed from the aforementioned association between arousal and anxiety: If one experiences anxiety over violations of social conventions and laws, one may be less likely to repeat such violations. In a prospective study, "at risk" adolescents who already had committed antisocial acts were measured at age 15 and again at age 29. The data supported the authors' hypothesis: Antisocial adolescents who did not become adult criminals had significantly higher levels of electrodermal and cardiovascular activity than those who subsequently became criminals. In other words, individuals who seemingly are at high risk for adult criminality—based on evidence of antisocial acts in adolescence—may be protected from committing subsequent crimes by experiencing significant levels of anxiety (Raine et al., 1995). These results again illustrate the potential costs of hypovigilance and extremely low levels of neuroticism.

A World Without Neuroticism?

As a thought exercise, consider what life might be like if human behavior were not shaped by negative (or positive) emotions. Recent advances in neuroscience have begun to provide a compelling illustration of what completely "aneurotic" behavior might be like, particularly with regard to decision making. Much of this research is based on Damasio's (1994) influential *somatic marker hypothesis*. This hypothesis provides a

> systems-level neuroanatomical and cognitive framework for decision making and the influence on it by emotion. The key idea of this hypothesis is that decision making is a process that is influenced by marker signals that arise in bioregulatory processes, including those that express themselves in emotions and feelings. This influence can occur

at multiple levels of operation, some of which occur consciously and some of which occur non-consciously. (Bechara, Damasio, & Damasio, 2000, p. 295)

Damasio and his colleagues have investigated this hypothesis by comparing individuals who have experienced a significant neurological event (e.g., traumatic brain injury, stroke, encephalitis) to control participants (i.e., individuals with intact cerebral function). Of particular interest are individuals who have suffered damage to the ventromedial prefrontal cortex (VM), the area of the frontal lobe that is considered by some to be the neural basis for personality (Tranel, Bechara, & Damasio, 2000). As such, this area is believed to represent a critical structure that facilitates a broad range of higher level social and cognitive activity, including decision making (Bechara et al., 2000).

Individuals with damage to the VM cortex often develop severe postinjury changes in their personality. These posttraumatic characteristics closely resemble the behaviors seen in antisocial personality and psychopathy (e.g., inability to organize future activity and hold gainful employment, diminished capacity to respond to punishment, display of inappropriate emotional reactions). Hence, the term *acquired sociopathy* has often been used to describe individuals with this type of brain lesion (Damasio, 1994; Tranel et al., 2000). These changes are made even more puzzling by the fact that individuals with this type of lesion tend to retain their premorbid levels of intelligence, language, memory, and perception. Phineas Gage—a railway worker who suffered massive frontal lobe damage following a gunpowder explosion in 1848—represents a well-known example of such an individual (see Damasio, 1994).

To explore such puzzling lesion effects, Damasio and his colleagues (e.g., Bechara et al., 2000; Bechara, Damasio, Damasio & Anderson, 1994; Tranel et al., 2000) have developed novel experimental procedures. One of these procedures is "the gambling task" (Bechara et al., 1994), in which participants are instructed to select cards from four different decks with the goal of maximizing their rewards. Two of these decks are advantageous in the short term (i.e., they are associated with larger immediate rewards) but disadvantageous in the long term (i.e., they produce larger delayed punishments and significant net losses). Conversely, the other two decks are less advantageous in the short term (i.e., they provide smaller immediate payoffs) but more advantageous in the long term (i.e., they yield smaller delayed costs and an overall net gain). Control participants (i.e., those with no neurological impairment) initially approach this task by sampling widely from all decks; however, they soon begin to concentrate primarily on those decks that are more advantageous in the long run. In contrast, individuals with damage to the VM cortex continue to sample from the disadvantageous decks without any regard for the long-range consequences of their behavior (Bechara et al., 2000).

The participants' psychophysiological arousal—as measured by SCR—is recorded while they complete this task. Analyses of these data have revealed that both control participants and VM individuals generate SCRs as an immediate reaction to reward or punishment. As they become familiar with the task, controls also begin to develop SCRs before the selection of any card. These are referred to as *anticipatory SCRs,* and they tend to vary in magnitude depending on whether individuals are about to choose from the advantageous or disadvantageous decks. It is interesting that these SCRs are more pronounced when control participants are about to sample from the disadvantageous decks, suggesting that they are experiencing a significant amount of anticipatory anxiety. However, anticipatory SCRs are completely absent in the VM individuals. On the basis of these results, Damasio and his colleagues (Bechara et al., 2000; Tranel et al., 2000) have concluded that VM individuals have a specific impairment in their ability to generate somatic markers, such as anticipatory SCRs; this, in turn, causes serious behavioral problems, including deficits in their decision-making skills. Indeed, Tranel et al. (2000) argued that

> A surprising conclusion from our work is that too little emotion has profoundly deleterious effects on decision making; in fact, too little emotion may be just as bad for decision making as excessive emotion has long been considered to be. (p. 1047)

Thus, these data again illustrate the adaptive problems associated with extremely low levels of neuroticism; negative emotions such as anticipatory anxiety are absolutely essential for our survival.

TOWARD A BALANCED VIEW: MODERATE NEUROTICISM AND THE GOLDEN SECTION

Taken together, the data we have reviewed suggest that extreme levels of neuroticism, whether high (e.g., generalized anxiety disorder, borderline personality disorder) or low (e.g., the cancer-prone personality) can have deleterious effects. In moderate amounts, however, neuroticism appears to be adaptive. This view that a moderate amount of neuroticism is healthy and adaptive is further supported by studies of the *states-of-mind* (SOM) *model,* which was developed by Schwartz (Schwartz, 1986; Schwartz & Garamoni, 1989).

The SOM model derives from the *golden section hypothesis* (Benjafield & Adams-Webber, 1976). The *golden section* is defined as

> the ratio that obtains between two parts when the smaller part (a) is to the larger part (b) as the larger part (b) is to the whole (a + b). This relation, a ÷ b = b ÷ (a + b), occurs when the both sides of the equation equal . . . .618. (Schwartz & Garamoni, 1989, p. 272)

This concept was initially applied in information-processing theory to posit that the minor element of the golden proportion (i.e., the remaining .382) provides maximally salient information (Berlyne, 1971). Later, personal-construct psychologists used the golden section proportion to investigate the balance between positive and negative interpersonal judgments (Schwartz & Garamoni, 1989).

Schwartz (1986) applied this concept of the golden section to the cognitive patterns of individuals classified as having functional or dysfunctional thoughts. Specifically, Schwartz argued that one could distinguish between these types of individuals by their ratios of positive to negative cognitions and the extent to which these ratios deviate from this golden section. The resulting SOM model hypothesizes that people monitor their thoughts and feelings to maintain a general balance, or set point, of positive and negative elements. In functional individuals, this set point is hypothesized to follow the golden section of a 62/38 ratio of positive to negative elements; significant variations from this set point—whether excessively negative or excessively positive—are associated with various types of psychopathology (Schwartz & Garamoni, 1989).

Several predictions of the SOM model have been supported (e.g., Michelson, Schwartz, & Marchione, 1991; William & Russell, 1997). For example, anxious and depressed individuals have been found to deviate from the aforementioned set point and engage in significantly more negative thinking than nonsymptomatic individuals (e.g., Garamoni, Reynolds, Thase, & Frank, 1991; McKellar, Malcarne, & Ingram, 1996). Conversely, excessively positive thinking (which Schwartz & Garamoni, 1989, label *the positive monologue*) is associated with bipolar disorder and disinhibited behavior (see Schwartz & Garamoni, 1989). In discussing the features of this positive monologue, Schwartz and Garamoni (1989) repeatedly emphasized that "Although immediately reinforcing, this SOM is not optimal in the long run" (p. 278). Thus, the SOM model emphasizes that emotional balance—a state of consciousness that is primarily positive but also includes a substantial component of negativity—is critically important for mental health. It is noteworthy that the optimal proportion includes such a sizable negative component (i.e., 38%). As discussed earlier, this makes considerable sense from an evolutionary perspective. Once again, we see that negative emotions are "part of a vital mechanism shaped by natural selection to help people survive in their environment" (Nesse, 1991, p. 37).

SUMMARY AND CONCLUSIONS

Neuroticism has emerged from its long past to become one of the most important and widely studied dimensions of human personality. As we have seen, neuroticism has strong and important associations with stress, distress, and dissatisfaction. Indeed, the accumulating data clearly indicate that high levels of neuroticism lead to prolonged and widespread misery, both in neurotic individuals themselves and in those close to them. These striking correlates have encouraged the erroneous view that neuroticism is inherently maladaptive. To correct this view, we have emphasized that neuroticism is an important component of a system (the BIS) that evolved to protect organisms from threat and danger. Because of the protective functions of this system, extremely low levels of neuroticism can be expected to increase the individual's vulnerability to various types of threat. Consistent with this argument, it appears that neuroticism actually may play an active and beneficial role in health-related awareness. In addition, neuroticism provides some protection against certain types of problem behaviors (e.g., recurrent antisocial behaviors and criminality). Finally, neuroticism plays a role in modifying our everyday behavior, as well as in providing us with cues that assist the decision-making process. Although extremely high neuroticism clearly exerts a heavy cost in certain individuals, the trait itself is essential: The price of survival is eternal vigilance.

REFERENCES

American Psychiatric Association. (1994). *Diagnostic and statistical manual of mental disorders* (4th ed.). Washington, DC: Author.

Bechara, A., Damasio, H., & Damasio, A. R. (2000). Emotion, decision making and the orbitofrontal cortex. *Cerebral Cortex, 10,* 295–307.

Bechara, A., Damasio, A. R., Damasio, H., & Anderson, S. W. (1994). Insensitivity to future consequences following damage to human prefrontal cortex. *Cognition, 50,* 7–15.

Benjafield, J., & Adams-Webber, J. R. (1976). The golden section hypothesis. *British Journal of Psychology, 67,* 11–15.

Berlyne, D. E. (1971). *Aesthetics and psychobiology.* New York: Appleton-Century-Crofts.

Block, J. (1965). *The challenge of response sets: Unconfounding meaning, acquiescence, and social desirability in the MMPI.* New York: Appleton-Century-Crofts.

Bolger, N. (1990). Coping as a personality process: A prospective study. *Journal of Personality and Social Psychology, 59,* 525–537.

Brief, A. P., Butcher, A. H., George, J. M., & Link, K. E. (1993). Integrating bottom-up and top-down theories of subjective well-being: The case of health. *Journal of Personality and Social Psychology, 64,* 646–653.

Brown, T. A., Chorpita, B. F., & Barlow, D. H. (1998). Structural relationships among dimensions of the *DSM–IV* anxiety and mood disorders and dimensions of negative affect, positive affect, and autonomic arousal. *Journal of Abnormal Psychology, 107,* 179–192.

Byrne, D. (1961). The Repression–Sensitization Scale: Rationale, reliability, and validity. *Journal of Personality, 29,* 334–349.

Clark, L. A., & Watson, D. (1999). Temperament: A new paradigm for trait psychology. In L. A. Pervin & O. P. John (Eds.), *Handbook of personality* (2nd ed., pp. 399–423). New York: Guilford Press.

Connolly, J. J., & Viswesvaran, C. (2000). The role of affectivity in job satisfaction: A meta-analysis. *Personality and Individual Differences, 29,* 265–281.

Costa, P. T. Jr., & McCrae, R. R. (1989). Personality, stress, and coping: Some lessons from a decade of research. In K. S. Markides & C. L. Cooper (Eds.), *Aging, stress, social support and health* (pp. 267–283). New York: Wiley.

Damasio, A. R. (1994). *Descartes' error: Emotion, reason, and the human brain.* New York: Grosset/Putnam.

DeNeve, K. M., & Cooper, H. (1998). The happy personality: A meta-analysis of 137 personality traits and subjective well-being. *Psychological Bulletin, 124,* 197–229.

Eysenck, H. J. (1994). Cancer, personality and stress: Prediction and prevention. *Advances in Behaviour Research and Therapy, 16,* 167–215.

Eysenck, H. J., & Eysenck, M. W. (1985). *Personality and individual differences: A natural science approach.* New York: Plenum.

Finkel, D., & McGue, M. (1997). Sex differences and nonadditivity in heritability of the Multidimensional Personality Questionnaire scales. *Journal of Personality and Social Psychology, 72,* 929–938.

Fowles, D. C. (1994). A motivational theory of psychopathology. In W. Spaulding (Ed.), *Nebraska Symposium on Motivation: Integrated views of motivation, cognition and emotion* (Vol. 41, pp. 181–238). Lincoln: University of Nebraska Press.

Fowles, D. C., & Kochanska, G. (2000). Temperament as a moderator of pathways to conscience in children: The contribution of electrodermal activity. *Psychophysiology, 37,* 788–795.

Friedman, H. S., Tucker, J. S., Tomlinson-Keasey, C., Schwartz, J. E., Wingard, D. L., & Criqui, M. (1993). Does childhood personality predict longevity? *Journal of Personality and Social Psychology, 65,* 176–185.

Garamoni, G. L., Reynolds, C. F., Thase, M. F., & Frank, E. (1991). The balance of positive and negative affects in major depression: A further test of the states of mind model. *Psychiatry Research, 39,* 99–108.

Gray, J. A. (1987). Perspectives on anxiety and impulsivity: A commentary. *Journal of Research in Personality, 21,* 493–509.

Hare, R. D. (1978). Electrodermal and cardiovascular correlates of psychopathy. In R. D. Hare & D. Schalling (Eds.), *Psychopathic behavior: Approaches to research* (pp. 107–144). New York: Wiley.

Judge, T. A., Locke, E. A., Durham, C. C., & Kluger, A. N. (1998). Dispositional effects on job and life satisfaction: The role of core evaluations. *Journal of Applied Psychology, 83,* 17–34.

Karney, B. R., & Bradbury, T. N. (1995). The longitudinal course of marital quality and stability: A review of theory, method, and research. *Psychological Bulletin, 118*, 3–34.

Kelly, E. L., & Conley, J. J. (1987). Personality and compatibility: A prospective analysis of marital stability and marital satisfaction. *Journal of Personality and Social Psychology, 52*, 27–40.

Kendler, K. S. (1996). Major depression and generalised anxiety disorder: Same genes, (partly) different environments—Revisited. *British Journal of Psychiatry, 168*(Suppl. 30), 68–75.

Krueger, R. F., Caspi, A., Moffitt, T. E., Silva, P. A., & McGee, R. (1996). Personality traits are differentially linked to mental disorders: A multitrait–multidiagnosis study of an adolescent birth cohort. *Journal of Abnormal Psychology, 105*, 299–312.

Lefcourt, H. M. (1966). Repression–sensitization: A measure of the evaluation of emotional expression. *Journal of Consulting Psychology, 30*, 444–449.

Loehlin, J. C. (1992). *Genes and environment in personality development.* Newbury Park, CA: Sage.

McCrae, R. R., & Costa, P. T. Jr. (1985). Comparison of EPI and psychoticism scales with measures of the five-factor model of personality. *Personality and Individual Differences, 6*, 587–597.

McCrae, R. R., & Costa, P. T. Jr. (1986). Personality, coping, and coping effectiveness in an adult sample. *Journal of Personality, 54*, 385–405.

McKellar, J., Malcarne, V. L., & Ingram, R. E. (1996). States-of-mind and negative affectivity. *Cognitive Therapy & Research, 20*, 235–246.

Michelson, L. K., Schwartz, R. M., & Marchione, K. E. (1991). States-of-mind model: Cognitive balance in the treatment of agoraphobia: II. *Advances in Behaviour Research & Therapy, 13*, 193–213.

Mineka, S., Watson, D., & Clark, L. A. (1998). Comorbidity of anxiety and unipolar mood disorders. *Annual Review of Psychology, 49*, 377–412.

Nesse, R. M. (1991, November–December). What good is feeling bad? The evolutionary benefits of psychic pain. *The Sciences*, 30–37.

Plomin, R., Corley, R., Caspi, A., Fulker, D. W., & DeFries, J. (1998). Adoption results for self-reported personality: Evidence for nonadditive genetic effects? *Journal of Personality and Social Psychology, 75*, 211–218.

Raine, A., & Venables, P. H. (1992). Antisocial behaviour: Evolution, genetics, neuropsychology, and psychophysiology. In A. Gale and M. W. Eysenck (Eds.), *Handbook of individual differences: Biological perspectives* (pp. 287–321). Chichester, England: Wiley.

Raine, A., Venables, P. H., & Williams, M. (1995). High autonomic arousal and electrodermal orienting at age 15 years as protective factors against criminal behaviors at age 29 years. *American Journal of Psychiatry, 152*, 1595–1600.

Roberts, J. E., Gilboa, E., & Gotlib, I. H. (1998). Ruminative response style and vulnerability to episodes of dysphoria: Gender, neuroticism, and episode duration. *Cognitive Therapy & Research, 22*, 401–423.

Schwartz, R. M. (1986). The internal dialogue: On the asymmetry between positive and negative coping thoughts. *Cognitive Therapy and Research, 10,* 591–605.

Schwartz, R. M., & Garamoni, G. L. (1989). Cognitive balance and psychopathology: Evaluation of an information processing model of positive and negative states of mind. *Clinical Psychology Review, 9,* 271–294.

Smith, T. W., Pope, M. K., Rhodewalt, F., & Poulton, J. L. (1989). Optimism, neuroticism, coping, and symptom reports: An alternative interpretation of the Life Orientation Test. *Journal of Personality and Social Psychology, 56,* 640–648.

Staw, B. M., Bell, N. E., & Clausen, J. A. (1986). The dispositional approach to job attitudes: A lifetime longitudinal test. *Administrative Science Quarterly, 31,* 56–77.

Tellegen, A. (1985). Structures of mood and personality and their relevance to assessing anxiety, with an emphasis on self-report. In A. H. Tuma & J. D. Maser (Eds.), *Anxiety and the anxiety disorders* (pp. 681–706). Hillsdale, NJ: Erlbaum.

Terman, L. M., & Oden, M. H. (1947). *Genetic studies of genius: IV. The gifted child grows up: Twenty-five years follow-up of a superior group.* Stanford, CA: Stanford University Press.

Tranel, D., Bechara, A., & Damasio, A. R. (2000). Decision making and the somatic marker hypothesis. In M. S. Gazzaniga (Ed.), *The new cognitive neurosciences* (2nd ed., pp. 1047–1061). Cambridge, MA: MIT Press.

Trull, T. J., & Sher, K. J. (1994). Relationship between the five-factor model of personality and Axis I disorders in a nonclinical sample. *Journal of Abnormal Psychology, 103,* 350–360.

Watson, D. (1999). Dimensions underlying the anxiety disorders: A hierarchical perspective. *Current Opinion in Psychiatry, 12,* 181–186.

Watson, D. (2000). *Mood and temperament.* New York: Guilford Press.

Watson, D. (2001). Neuroticism. In N. J. Smelser & P. B. Baltes (Eds.), *International encyclopedia of the social and behavioral sciences* (10609–10612). Oxford, England: Elsevier.

Watson, D., & Clark, L. A. (1984). Negative affectivity: The disposition to experience aversive emotional states. *Psychological Bulletin, 96,* 465–490.

Watson, D., Clark, L. A., & Harkness, A. R. (1994). Structures of personality and their relevance to psychopathology. *Journal of Abnormal Psychology, 103,* 18–31.

Watson, D., David, J. P., & Suls, J. (1999). Personality, affectivity, and coping. In C. R. Snyder (Ed.), *Coping: The psychology of what works* (pp. 119–140). New York: Oxford University Press.

Watson, D., & Hubbard, B. (1996). Adaptational style and dispositional structure: Coping in the context of the five-factor model. *Journal of Personality, 64,* 737–774.

Watson, D., Hubbard, B., & Wiese, D. (2000). General traits of personality and affectivity as predictors of satisfaction in intimate relationships: Evidence from self- and partner-ratings. *Journal of Personality, 68,* 413–449.

Watson, D., & Pennebaker, J. W. (1989). Health complaints, stress, and distress: Exploring the central role of negative affectivity. *Psychological Review, 96,* 234–254.

Watson, D., & Slack, A. K. (1993). General factors of affective temperament and their relation to job satisfaction over time. *Organizational Behavior and Human Decision Processes, 54,* 181–202.

Widiger, T. A., & Costa, P. T. Jr. (1994). Personality and the personality disorders. *Journal of Abnormal Psychology, 103,* 78–91.

Widiger, T. A., & Trull, T. J. (1992). Personality and psychopathology: An application of the five-factor model. *Journal of Personality, 60,* 363–393.

Widiger, T. A., Verheul, R., & van den Brink, W. (1999). Personality and psychopathology. In L. A. Pervin & O. P. John (Eds.), *Handbook of personality* (2nd ed., pp. 347–366). New York: Guilford Press.

William, N., & Russell, M. (1997). Posttraumatic stress disorder and the states-of-mind model: Evidence of specificity. *Cognitive Therapy & Research, 21,* 117–133.

Zahn, T. P., Nurnberger, J. I., Berrettini, W. H., & Robinson, T. N. (1991). Concordance between anxiety and autonomic nervous system activity in subjects at genetic risk for affective disorder. *Psychiatry Research, 36,* 99–110.

III

FURTHER THOUGHTS

10

GOING BEYOND (WHILE REMAINING CONNECTED TO) PERSONALITY AS VIRTUE AND VICE

HOWARD TENNEN AND GLENN AFFLECK

This volume represents a refreshing effort to bring balance to psychology's recent fervor concerning personal qualities that promise to heal or strengthen. We were asked to offer approaches to the study of virtues and vices that go beyond personality. To this end, we begin this chapter by suggesting ways to go beyond trait conceptualizations of personality. Yet we believe that there is much to be gained by examining virtues (and vices) from the perspective of modern personality theory, which has moved beyond traits. Next, we offer a challenge to investigators to question their most cherished assumptions regarding virtues and the mechanisms through which they exert their healing powers. We then turn to the phenomenon of abrupt positive change as an important but largely ignored context in which to evaluate the transformation of vices to virtues. Finally, we offer a compelling example of how the heralded virtue of optimistic expectations can in the long run diminish life quality and dignity in the final stage of life. Our goal is to offer ways to move the study of virtues beyond traditional personality theory while retaining the most promising features of the field's recent advances.

MOVING BEYOND TRAIT CONCEPTUALIZATIONS OF PERSONALITY, VIRTUE, AND VICE

Before deciding to move beyond personality, we should be certain that we have fully exploited all domains of personality as potential guides to our understanding of virtue and vice. McAdams (1994) distinguished three levels of personality: (a) *dispositional traits* (Level 1), (b) *personal concerns* (Level 2), and (c) *life narratives* (Level 3). Traits are "relatively nonconditional, relatively decontextualized, generally linear, and explicitly comparative dimensions of personality" (McAdams, 1994, p. 300). Self-esteem (Kernis, chap. 1, this volume), intelligence (Sternberg, chap. 3, this volume), perfectionism (Chang, chap. 8, this volume) and neuroticism (Watson and Casillas, chap. 9, this volume) have been viewed as personality traits. *Personal concerns* refers to what a person wants at a particular point in life and how one plans to get what one wants (see King and Burton, chap. 4, this volume). These are not traits, neither are they epiphenomena of a more "fundamental" aspect of personality. People are quite aware of this second level of their personalities, because personal concerns guide everyday activities. Unlike Level 1, Level 2 is contextual and motivated.

When the contributors to this volume describe virtues in terms of "strategies," they are implicitly working within this second level of personality, although, as we soon argue, a third level of personality may also be important to our understanding of virtues. A research participant who states that, since she received a life-threatening medical diagnosis, personal relationships have become a focus of her everyday life in a way that is new and rewarding, is describing both a change in personality at Level 2 and what others are likely to see as a virtue. Or consider a young man who notes how since his son's death he has shifted his priorities toward community programs for chronically ill children and shares freely his time and expertise with the town Little League. These generative efforts capture both the commendable qualities required by most dictionary definitions of a virtue and more recent psychological definitions of virtues as personal qualities that bring "happiness, productivity, and harmony to both the individual and the society more generally" (McCullough & Snyder, 2000). They also reflect a change in personality at Level 2.

Personality at Level 3 concerns the individual's attempt to shape an identity by finding unity and purpose in life. McAdams and others who draw on the narrative tradition to understand personality consider identity an "evolving story that integrates a reconstructed past, perceived present, and anticipated future into a coherent and vitalizing life myth" (McAdams, 1994, p. 306). Personal myth cannot be reduced to traits or personal concerns; it is an internalized, unfolding narrative that is revised so as to give life a sense of direction, meaning, and continuity. McAdams (1993) speculated that whereas traits remain stable throughout adulthood and personal concerns change in response to circumstances and life stage, identity is continuously being shaped—both consciously and without awareness—to provide narrative coherence and a sense of meaning and purpose to life, and to fit personal experiences into this coherent account.

Drawing on literary scholarship, McAdams (1993) distinguished among four narrative forms: comedy, romance, tragedy, and irony. Comedy and romance supply a hopeful, optimistic narrative tone, whereas tragedy and irony offer a more hopeless, pessimistic tone. Comedy as personal narrative need not be funny; rather, it is based on the notion that happy endings are possible and that pain can be avoided. Comedy as a narrative form of this third level of personality has much to offer investigators who are interested in virtues such as optimism and hope (see Peterson and Vaidya, chap. 2, this volume). Romance, like comedy, is optimistic, but rather than emerging from life's obstacles happy, the romantic hero emerges "wiser and more virtuous" (McAdams, 1993, p. 51). The romantic form of personality at Level 3 may have the most to offer conceptually to investigators and theorists involved in the study of virtues.

An important implication of these distinctions among dispositional traits, personal concerns, and life narratives is that investigators involved in the study of virtues and vices should not be too quick to jettison personality constructs or move too far beyond personality, especially personality construed as personal concerns or life narratives. Whereas McCullough and Snyder (2000) distinguish between virtue and personality by pointing to virtue's moral relevance and its amenability to change, we contend that these distinctions apply only to personality at the level of dispositional traits. Personality at the level of personal concerns and life narratives is both morally relevant and potentially malleable.

CHALLENGING OUR CHERISHED ASSUMPTIONS REGARDING VIRTUES

In order for the empirical study of human virtues to fulfill its promise of advancing our knowledge of individual characteristics and processes that heal or strengthen, investigators must be willing to challenge their cherished assumptions about virtues and the mechanisms through which they assert their healing powers. The recent burgeoning in the study of physical and psychological health advantages associated with finding benefits in adversity provides, we believe, an illustration of how uncritically we attach our findings to existing conceptual frameworks and how reluctant we are to consider alternative formulations. The phenomenon of benefit finding is intimately linked to virtues in that the most commonly cited benefits reported by individuals in threatening situations include the most widely studied virtues, including the development of gratitude, wisdom, patience, tolerance, empathy, courage, and positive self-concept (Tennen & Affleck, 1998).

In both cross-sectional and longitudinal studies, benefit finding has been linked consistently to psychological well-being and protection against the development of posttraumatic stress disorder among disaster victims (McMillen, Smith, & Fisher, 1997) and to health outcomes, including high-risk infants' developmental outcomes (Affleck, Tennen, & Rowe, 1991), the probability of experiencing a second heart attack (Affleck, Tennen, Croog, & Levine, 1987), AIDS related mortality (Bower, Kemeny, Taylor, & Fahey, 1998), and activity limitations among individuals experiencing chronic pain (Tennen, Affleck, Urrows, Higgins, & Mendola, 1992). The consistency of these findings is impressive and supports the notion that benefit finding is a virtue in the face of threatening encounters. Perhaps bolstered by these consistent findings, investigators have accepted unequivocally the assumption that benefit finding is either a selective evaluation (Taylor, Wood, & Lichtman, 1983) or a coping strategy (Tedeschi, Park, & Calhoun, 1998). We urge theorists and investigators studying human virtues to question these and similar assumptions. Testable alternative perspectives are abundant (Tennen & Affleck, 2002).

As an example of how we hope all professed virtues might be evaluated conceptually, we briefly entertain five alternative views of the virtues reported regularly among individuals facing misfortune, each of which we believe warrants empirical examination. First, consider the possibility that people with the greatest psychological resources may also be the ones who describe episodes in which adversity ultimately leads to the development of virtuous qualities. This hypothesis is consistent with McAdams's (1993) conjecture that some individuals characteristically provide narrative in which misfortune contains a positive aspect, and if this is so, then perhaps the adaptational advantages interpreted by investigators as *consequences* of the capacity to identify virtues are actually a characteristic of those individuals who are more likely to generate "redemptive sequences" (McAdams, 1993) in response to loss or threatening encounters.

A second possibility is that the benefits/virtues reported by research participants are not cognitive constructions or strategies designed to protect threatened worldviews but rather indicators of genuine positive change. We know of only one study (Park, Cohen, & Murch, 1996) in which participant reports of positive change in the aftermath of negative events were corroborated by informants, and in that study participants and informants showed significant agreement. We believe that the psychological study of virtues needs to carefully distinguish self-perceptions and strategies created from illusory whole cloth from positive personal attributes confirmed by close friends and relatives.

Third, a virtue may also represent a way in which individuals facing difficult circumstances explain their characteristic hedonic level (Tennen &

Affleck, 2002). A well-adjusted extrovert may find herself feeling happy despite a life crisis. To make sense of her continued positive emotional state—which does not fit our expectations of someone in the aftermath of crisis—she may attribute it to a newfound capacity to feel grateful for past good fortune. This self-reported sense of gratitude is likely to be seized on by the investigator as a virtue, especially because for this individual it is associated with positive adjustment. However, the participant may be doing nothing more than providing a satisfying explanation for her temperament. We believe that this possibility presents a genuine challenge to researchers who study virtues in the context of adjustment to adversity. It also demonstrates the complexities involved in studying personality in relation to virtue and vice.

A fourth alternative perspective on virtues that emerge following misfortune turns on how people reconstruct the past. By its very nature, the report of a new-found virtue in the aftermath of an untoward event requires an individual to compere her current status on that virtuous quality with her status on the same quality prior to the event. Thus, for someone who is facing adversity to determine that she has gained wisdom or generativity from the experience, she must compare her current standing on these qualities with a recalled version of a former self. This comparison process invites distortion and bias, because, as Ross (1989) explained, people possess implicit theories of change, and these theories often lead them to overestimate how much they have changed. Such overestimation is most likely to occur when pertinent information cannot be fully recalled, because the individual then turns to his or her implicit theory and present status on the virtuous quality to create a plausible past.

A long and widely held premise in Western culture is that people gain wisdom and moral strength in the aftermath of threatening encounters. Indeed, attaining virtuous qualities from having faced misfortune has been a central theme in Western literature and poetry and, more recently, in widely read accounts of traumatic experiences, social commentaries, self-help manuals, and commencement speeches. We should therefore not be surprised that such virtues are also commonly reported in studies of adjustment to adversity. Whereas the commonly used constructivist explanation of such perceived virtues views them as motivated or strategic explanations of the present, the implicit-theory approach views such self-reported virtues as the natural consequence of a "dispassionate" reconstruction of the past (Ross, 1989). Ross's (1989) theory and experimental findings suggest that an exaggeration of increases in virtuous qualities should occur when a person's theory of change leads him or her to anticipate such change when little or no change has actually occurred. It is unfortunate that neither emerging models of virtue that accept individuals' own reports, nor models of adaptation to adversity that assume a motivated or strategic origin to perceived changes in virtuous qualities, consider the role of memory processes in self-reports of virtue. This, we believe, is a significant oversight.

Finally, reports of virtue among individuals experiencing major threats may be construed as manifestations of temporal comparisons. Serious illness and other misfortunes are likely to increase the salience of one's own past. Indeed, a central tenet of temporal comparison theory is that people are most likely to compare their current situation with the past during critical life events, and when efforts to reduce negative discrepancies between the past and the present are unsuccessful, temporal comparison theory predicts that people will construct positive changes, including subjective evidence of qualities typically interpreted as virtuous.

We do not mean to imply that self-reported virtues, especially among individuals facing misfortune, are "nothing more than" a tendency to structure one's life story with coherence and meaning in the form of redemptive sequences, or an explanation of one's temperament, or a manifestation of efforts to reconstruct the past, or a temporal comparison. Neither do we mean to imply that when reported by research participants, such reports are never selective evaluations. But how do we know if any or all of these processes are at play unless we examine them? Our message, simply stated, is that there are many roads to self-reported virtues, and for theorists and investigators the road itself should be as important as the destination. Also, although a self-reported virtue verified by an informant may not be as sexy as a perceived virtue derived from self-protective cognitive somersaults, we need to distinguish one from the other to fully comprehend virtue as a psychological phenomenon.

ABRUPT PERSONAL CHANGE: A RARELY EXAMINED CONTEXT FOR VICE TURNED VIRTUE

The contributors to this volume have gone to considerable lengths to demonstrate how a virtue can serve as a vice and how a vice may become a virtue. We believe that abrupt personal transformations create a unique context in which to study how vices can turn into virtues. The literature on personal change processes suggests a gradual pace and tempo. Adaptation to misfortune and trauma is described in terms of "working through" and moderated "dosing" of threatening material into awareness. The very notion of "rebuilding" shattered assumptions (Janoff-Bulman, 1992) reflects well this sense of gradual change. Individuals "pace their recovery" (Janoff-Bulman, 1992, p. 100) "over the course of coping and adjustment" (Janoff-Bulman, 1992, p. 110). Some theories of personal change are explicit about its protracted course—indeed, the literature on coping has come to equate the term *process* with something that requires time to unfold.

Yet there exists a rather compelling theoretical and empirical literature on dramatic transformations that occur abruptly and through mechanisms that are not fully appreciated. On the basis of their fascinating review of what is known about abrupt personal changes, Miller and C'deBaca (1994, 2001) concluded that dramatic change, including what appears to be fundamental personality change, sometimes occurs quite abruptly. Such changes are typically associated with the development of virtuous values, including forgiveness, generosity, helpfulness, honesty, and humility. It is interesting that participants in Miller and C'deBaca's study experienced only a modest degree of personal control of their lives prior to their conversion. Although in direct contrast to current theorizing about the appraisals and personality characteristics associated with incremental transformation, this finding is perfectly consistent with William James's (1902) contention that the "perception of external control" (p. 195) is essential to abrupt positive personal transformations. Thus, the vice of experiencing little control over one's life can set the stage for abrupt positive personal changes.

Although formal indicators of optimism and hope (see Peterson & Vaidya, chap. 2, this volume) were not available, most participants in Miller and C'deBaca's (1994) study noted that they were at a relatively low point in their lives. Whereas current conceptualizations of crisis-related growth associate the virtue of optimism with positive change in the face of adversity, James (1902) suggested that such change, at least abrupt change, is often preceded by despair, and Premack (1970) suggested that a sense of humiliation and conscience pangs may trigger abrupt positive personal changes. It is interesting that humiliation and conscience pangs are more common among field-dependent individuals (Lewis, 1971). We find appealing the idea that a personality characteristic such as field dependence, which increases the likelihood of rumination (see Sanna, Stocker, & Clarke, chap. 7, this volume) and distress during times of relative stability might at stressful times trigger abrupt personal growth. Taken together, these admittedly limited empirical findings suggest that qualities we would typically consider vices—including perceived lack of control (Strube, Hanson, & Newman, chap. 5, this volume), pessimism (Norem, chap. 6, this volume), and field dependence—can trigger abrupt positive personal changes, that is, these vices can become virtues. We therefore urge investigators to move beyond notions of gradual change to embrace the potential for abrupt change triggered by qualities we commonly consider vices.

HOW SHOULD WE DEFINE A STRATEGY?

This volume was guided by the notion that virtues and vices can be conceptualized in terms of *strategies*. In what appears to be an evolving shift across many areas of personality, social and health psychology, investigators now use the term *strategy* to describe aspects of individual functioning that have traditionally been construed as personal characteristics or beliefs (Tennen, Eberhardt, & Affleck, 2000).

A strategy is a plan of action designed to achieve a goal. The intentional and goal-directed nature of strategies are particularly well suited to the study of virtues as personal concerns, that is, McAdams's (1994) second level of personality. But can all virtues be construed in terms of strategies? We think not. The concept of strategic behavior excludes both higher order beliefs and well-learned behavior that requires neither concentration nor effort. Moreover, if a virtue is conceptualized as a strategy, it should be measured so as to capture its effortful, intentional, and goal-directed qualities. In coping research, investigators explicitly define and assess the effortful and strategic aspects of the coping dynamic. Lazarus's (1993) definition of coping as "cognitive and behavioral efforts to manage psychological stress" (p. 237) fits well with what we usually consider a "strategy," as does Stone and Neale's Daily Coping Inventory (1992), which "asks if anything was thought or done with the intention of accomplishing the function" (Stone, Neale, & Shiffman, 1993, p. 9). The empirical study of virtues and vices demands comparable definitional and measurement clarity. Although virtues, particularly those conceived in terms of personal concerns, can be effortful and goal directed, they need not be effortful or goal directed.

Some readers may be inclined to view our definition of strategies as excessively restrictive or a form of academic hairsplitting. We have, however, demonstrated that theoretical and measurement distinctions among appraisals, beliefs, and strategies are not trivial (Affleck & Tennen, 1993). Others may argue that a virtue itself does not need to be defined in terms of a strategy. Rather, investigators might simply examine the virtue-relevant strategies used by those individuals who manifest virtuous personal qualities or behaviors. We agree. Still, relatively few investigations have examined the strategies—that is, the virtue-relevant, goal-directed efforts—of virtuous people.

In a study of women with fibromyalgia (Tennen & Affleck, 1999), a chronic pain syndrome, we examined the daily strategic use of what we refer to here as *virtue-reminding*, that is, efforts to remind oneself of the virtues derived from the illness. These virtues, which we framed in the study as "benefits," included the development of compassion for others, social concern, wisdom, and courage. The time-intensive self-monitoring methodology used in this study involved a combination of a nightly structured diary with a computer-assisted real-time assessment of pain intensity and mood several times each day. One item on the nightly questionnaire asked participants to describe how often that day they had reminded themselves of some of the benefits that have come from living with their chronic pain. Prior to the daily self-monitoring segment of the study, they had completed a questionnaire that assessed the benefits/virtues they believed they had gained from living with chronic pain. We refer to their questionnaire responses as *virtue-finding*.

Although there was a moderate correlation between virtue finding and virtue-reminding, some participants who had cited many virtues apparently never reminded themselves of these during the month of daily monitoring. Others, who had cited only one virtue on the questionnaire, reported virtue-reminding on many days. We discovered that days characterized by more virtue-reminding did not differ in pain intensity, but they were accompanied by improved mood; that is, on days when these chronic pain sufferers made greater efforts to remind themselves of the virtues they had derived from their illness, they were especially more likely to experience pleasurable mood, regardless of their pain intensity on these days. Thus, the daily unfolding of a virtue-related strategy (i.e., virtue-reminding) had adaptive significance. We urge investigators who are hoping to complement a personality conceptualization of virtues with a strategy conceptualization to measure strategies as they unfold day to day and to maintain in their measurement the intentional qualities inherent in a strategy.

WHEN MIGHT VIRTUES *DIMINISH* LIFE QUALITY AND WELL-BEING?

The contributors to this volume have carefully distinguished ways in which virtues can turn to vices and how vices can be transformed into virtues. Our impression of this literature is that the best evidence for these transformations comes from laboratory studies, which by their nature focus on short-term outcomes. Yet in the real world, short-term virtues may become vices in the long run. This is why we urge investigators to turn to longitudinal designs to gain a balanced view of vice and virtue. We are particularly concerned with the growing consensus that optimistic expectancies represent an unalloyed virtue, an opinion that has been endorsed by the National Institute of Mental Health. We find it curious that investigators have paid little attention to circumstances in which positive expectancies might also diminish well-being (Tennen & Affleck, 1987, 2000). Although theorists have speculated that positive expectancies can promote inappropriate persistence, and may thus diminish rather than enhance life quality (Armor & Taylor, 1998), until recently this phenomenon has been confined to laboratory demonstrations (Aspinwall & Taylor, 1997). Evidence from field studies seems to consistently support the idea that individuals with the most positive outcome expectancies experience the most positive outcomes.

At least one longitudinal study has found compelling support for the idea that in certain critical life situations, positive expectations can have harmful effects. Weeks et al. (1998) followed a cohort of patients with advanced lung and colon cancer. Patients in their study who believed that they would survive at least 6 months favored life-extending therapy rather than comfort care at more than twice the rate of individuals who believed that there was at least a small chance that they would not live 6 months. Yet those who preferred life-extending therapy rather than pain relief were more likely to be rehospitalized, to experience attempted resuscitations, to die while receiving ventilation, and to face other untoward consequences of aggressive treatment—without the benefit of living longer. Weeks et al. found that, controlling for known prognostic factors, the 6-month survival of patients who received more aggressive treatment was not better than it was for those who received comfort care. We hope that findings such as these stimulate investigators to seek research contexts in which the potential costs and benefits of positive outcome expectancies, and other professed virtues, can be fully explored.

RESTRAINING THERAPEUTIC ZEAL

A theme that runs through this volume is that virtues can be construed as strategies as well as personal characteristics. It is a short step from defining a virtue as a strategy to creating interventions to induce that strategy. Indeed, McCullough and Snyder (2000) posited that because virtues are malleable, "education and other interventions should have the potential to shape a person's . . . virtues" (p. 4). We take the position that only some virtues studied by psychologists can be reasonably construed as strategies in the sense of intentional, goal-directed efforts (Tennen & Affleck, 1999), and this may be why research participants facing threatening circumstances mention frequently that they view even well-intentioned attempts to encourage such virtues as optimism, courage, and wisdom as insensitive and inept. These efforts are almost always interpreted as an unwelcome attempt to minimize the unique burdens and challenges that need to be overcome (Affleck et al., 1991). A number of investigations have demonstrated that hope and the perception of benefits in negative life events can be induced with positive adaptational consequences (e.g., King & Minor, 2000). Still, we remain concerned that until we know more about when virtues turn to vices and when a virtue has strategic qualities, our attempts to induce virtues in educational and clinical trials may be premature. We suspect, in fact, that the emergence of some virtues requires a spontaneous (nonintentional) process and that efforts to turn this process into an effortful task may itself become a "problem maintaining solution" (Watzlawick, 1978). Thus, we urge investigators to focus on theory, measurement, and study design. Interventions will then follow naturally.

REFERENCES

Affleck, G., Tennen, H. (1993). Cognitive adaptation to adversity: Insights from parents of medically fragile infants. In A. P. Turnbull, J. M. Patterson, S. K. Behr, D. L. Murphy, J. G. Marquis, & M. J. Blue-Banning, (Eds.), *Cognitive coping, families, and disability: Participatory research in action* (pp. 135–150). New York: Brooks.

Affleck, G., Tennen, H., Croog, S., & Levine, S. (1987). Causal attribution, perceived benefits, and morbidity following a heart attack: An eight-year study. *Journal of Consulting and Clinical Psychology, 55,* 29–35.

Affleck, G., Tennen, H., & Rowe, J. (1991). *Infants in crises: How parents cope with newborn intensive care and its aftermath.* New York: Springer-Verlag.

Armor, D. A., & Taylor, S. E. (1998). Situated optimism: Specific outcome expectancies and self-regulation. In M. P. Zanna (Ed.), *Advances in experimental social psychology* (pp. 211–238). San Diego, CA: Academic Press.

Aspinwall, L. G., & Taylor, S. E. (1997). A stitch in time: Self-regulation and proactive coping. *Psychological Bulletin, 121,* 417–436.

Bower, J. E., Kemeny, M. E., Taylor, S. E., & Fahey, J. L. (1998). Cognitive processing, discovery of meaning, CD4 decline, and AIDS-related mortality among bereaved HIV-seropositive men. *Journal of Consulting and Clinical Psychology, 66,* 979–986.

James, W. (1902). *The varieties of religious experience.* Cambridge, MA: Harvard University Press.

Janoff-Bulman, R. (1992). *Shattered assumptions: Towards a new psychology of trauma.* New York: Free Press.

King, L. A., & Miner, K. N. (2000). Writing about the perceived benefits of traumatic events: Implications for physical health. *Personality and Social Psychology Bulletin, 26,* 220–230.

Lazarus, R. S. (1993). Coping theory and research: Past, present and future. *Psychosomatic Medicine, 55,* 234–247.

Lewis, H. B. (1971). *Shame and guilt in neurosis.* New York: International Universities Press.

McAdams, D. P. (1993). *The stories we live by: Personal myths and the making of the self.* New York: Morrow.

McAdams, D. P. (1994). Can personality change? Levels of stability and growth in personality across the life span. In T. F. Heatherton & J. L. Weinberger (Eds.), *Can personality change?* (pp. 299–313). Washington, DC: American Psychological Association.

McCullough, M. E., & Snyder, C. R. (2000). Classical sources of human strength: Revisiting an old home and building a new one. *Journal of Social and Clinical Psychology, 19,* 1–10.

McMillen, J. C., Smith, E. M., & Fisher, R. H. (1997). Perceived benefit and mental health after three types of disaster. *Journal of Consulting and Clinical Psychology, 65,* 733–739.

Miller, W. R., & C'deBaca, J. (1994). Quantum change: Toward a psychology of transformation. In T. F. Heatherton & J. L. Weinberger (Eds.), *Can personality change?* (pp. 253–280). Washington, DC: American Psychological Association.

Miller, W. R., & C'deBaca, J. (2001). *Quantum change*. New York: Guilford.

Park, C. L., Cohen, L. H., & Murch, R. L. (1996). Assessment and prediction of stress-related growth. *Journal of Personality, 64*, 71–105.

Premack, D. (1970). Mechanisms of self-control. In W. A. Hunt (Ed.), *Learning mechanisms in smoking* (pp. 107–123). Chicago: Aldine.

Ross, M. (1989). Relation of implicit theories to the construction of personal histories. *Psychological Review, 96*, 341–357.

Stone, A. A., & Neale, J. M. (1982). Development of a methodology for assessing daily experiences. In A. Baum and J. E. Singer (Eds.), *Advances in environmental psychology: Environment and health* (Vol 4, pp. 49–83). Hillsdale, NJ: Erlbaum.

Stone, A. A., Neale, J. M., & Shiffman, S. (1993). Daily assessments of stress and coping and their association with mood. *Annals of Behavioral Medicine, 15*, 8–16.

Taylor, S. E., Wood, J. V., & Lichtman, R. R. (1983). It could be worse: Selective evaluation as a response to victimization. *Journal of Social Issues, 39*, 19–40.

Tedeschi, R. G., Park, C. L., & Calhoun, L. G. (1998). Posttraumatic growth: Conceptual issues. In R. G. Tedeschi, C. L. Park, & L. G. Calhoun (Eds.), *Posttraumatic growth: Positive changes in the aftermath of crisis* (pp. 1–22). Mahwah, NJ: Erlbaum.

Tennen, H., & Affleck, G. (1987). The costs and benefits of optimistic explanations and dispositional optimism. *Journal of Personality, 55*, 377–393.

Tennen, H., & Affleck, G. (1998). Personality and transformation in the face of adversity. In R. G. Tedeschi, C. L. Park, & L. G. Calhoun (Eds.), *Posttraumatic growth: Positive changes in the aftermath of crisis* (pp. 65–98). Mahwah, NJ: Erlbaum.

Tennen, H., & Affleck, G. (1999). Finding benefits in adversity. In C. R. Snyder (Ed.), *Coping: the psychology of what works* (pp. 279–304). New York: Oxford University Press.

Tennen, H., & Affleck, G. (2000). The perception of control: Sufficiently important to warrant careful scrutiny. *Personality and Social Psychology Bulletin, 26*, 152–156.

Tennen, H., & Affleck, G. (2002). Benefit-finding and benefit-reminding. In C. R. Snyder & S. Lopez (Eds.), *Handbook of positive psychology* (pp. 584–597). New York: Oxford University Press.

Tennen, H., Affleck, G., Urrows, S., Higgins, P., & Mendolar, R. (1992). Perceiving control, construing benefits, and daily processes in rheumatoid arthritis. *Canadian Journal of Behavioral Science, 24*, 186–203.

Tennen, H., Eberhardt, T., & Affleck, G. (2000). Social comparison processes in health and illness. In J. Suls & L. Wheeler (Eds.), *Handbook of social comparison* (pp. 443–483). New York: Plenum.

Watzlawick, P. (1978). *The language of change*. New York: Basic Books.

Weeks, J. C., Cook, F., O'Day, S. J., Peterson, L. M., Wenger, N., Reding, D., Harrell, F. E., Kussin, P., Dawson, N. V., Connors, A. F., Lynn, J., & Phillips, R. S. (1998). Relationship between cancer patients' predictions of prognosis and their treatment preferences. *Journal of the American Medical Association, 279*, 1709–1714.

11

BEYOND VIRTUE AND VICE IN PERSONALITY: SOME FINAL THOUGHTS

LAWRENCE J. SANNA AND EDWARD C. CHANG

There should be summer and winter,
And plenty and dearth,
And vice and virtue, and all such opposites,
For the harmony of the whole.

—*Epictetus* (ca. 55–135 CE)

The chapters in this volume give testimony to the use of considering a balanced view of virtue and vice in personality. As the various contributors have so eloquently suggested, what some researchers and theorists might routinely perceive to be strictly positive or virtuous personality characteristics (i.e., self-esteem, optimism, intelligence, goal pursuit, and control) can also have some negative or vicious aspects. In an analogous yet opposing fashion, what some might routinely perceive to be strictly negative or vicious personality characteristics (i.e., pessimism, rumination, perfectionism, and neuroticism) can have some positive or virtuous aspects. In short, virtues can become—or can be—vices, and the opposite holds true as well.

It is not our purpose with these closing remarks to summarize all that is contained within the preceding chapters. The authors of those chapters have already proffered their own intriguing suggestions about future research directions and have articulated well areas that are in need of more attention. However, we did want to end our book by making a few final observations.

We began with the idea of moderation, referring to classical notions of virtue and vice as delineated in treatises such as Aristotle's *Nicomachean Ethics* (1908/350 BC). By viewing personality simply in terms of dichotomies, we argued, psychology professionals may be engaging in a perilous oversimplification. We would like to make absolutely clear, however, that the objective of this book is not to attempt to refute the voluminous literature that already relates various personality traits and strategies to either good or bad qualities; rather, our objective is to explicitly embrace the fact that in actuality there is much more complexity in the existing literature and findings. It is our view that focusing exclusively on only one perspective or the other merely leads to an unnecessarily myopic portrayal of the field. Openly accepting this complexity and recognizing any gaps in our knowledge is the first step in the much larger endeavor of understanding the full range and broad spectrum of personality and human behavior.

It appears to us to be particularly interesting that the field of psychology as a whole has itself wavered between a focus on virtue or vice. There was an early emphasis on the negative side of human nature, such as on people's illicit impulses and motives. This view was subsequently criticized for a pessimistic orientation by those who wanted to call attention to a more humanistic and positively oriented outlook, one that conceptualized people as striving to be all they could be, realizing all of their human potentialities. The positive psychology movement that currently is in vogue is again a call to focus on the good or virtuous, which is itself partly in response to a perceived overemphasis on the bad or vicious side of personality (Sheldon & King, 2001). In other words, the pendulum has swung this way before, and calls to emphasize the positive can give one a somewhat notoriously eerie sense of déjà vu.

As researchers in this area, we ourselves are especially sensitive to these waxing and waning trends and to a *zeitgeist* that tends to present qualities as uniquely and completely positive or negative. We believe strongly that instead, the picture is multicolored. The virtues and vices of each individual personality characteristic depend on, among other things, the specific trait about which one speaks; on the kinds of outcomes on which one focuses; and on the particular social, cultural, and life span contexts. A thorough and balanced consideration of this should lead to more insightful research into the costs and benefits of each characteristic as well as to more effective use of knowledge gained from that research for the betterment of all people. We need to acknowledge virtue and vice, good and bad, positive and negative, *simultaneously*.

We hope the chapters in this volume express the vigor and excitement of the field that we ourselves felt when embarking on this endeavor. We feel even more strongly about this now. The chapter authors, while advancing knowledge, also help focus attention on issues that remain, and they suggest new and intriguing problems to be addressed. We believe that the chapters get to the very heart of what it means to move beyond conceptions of personality as either virtue or vice. It is only then that a greater understanding of the "harmony of the whole" can be achieved.

REFERENCES

Aristotle. (1908). *Nicomachean ethics* (W. D. Ross, Trans.). Oxford, England: Clarendon Press. (Original work written ca. 350 BC)

Epictetus. (1909–1914). The golden sayings of Epictetus (H. Crossley, Trans.). In C. W. Eliot (Series Ed.), *The Harvard classics* (Vol. 2, Part 2). New York: P. F. Collier (original work written ca. 50–138 CE)

Sheldon, K. M., & King, L. A. (2001). Why positive psychology is necessary. *American Psychologist, 56*, 216–217.

INDEX

Repression—Sensitization Scale, 148
"Repressors," 147
The Republic (Plato), 126
Respondent thoughts, 110
Retrospective mental simulations,
112–114
Retrospective simulations, 110
Richter, L., 30
Risk perception, optimistic bias in, 30
Romance, 167
Rosenman, Ray, 74
Ross, M., 169
RRI. *See* Relationship Reaction Inventory
Ruminations
variation in, 119
Rumination(s), 105–119
bad aspects of, 107–108
good aspects of, 106–107
and IGoA, 109–112
individual difference in, 117
and repetitive thought about goals, 56
Ryan, R. M., 9, 63

Sadness, 94
Saxon, J. L., 55
Scheier, M. F., 26
Schindler, Oscar, 46
Schopenhauer, Arthur, 24
Schwartz, R. M., 156
SCR. *See* Skin conductance response
SDT (self-determination theory), 63
Secondary control, 73
Secure high self-esteem, 4–5
Self-aggrandizing strategies, and high self-
esteem, 7, 8, 12, 15
Self-concordance model, 63
Self-criticism, 126, 128
Self-definition, control strivings as
elements of, 80–81
Self-determination theory (SDT), 63
Self-esteem. *See also* High self-esteem
and mental simulations, 117
stability vs. level of, 11
in Type A individuals, 76
Self-Esteem Scale, 4–5
Self-handicapping, 14–15, 114–115
Self-improvement, 114
Self-oriented perfectionism, 127, 128
Self-protection, 114–115
Self-protective strategies, and high self-
esteem, 7, 9, 12, 15

Self-regulation
in goal pursuit, 58
goals in, 54
Self-reported virtues, 170
Self-serving behaviors, of Type A
individuals, 76
Self-serving responses, and implicit vs.
explicit self-esteem, 8, 9
Self-worth, feelings of
conscious vs. nonconscious, 7–9
contextually-based, 11–14
and effective functioning, 12
and fragile high self-esteem, 4–5
and secure high self-esteem, 4, 5
Seligman, M. E. P., 29–30
"Sensitizers," 147
September 11, 2001 terrorist attacks, 99
Shaping (of environment), 46
Sheldon, K. M., 61–62
Situated optimism, 33
Skill maintenance costs, of control, 80
Skin conductance response (SCR), 153,
155
Slaney, R. B., 136–137
Snyder, C. R., 167, 174
Socially prescribed perfectionism, 127,
128
Social problem solving, 130–134
Social Problem-Solving Inventory—
Revised, 131
Sociopathy, acquired, 154
Solomon, King, 45
Somatic marker hypothesis, 153–154
Sommers, S. R., 10
SOM model. *See* States-of-mind model
Spontaneity, 119
Stable high self-esteem, 6, 11–14
Stang, D., 25
States-of-mind (SOM) model, 155–156
Stone, A. A., 172
Strategic optimism, 33, 97
Strategies, 171–173
Stress, 75, 77–78
Stumpf, H., 135
Success
and IQ, 41–42
perceived, 55
for Type A individuals, 74
Successful intelligence, 41
Suicidal ideation, 131–133
Susceptibility to cues for punishment,
94

ABOUT THE EDITORS

Edward C. Chang is an assistant professor of clinical psychology and a faculty associate in Asian/Pacific Islander American Studies at the University of Michigan. He received his MA and PhD from the State University of New York at Stony Brook and completed his clinical internship at Bellevue Hospital Center–New York University Medical Center. Dr. Chang is on the editorial boards of several journals, including the *Journal of Personality and Social Psychology*, *Cognitive Therapy and Research*, the *Journal of Social and Clinical Psychology*, and the *Asian Journal of Social Psychology*. He has published numerous articles and chapters on optimism and pessimism, perfectionism, social problem solving, and cultural influences on behavior. Dr. Chang is the editor of *Optimism and Pessimism: Implications for Theory, Research, and Practice* (American Psychological Association, 2001).

Lawrence J. Sanna is an associate professor in social psychology at the University of North Carolina at Chapel Hill. He received his MS and PhD from Pennsylvania State University. Dr. Sanna has previously held positions at Bucknell University and Washington State University and was a visiting scholar at the University of Michigan. He has taught a variety of courses related to social and personality psychology, and he has published numerous articles in the areas of social cognition, personality processes, social judgment, and group influences. Dr. Sanna is coauthor of *Group Performance and Interaction* (1999) and serves on the editorial boards of the journals *Personality and Social Psychology Bulletin*, *European Journal of Social Psychology*, and *Basic and Applied Social Psychology*.